Doing Better with Less? The Future of the Government Workforce

Christoph Demmke

Doing Better with Less? The Future of the Government Workforce

Politics of Public HRM Reforms in 32 Countries

PL ACADEMIC RESEARCH

Bibliographic Information published by the Deutsche Nationalbibliothek

The Deutsche Nationalbibliothek lists this publication in the Deutsche Nationalbibliografie; detailed bibliographicdata is available in the internet at http://dnb.d-nb.de.

Library of Congress Cataloging-in-Publication Data

Names: Demmke, Christoph, author.
Title: Doing better with less? : the future of the government workforce : politics of public HRM reforms in 32 countries / Christoph Demmke. Description: Frankfurt am Main : Peter Lang, [2016] | Includes bibliographical references.
Identifiers: LCCN 2016035518 | ISBN 9783631677001
Subjects: LCSH: Civil service--Cross-cultural studies. | Public administration--Cross-cultural studies. | Government employees--Dismissal of--Cross-cultural studies.
Classification: LCC JF1601 .D374 2016 | DDC 352.6/2367--dc23 LC record available at https://lccn.loc.gov/2016035518

ISBN 978-3-631-67700-1 (Print)
E-ISBN 978-3-653-07180-1 (E-Book)
E-ISBN 978-3-631-69552-4 (EPUB)
E-ISBN 978-3-631-69553-1 (MOBI)
DOI 10.3726/ 978-3-653-07180-1

PL Academic Research is an Imprint of Peter Lang GmbH.

Peter Lang – Frankfurt am Main · Bern · Bruxelles · New York · Oxford · Warszawa · Wien

This publication has been peer reviewed.

www.peterlang.com

Table of contents

Figures

Tables

1. Introduction

The study of public management and HRM has long concentrated on the state as a sovereign authority—"the Leviathan". The word "leviathan" has become a synonymous with any large monster or creature. Since Thomas Hobbes' *Leviathan*, published in 1651, it has also become a synonym for a powerful state with a strong, undivided government run by an absolute sovereign who rules and protects the country and is separated from the society. Indeed, for a long time, public employment features were characterized by hierarchical organisational structures, centralized approaches, standardized and highly-regulated HR policies, specific recruitment systems, clear and rigid career paths, lifetime tenure and seniority in pay and pension systems. Overall, HR policies were designed to meet the needs of a sovereign state that is exercising public powers and safeguarding the national interest. Also the (claimed) results of the Hawthorne-experiments in the 1920's led to few changes in public personnel administration. At least until the second world-war, the concept of public HRM was based on the traditional nation-state philosophy, the concepts of taylorism, fordism and bureaucracy, the rule of law and the social-contract doctrine according to the "leviathan" model. Even long after the second-world war, the popularity of the Human Resource Movement did not change most HR practices, which continued to focus on extrinsic motivators.

Nowadays, the concepts of the social-contract doctrine, sovereignty, the nation-state, nationality, public powers, safeguarding general interests, public tasks, carrying out public tasks, high performance work systems and public values have changed. Moreover, new management and public policy concepts have predicted the end of the "leviathan" and the beginning of a new era characterized by new forms of cooperation between the public and private sectors and the citizenry: a lean state, a digital society, a new public management, a networking society, or a state of Good, Smart, Multi-Level and/or European governance.

Experts observe a process of blurring of boundaries between the state and the society, the public and the private sector, the overlapping of public and private sector values, the alignment of public and private employment conditions, an increased interaction between public administration and politics and the weakening of the nation-state through processes of globalisation. Also, the concept of public service has developed from a centralised to a decentralised and fragmented conception, which includes a myriad of different services and providers from the public, semi-public and private sectors. Public policies are also administered through increasingly complex networks, decentralised governance structures, public-private partnerships and cooperative ventures between NGOs, consultants, citizens, public companies and governments. Many waves of externalisation, delegation and agencification have created a more complex picture of public service providers. Furthermore, most public administrations include or are closely linked to public institutions which, for the execution of specific tasks, are relatively independent from government. However, modern technologies have changed communication styles. Values have changed. Public employees are better educated than ever and can now challenge the authority of their governments, leaders, politicians and superiors. Line managers are given more individual responsibilities which threaten classical hierarchical decision-making procedures. Citizen orientation and principles of good administration are at the top of all administrative reform agendas. In many countries, civil servants are recruited "on the market" and employed at mid-career levels. Overall, HRM is becoming more fragmented and individualised.

On another more micro level, sociologists have been observing the blurring of boundaries in different parts of societal systems. For example, in *Elsewhere U.S.A.* Conley describes the change of the modern world "where modernist distinctions like home-office, work-leisure, public-private… no longer hold fast. In the twenty-first century, the boundary between work and home has largely disappeared, technological gadgets structure family life, business often intrudes on leisure…"[86]

Everywhere, civil servants will be working in a digital environment and are required to be more mobile and flexible. Increasingly, civil servants are working on a part-time basis or making use of offers to work from home ("teleworking"). In the future, social media and virtual networks will further challenge leadership and communication styles. According to Margetts, in the future traditional public organisations will change into virtual organisations[1]. In fact, increasingly, classical civil service tasks (which also involve the exercise of public powers) are carried out at home, in social networks, in trains, on airports or on the street with the mobile smartphone. The digital era will further erode the boundaries between the state, civil service and the society, as well as between the public and private sectors, between professional and private life and between the different

1 Helen Margetts.: Virtual Organisations. In: Ewan Ferlie/Lawrence Lynn/Christopher Pollitt, The Oxford Handbook of Public Management, Oxford University Press, Oxford.2007, pp. 305–326.

professions[2]. Because we have flexitime and improved information, work is becoming more intensive, "faster" and less restricted by place and time.

All of these trends have an important – but uncertain – impact on public organisational structures, employment features and HR policies. For example, governments have started to shy away, through politics or law, from imposing any particular conception of a specific public service organisational and employment structure that differs from private sector practices. This modernist trend towards more neutrality and more moral restraints in employment matters has opened central public employment for employment concepts in the private sector.

Paradoxically, contrary to these developments towards increased diversity and fragmentation, public views about the definition, role and tasks of the public service are still very much grounded in the existence of a "leviathan", the belief that public management differs to private sector management and in a centralised and unified public administration which is clearly separated from the private sector. The civil service is still often seen as a closed and apolitical apparatus which is separated from the private sector. In fact, citizens, media and politicians often express dissatisfaction with the too big and costly public sector and with civil servants in general, as well as campaigning against "bureaucrats" and the slow, inefficient, unresponsive and expensive bureaucracies[3].

These perceptions are (indirectly) supported by expectations as regards a specific civil service ethos, and ethical, neutral, loyal and impartial state servants with specific public sector values, a specific public service motivation and the call for specific employment features in central public administration[4].

Also concepts of government and good governance are becoming broader, and expectations for the quality of state policies are increasing. Likewise, the concepts of integrity and ethical government are also becoming more complex and expanded from an early focus on anti-corruption and fraud to many other fields. Thus, ethics policies share a number of features with the field of anti-discrimination (and/or diversity). Whereas in the past the concept of anti-discrimination focused on equal opportunities, equal treatment and equal pay, today it encompasses a much wider field and includes the fight against discrimination based on sex, racial or ethnic origin, religion or belief, disability, age or sexual orientation (Art. 10 TFEU). The case law of the EJE in the field of

---

2 Dalton Conley.: Elsewhere U.S.A. Pantheon: New York 2008.

3 In reality, in some countries the civil service with its (still) typical bureaucratic features represents only 4% of the total workforce (Germany). In Japan, it is even smaller.

4 Torben Beck Jørgensen &Barry Bozeman: Public Values, An Inventory.*Administration & Society*, Volume 39 Number 3, May 2007, pp. 354–381.

age discrimination includes an impressive number of important and complex judgements.

Thus, despite all trends towards individualisation, fragmentation, privatisation, blurring and alignment of policies and structures, citizen engagement we are also moving from a minimalist concept to a maximalist concept of (good) governance. Increasingly, governments promise better governance, less red tape, fewer administrative burdens, more security and protection, lower levels of corruption, professional HRM, better leadership, representative and diverse administrations, more flexibility, less hierarchy, more job autonomy, participatory management, effective anti-discrimination rules, more performance, better accountability structures, more transparency, more openness and more citizen-orientation.

Next to the popularity of the good governance concept we are also witnessing that state capitalism will not disappear and elements of the traditional Leviathan state are even returning. In public policies, "security" is a top issue on the political agenda. Still, after the financial crash of 2008 and numerous bailout policies, the management of the Greek financial crisis, the refugee crisis and state responses to numerous terrorist attacks everywhere in the world, government reactions have demonstrated that the "Leviathan" is not dead. Although the boundaries between the state and societies are further eroding, the state has re-appeared in many public policies: in the fight against terrorism, cyber-crime, security issues, data protection etc. Also, in the field of HRM, too much managerial thinking and too strong of a focus on rational choice theories have brought an end to the New Public Management euphoria, a certain revival of the bureaucratic concept combined with new forms of individualized HRM. Thus, the blurring of boundaries between the different "system spheres" is quite ironic, as many traditional public tasks are not changing, and are even returning. Protecting the common good and ensuring liberty, freedom and human rights remain the prime goals of government, public policies and the public sector.

In fact, as it seems, Leviathan is dead—long live Leviathan!

In the meantime, experts in the field of public policy have very different opinions about the developments of future governance reforms; for example, whereas Sandel[5] and Crouch[6] predict the total marketization of societies and public policies, Rifkin observes trends towards a shared (collaborate commons

---

5 Michael J. Sandel.: What Money Can't Buy: The Moral Limits of Markets, Farrar, Straus and Giroux.2012.

6 Colin Crouch.: The Knowledge Corruption, Hidden Consequences of the Financial Takeover of Public Life, John Wiley.2015.

citizen-oriented) economy[7] and Gros[8] towards the return of the strong state, Leviathan, as security issues become ever more dominant in our societies. Whereas in the European discourse, the scientific community discusses the dangers of a new nationalism and the future of differentiated (EU) integration, the wider OECD-world wonders about the return of Keynesianism, the growing influence of state capitalism in the (financial) world-order[9], and discuss the popularity of good governance and neo-institutional approaches.

As it seems, "Techniques for organisational engineering come and go with remarkable rapidity. New techniques come into fashion and old ones go out, much like the outfits modelled in Paris, Milan, and New York"[10]. During the last decades, public management reform was defined as a move towards a "lean state", an "activated state", a "collaborative government", a "digital government", a "networking society", "multilevel governance", "good governance", a "smart government", a "security state" and other numerous new reform concepts. Moreover, the "evolving models of government are not intrinsically liberal or conservative, effective or not effective – they are simply different and new and thus require some careful thought on the part of those who care about good governance and well-functioning public administration"[11].

The problem with the design of HRM in this turbulent public administration in the 21st century is obvious. Whereas the term "Leviathan", "bureaucracy" or "modernity" can be defined and broken down into concrete HR contents, concepts and principles, this is much less the case with the terms "post-bureaucratic", "digital government", "networking society" or "bureaucracy-lite" (Hayle) and the translation of these concepts into current HRM strategies. Present governance concepts represent fluid notions and neither offer a clear definition nor orientation for HR policies. Although these terms may be an adequate description of the

7 Jeremy Rifkin.: The Zero Marginal Cost-Society: The Internet of Things, The Collaborative Commons and the Eclipse of Capitalism, MacMillan.2015.

8 Frederic Gros.: Die Politisierung der Sicherheit, Matthes & Seitz.2015.

9 J. Kurlantzick.: State-Capitalism – How the return of statism is transforming the world, Oxford University Press: Oxford.2016.

10 Joel D. Aberbach/Bert A. Rockman, In the Web of Politics – Three Decades of the U.S. Federal Executive, Brookings Institution, Washington D. C. 2000, p. 9., Christopher Hood.; The Art of the State, Clarendon Press, Oxford University Press, Oxford 2000, p. 199.

11 Elaine Ciulla Kamarck.: Public Servants for Twenty-First-Century Government. In: John D.Donahue/Joseph S. Nye (eds.).: For the People, Can We Fix Public Service, Brookings Institution Press, Washington D. C. 2003, p. 134.

current change processes, they leave those in charge of introducing change processes in the field of HRM puzzled. Notions of postmodern, post-bureaucratic organisation or post-public service also illustrate that we lack an understanding of what could be a (universal) HRM alternative to the bureaucratic form of organisation.

Still, this difficulty is not the only challenge.

Everywhere within the OECD world, high corruption levels, increasing levels of (income and capital) inequality, stagnating social mobility and low trust levels, a certain crisis of the system of representative democracy[12], political parties also put civil service systems under pressure. Because of rising levels of inequality in many OECD countries, what also seems to be an emerging challenge is the disaggregation of societies and a growing disagreement with the social contract. In the central administration, this can be best seen by changes in established forms of formalised social dialogue and the role of the trade unions. What will be the effects of future forms of employee participation on working conditions and employee well- being?

The challenge of balancing conflicting objectives and managing "scarcity and public sector contraction to the viability of our political and administrative systems should be obvious"[13].Consequently, HRM policies are also confronted with a new challenge: how to maintain merit, fairness and equal treatment in a fragmented, decentralised, ever more competitive and individualised context?

In the meantime, the influence of (behavioral) economics, organizational theory, new technologies and politics has been further increasing in the field of public management and in HRM. At the same time, the influence of law is decreasing but evidence is missing as regards the effects of new instruments (such as nudging) on rational administrative behavior, classical administrative law and the future of the rule of law doctrine as such. Human Resource Management (as a discipline) is gaining in importance as regards trends towards the "psychologization of HRM" and an increased attention to isolated HR issues like Leadership, Coaching and Competency Management. Standardisation is "out" with all its positive and negative implication. We will come back to this issue later on.

In fact, at least the growing influence of economics in HRM in the context of budgetary constraints is well researched. Also, studies on the effects of financial constraints on public management reforms have become increasingly popular

12 Helmut Wilke, Dezentrierte Demokratie, Frankfurt/M., Suhrkamp.2016.

13 Levine, Charles H.: More on Cutback Management: Hard Questions for Hard Times. In: Public Administration Review, Vol. 39, No. 2 (Mar. – Apr., 1979), p. 180.

(Kickert/Randma-Liiv 2015[14]; Van der Voet/van de Walle, 2014[15]). However, the impact of governance reforms, public management reforms and budgetary constraints have not been a subject of rigorous comparative empirical scrutiny as regards the impact on different HR policies and in different areas of HRM. Similarly, the effects of financial constraints on work systems and on workplace behaviour in public administration have not been studied either. Thus, neither the growing influence of politics and economics nor the change of governance and their effects on HRM policies are sufficiently researched, although Levine wrote in 1979, "I have no ready solutions for these hard questions. I do not know of anyone else with solutions either"[16]. Moreover, OECD countries are not "in the same boat". While all countries may be said to have a common interest in avoiding global financial meltdown, there are also striking variations in financial vulnerability across the OECD that might be expected to lead to different pressures for the reshaping of public services in matters of pay, competency, and responsibility. To this should be added the existence of different institutional configurations, the power of history, culture and politics.

In all countries, there is only agreement that new ways of managing HRM are needed in this turbulent and contradictory socio-economic context: "We are entering a new era of public budgeting, personnel, and program management. It is an era dominated by resource scarcity. It will be a period of hard times for government managers that will require them to manage cut-backs, trade-offs, reallocations, organisational contractions, program terminations, sacrifice, and the unfreezing and freeing up of grants and privileges that have come to be regarded as unnegotiable rights, entitlements, and contracts. It will be a period desperately in need of the development of a methodology for what I call 'cutback management'[17]."

- Governments need to balance budgetary constraints with the need to have productive, satisfied, innovative and high-performing employees.
- Organisations are required to become more efficient while also needing legitimacy amongst the workforce.

---

14 Kickert, W.J.M. & Randma-Liiv, T.: Europe Managing the Crisis. The Politics of Fiscal Consolidation. London: Routledge.2015.

15 Joris Van der Voet & Steven van de Walle.: How cutbacks and job satisfaction are related: The role of top-level public managers' autonomy, FP7 COCOPS Final Academic Conference: Leuven, Belgium (2014, June, 10–2014, June 11).

16 Charles H. Levine, More on Cutback Management, op cit, p. 180.

17 Charles H. Levine, More on Cutback Management, op cit, p. 179.

- Finally, HRM is about the need to be both a cultural guardian and an architect of a new culture[18]. Currently, HRM tries to distance itself from its stuffy and traditional welfare image and confirms its significance for corporate profitability, performance and innovation[19] while trying to balance different employee and employer interests with the need for change, discipline and stability.

Of course, all of this yields a number of paradoxes and tensions that must be acknowledged. Obviously, change as such does not mean that we are taking a step forward towards solving problems and offering better solutions. In fact, more empirical evidence is needed on the effects of HR reforms in the context of budgetary constraints.

Filling this important gap, this survey attempts to assess the effects of these developments in public employment in the central public administrations of the OECD countries. It is therefore a study about the management of strategic tensions, complexities and contradictions.

Consequently, our interest in this survey can be divided in four objectives:

- First, one objective is to compare what kind of reforms are being implemented as a consequence of new economic pressures.
- Second, a crucial objective is to generate empirical evidence on the effects of reforms on motivation, trust levels, job satisfaction, job commitment and so forth.
- Third, another interest is to generate evidence as to the link between budgetary constraints, the choice of HR reform instruments (HR bundles) and reform effects. Is it possible to categories countries as to the choice of measures and the effects of reforms?
- Fourth, is it possible to identify best practices (for example, countries that have succeeded in managing budgetary constraints while maintaining job satisfaction and job commitment and by introducing smart HR bundles)? Do countries exist that *do better with less*?

As we will see in this study, the reform of central HR policies is actually a fascinating subject. It challenges many popular assumptions and increasingly calls

---

18 Dave Ulrich.: Human Resource Champions, Harvard Business Review Press, Boston.1997. p. 47.

19 Ashly Pinnington/Rob Maqcklin/Tom Campbell.: Introduction: Ethical human resource management. In: Ashly Pinnington/Rob Maqcklin/Tom Campbell (eds.).: Human Resource Management, Ethics and Employment, Oxford University Press, Oxford.2007, p. 1.

into question traditional characteristics of public administration systems, but leaves us puzzled as to the outcomes of all reforms. Whereas most OECD countries continue to move away from classical bureaucratic systems, the current development is not towards the return of the big state or "Leviathan", but also not towards a new universal best-practice organisational model, or the "privatisation" of Government. Instead, new reforms indicate trends towards different laboratories of innovation, many new best-fit practices and organisational diversity. The latter can be best seen by the share of employment in the public sector as a percentage of total employment, which ranges from 7.6% in South Korea up to almost 35% in Denmark and in Norway[20]. Despite globalisation, different historical traditions and cultures as well as different budgetary pressures continue to have a considerable impact on the way HR reforms are implemented and also on the outcomes of HR reforms. As a side effect, this study gives a fascinating picture about the differences and similarities of the HR systems in the OECD world. This relevance of context and diversity in public administrations has important implications for the concept of mutual learning and good practice. Therefore, this publication is also supposed to contribute to a discussion on meaningful state- and HR-concepts, typologies, country classifications, convergence theories and the possibility to deliver best practices, as we will not only observe "discursive" but also "result convergence" (Pollitt).

I would like to thank Jan Warode for his valuable help with the "statistical challenge".

20 OECD.: Governance at a Glance, Public Employment. Data for 2013, http://stats.oecd.org//Index.aspx?QueryId=66856.

2. Theoretical Part

2.1 Public Management and the reform of HRM

Unfortunately, until today no public management theory offers a comprehensible theory and explanation of changing processes. When looking from the past to the present, however, it seems more likely that change will not result in a linear progress for the better, but rather to failures, successes, paradoxes, dilemmas and simple alternation. Choices must therefore be made very carefully. Recent public management theories suggest that some reforms in the public sector are following the same path, whereas others are not. Some claim that partial convergence exists, whereas others are of the opinion that even among the most similar countries, convergence has been exaggerated. Mostly, management science promotes the linear development belief that there is always a better way to do things. Management theory therefore often matches our own cultural belief that anything new is better and promising. For example, the introduction of new information technologies is generally seen as a very positive development which will enhance the transparency, efficiency and effectiveness of public services. Modernisation and change is a Western concept that promises change, progress and a way to improve things. The best known claim for modernisation is the book from Osborne and Gaebler (1992)[43] in which the authors state that Western societies are moving to a new "entrepreneurial" paradigm of public management, replacing outdated turn-of-the-century rule-bound design. It is precisely because of this promise, it seems, that new public management theories were so popular.

In reality, public management reforms are inherently ambivalent. In fact, public management reforms are always about balancing conflicting values and principles and about setting priorities in the reform process.

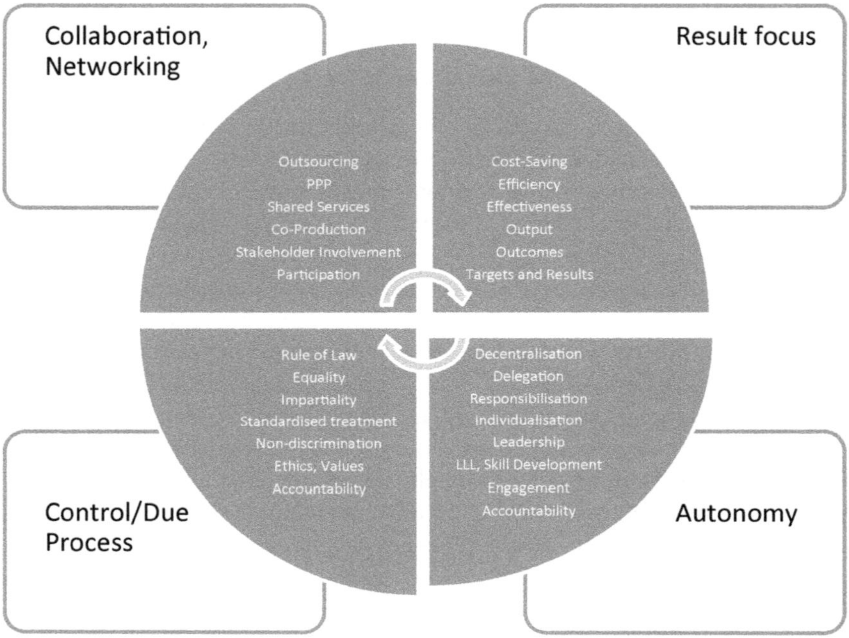

Overall, there is "more reform" than evidence about reform outcomes and whether the changing processes will produce better results. Today, it is widely accepted that evidence about the impact and results of many reforms is still insubstantial. Many methodological problems still exist in measuring the outcomes of reforms. Also, many national and comparative studies on performance management and performance measurement studies are more "preoccupied with describing the new measures, comparing measures from various countries and assessing the impact on accountability"[21]. However, little effort has been devoted to rigorous empirical verification of claimed results or to the identification of the causal relationships underlying them.

21 Melissa Forbes & Laurence E. Lynn Jr..: How Does Public Management Affect Government Performance? Findings from International Research, Bush School Working Paper, No. 420, October 2004, p. 2.

In the past, a standard criticism towards New Public Management has been its focus on results and cost saving (Hood/Dixon, 2012[22]) and a tendency to downplay the importance of other values and principles such as quality, fairness, sustainability and impartiality. This again would result in many (un-) intentional reform effects, such as more demotivation, less engagement and less trust of the workforce in leadership. On a more macro-economic level, inequality is increasing in many countries[23], which is also reflected by rising levels of pay differentiation in the private and public sector[24]. Consequently, in many countries with high budgetary pressures and a strong focus on cost saving, this could increase the probability of rancorous conflict, decrease the prospects for innovation by consensus, and complicate the processes for building and maintaining support for administrative systems and democratic processes[25]. Unfortunately, many of these claims have not been tested empirically and in a comparative setting. One of the objectives of this survey will be to test these assumptions.

The link between HRM and central public administration is specific[26]. Central public administration is a constituent part of the system of government. Until today, no government has been completely privatised and no public administration works like a private company. One reason for this is that, still, most experts claim that there are important differences between the public and the private sector and between public and private HRM. In fact, the quality of life of whole populations depends in many ways on those who work for government and on how government works as such. Furthermore, public administrations have a democratic and ethical function; they should serve the society and the law, protect the population as well as function in a sustainable manner. For all of these tasks and duties many OECD countries are reluctant to outsource or to privatize core governmental tasks and to completely reverse established specific employment features and HR policies that were founded in the 19th century in order to protect the democratic and liberal state.

---

22 Christopher Hood/Ruth Dixon.: A Model of Cost-Cutting in Government? The Great Management Revolution in UK Central Government Reconsidered. In: *Public Administration*, Vol. 91, No. 1. 2013, pp. 114–134.

23 Thomas Pickerty.: Capital in the Twenty-First Century, Harvard University Press. 2014.

24 Dorothea Brunner.: Die Wahrnehmung der Lohndisparität im Unternehmen und deren Wirkung auf die Kündigungsabsicht, Rainer Hamp, München. 2009; See also OECD.: OECD Study on Compensation in the Public Sector, OECD Publisher, Paris.2014.

25 Charles Levine, More on Cutback Management, op cit, p. 180.

26 Christoph Demmke & Timo Moilanen.:, Government Transformation and the Future of Public Employment, Peter Lang, Frankfurt/M. et al.2013.

Therefore, in all countries worldwide, Government employment frameworks are *specific* and *different* compared to private sector features. They are also very *ambitious*. They want employment systems that guarantee observation of the fundamental values, administrative law principles and ensure a focus on effectiveness, efficiency and accountability. Government policies should also ensure equal treatment and fairness, be attractive and competitive with respect to the private sector policies while managing tax payers' money as prudently and while also rewarding individual performance. Increasingly, employment structures should also be diversified and representative while ensuring the merit principle, the equality of chances and the principle of non-discrimination (which is being defined much broader than decades ago).

Consequently, a number of differences between public and private sector employees have been maintained in many OECD countries. In most cases, these relate to job security, remuneration systems and recruitment procedures.

However, this survey shows that central public organisations are, by far, not as specific, different, ambitious, old-fashioned and traditional as is often suggested. Also, common accusations that central administrations are not innovative, not ready for reform and suffer from reform inertia are clearly wrong[27]. The findings in this survey contradict with popular perceptions and long-established clichés to which the public sector is reform-resistant and public employees inflexible[28]. We are therefore not surprised by evidence from new studies that point to the fact that many public sector organisations have higher levels of organisational learning and innovation than private sector companies[29]. For example, evidence by Eurofound shows that "learning community and professional models, both characterised by high level of learning, problem-solving and discretion in work, tend to be characteristic of public services and of the more knowledge-intensive private sector services"[30]. These findings are in clear contrast to established clichés and, for many observers, it seems even hard to believe them.

---

27 Mariana Mazzucato.: The Entrepreneural State, Anthem Press, London.2014.

28 Christoph Demmke/Timo Moilanen (2013), Governmental Transformation and the Future of Public Employment, op cit.

29 OECD.: Innovative Workplaces, Making better use of skills within organisations, OECD Publishing: Paris.2010; European Foundation for the Improvement of Living and Working Conditions.: Work Organisation and Innovation, Dublin 2012; Mariana Mazzucato.: op cit.

30 OECD (2010), Innovative Workplaces, op cit; see also: European Foundation for the Improvement of Living and working Conditions.:, Working Conditions in the European Union: Work Organisation, Dublin. 2009; Anthony Arundel/Edward Lorenz/

Thus, today, the problem with HR reform is not that there are too few reforms or too little innovation. In fact, the real challenge may be the lack of evidence on the effects of reforms, a neglected role of HRM as such and the ongoing importance of perceptions and clichés.

However, the question "where do reforms lead to?" is difficult to answer: The question of what has resulted from the many reforms is obviously an absolutely fundamental one. Yet it is not at all simple. In reality, even experts have no clear understanding of how public administration is changing. There is also little evidence as to whether change processes produce better results. And if so, which change processes and which reform instruments?

The Coordinating for Cohesion in the Public Sector of the Future (COCOPS), a public management research consortium grouping eleven universities from ten different countries, made a meta-analysis of all the academic empirical data evaluating the impacts of the NPM reforms in Europe. COCOPS' concern was that, highly surprisingly, many academic writings, governmental works or consultancy evaluations did not focus on the outcomes obtained by the implementation of NPM reforms. Most of them consisted of a description of the reforms implemented and the impact on activities and processes: "A full discussion of 'results' therefore embraces the wider question of 'results for whom, defined by whom, against what objectives?'"[31].

Notwithstanding that, it is highly unwise to have spread those kinds of reforms through most of the OECD countries without having a clear understanding of their impact; it is hard to assess the results today due to the lack of empirical analysis. Whatever is the right diagnosis of "change", the evolving models of government are not intrinsically liberal or conservative, left or right, effective or not effective—they are simply different as the traditional forms of public administration and thus require some careful thought on the part of those who care about well-functioning public administration.

Ideally, given the legal, political and economic importance of central public administration, reforms of these features should be supposed to be the outcome of a rational decision making process. In reality, the term *bounded rationality* (Simon) has become a buzz word and *nudging* (Thaler and Sunstein), which is based on behavioural economy insights, a new fashion.

Bengt-Åke Lundvall/Antoine Valeyre (2007), The Organisation of Work and innovative Performance, Paper prepared for the Blue Sky II Indicators Conference, Statistic Canada, 25–27 September, Ottawa, p. 11.

31 Geert Bouckaert &Christopher Pollitt.: Public Management Reform: A Comparati Analysis, Third edition, Oxford University Press, Oxford. 2011, p. 126.

Unfortunately, the field of public management reform is loaded with theories that reflect personal opinions, images and perceptions. Moreover, public perceptions and also expectations as to administrative reforms are full of paradoxes.

- Whereas people and media demand more efficient and better performing public services, they allow for the emergence of a new performance management bureaucracy.
- While people place higher demands on the quality of service delivery, they agree to public budgets being reduced.
- While observers pledge for administrative simplification, deregulation and the reduction of administrative burdens, people are constantly asking for new laws and rules (e.g., in the fight against terrorism, data protection, climate change, anti-corruption etc.).
- While people criticize the existence of specific pay systems in the public sector, they agree that rising pay disparities and pay flexibility in the private sector led to a number of perverse developments.

In the eyes of the public, central public administrators still work in an environment which is clearly separated from the private sector and are perceived as a protected group set apart from the outer world. They enjoy privileges, are not performing well enough, are not innovative, are too costly and risk averse because of too much job protection and hierarchical thinking. Consequently, many people require that public employees should also not be treated differently than private sector employees.

In reality, government has shifted towards collaborative government, working conditions have been aligned with the private sector and public services are delivered by many forms of public, public-private or private actors or in co-production with citizens and NGOs.

Consequently, for some observers, the reform of public administration and nagement seems to be a simple story: the transformation from an old paradigm ublic administration = bureaucracy) to a new universal high-performance re.[32] Generally, the old paradigm is dismissed as being too hierarchical, nflexible, hostile to discretion, closed and non-transparent, not focused y and not enhancing (organisational or individual) performance. Or -study puts it: "The rhetoric of the times had identified government

---

yth of the Bureaucratic Paradigm: What Traditional Public Admi- ood for. *Public Administration Review*, March/April 2001, Vol. 61,

as "the problem" rather than "the solution"[33]. In the meantime, experts are wondering whether new forms of public management are less bureaucratic and delivering better results. Authors like Mungiu-Pippidi come to the conclusion that the "Quest for Good Governance" was not a success story and corruption levels increased in many countries since 2008[34]. Thus, in the meantime, more experts doubt that there is a new universal paradigm. But few still doubt that there was an old universal paradigm.

The discussions about the old and new paradigm also show that our culture is deeply influenced by the concept of positive change and the restless search for better models, ideas and solutions. Management science promotes the linear development belief that there is always a better way to do things. Management theory therefore often matches our cultural belief in most OECD countries that anything new is better and promising. For example, the introduction of new information technologies is generally seen as a very positive development that will enhance the transparency, efficiency and effectiveness of public services. Modernisation and change is a western concept that promises change, progress and a way to better things. The best known claim for modernisation is the book *Reinventing Government* by Osborne/Gaebler (1992)[35] in which the authors state that Western societies are moving to a new "entrepreneurial" paradigm of public management, replacing the outdated turn-of-the-century rule-bound design. It is precisely because of this promise, it seems, that new public management theories were so popular. More recently, discussions about innovation in the public sector have taken a similar direction and have been regarded as potentially obligatory and as an innovation imperative[36].

In reality, however, "modernisation" is also an inherently ambiguous idea[37] since "much depends on which meaning of "modernisation" is at issue"[38]. Today,

33 Alex Matheson & Hae-Sang Kwon.: Public Sector Modernisation: a New Agenda, in: OECD Journal on Budgeting – Vol. 3, No. 1, Paris.2003, p. 9.

34 Alina Mungiu-Pippidi.: The Quest for Good Governance, Cambridge University Press.2016.

35 David Osborne & T.Gaebler.:, Reinventing Government, Cambridge M.A.1992.

36 Sara R. Jordan.:, The Innovation Imperative: an analysis of the ethics of the imperative to innovate in public sector delivery. *Public Management Review*, Vol. 16, No. 1.2014, pp. 67–89.

37 Hood, The Art of the State, op cit, p. 195.

38 Hood, The Art of the State, op.cit, p. 219.

some observers even claim that public administration in the 21st century has arrived in a new era of post-modernity[39].

However, current reforms are embedded in a turbulent environment which makes it difficult to follow a clearly defined, rational reform trajectory. Most reform strategies are characterized by competing values and reform objectives, ever-changing reform pressures and new reform priorities on the political agenda. In addition, the financial crisis has led to the introduction of many ad hoc and hasty reforms. Consequently, Pollitt claims that "Overall, therefore, it appears that for most EU and OECD management reform programmes, most of the time, we have precious little good information about results. There is an ocean of literature but only a trickle of high quality data on efficiency and effectiveness… To put it another way, humility is undersung as a management reform virtue – globally"[40].

In all countries, reforms are only rarely the product of well-designed and carefully implemented strategies. Because of this, Pollitt and Bouckaert wonder about the differences between "large optimism about the potential of public sector reforms" and the results: trade-offs, balances, limits, dilemmas and paradoxes. Other authors are worried about the instability that seems to reign in public organisations, and point to several negative consequences of current HR reforms, especially the danger that they will destroy institutional memory as well as negatively affecting morale and trust. One has to deal with the goal of motivating staff and the promotion of cultural change, while at the same time tenure is weakened and downsizing projects are going on.

After years of new public management euphoria, Hood states: "Slowly, however, the euphoria starts to wear off, then new heaven and new earth start to look all too much like the old ones, and the cycle of disappointment begins again"[41]. In the meantime, New Public Management doctrines have lost much of their appeal, as their focus was "too much" on rational choice theories.

However, current budgetary constraints have also encouraged a renewed focus on the dominance of economic thinking in the field of HRM. When public resources are scarce, there will be an increased demand for aggressive cost-cutting management that concentrates on squeezing inputs rather than pursuing more intangible and collegial objectives. "That means putting primary emphasis on cutting headcounts, reorganizing services into structures that are more readily

---

39 See Ellen Mastenbroek.: De postmoderne overheid: wens of werkelijkheid?. Bestuurswetenschapen, No. 2.2003.

40 Christopher Pollitt.: Back in the OECD…An Oblique Comment on the World Bank's "Better Result from Public Institutions". 2012, p. 4 and 5.

41 Christopher Hood, The Art of the State, op cit, p. 190.

cost controllable, axing activities with no immediate apparent payoff (such as blue-sky thinking, long-term maintenance, training and staff development), on more outsourcing if it can deliver short-term cost savings—in short, a return to precisely the kind of early NPM style associated with the Thatcher (United Kingdom) government"[42].

Today, public management reforms in central public administration are entering into a new digital phase. Everywhere in the OECD, the digitalisation of HRM brings new opportunities and new risks, the emergence of new forms of hybrid organisations, new challenges to the concept of data management, shared services, privacy, decentralization and individualization[43].

Long-standing features such as the existence of hierarchical decision-making, centralized HR practices, little job autonomy and the existence of rigid careers combined with the principle of seniority, the nature of work, public service motivation and work ethos, the values of public servants, skills, the composition of the workforce, contractual arrangements and age structure of the workforce are changing. To this should be added a different understanding of the underlying reasons for organisational performance, the link between HR and organisational success, leadership success and innovation.

Despite these complex trends in many different HR policies, and as regards many different instruments, in popular public management literature, often, whole countries are praised as being reform-oriented countries, whereas others are seen as reform laggards although it remains unclear as to the basis on which these general judgements and value statements are based. Still, public sector benchmarking, rating public performance and comparing the performance of countries as such is becoming ever more popular although evidence is increasing that trends towards digitalisation allow for more effective fine tuning and differentiation of individual situations. In the field of HRM, the identification of "best practices" or "universal solution" is also a difficult exercise in times of searching for "organisational best-fits".

Thus, even if—so —the best of both worlds could not be achieved in the field of public management and HRM, it is always worth searching for it. The fact that this search will be endless is no reason to be pessimistic.

---

42 Martin Lodge & Christopher Hood.: Into an Age of Multiple Austerities? Public Management and Public Service Bargains across OECD Countries. *Governance: An International Journal of Policy, Administration, and Institutions*, Vol. 25, No. 1, January 2012, p. 83 and 84.

43 See for a good overview: Mark Bevir (Editor), The SAGE Handbook of Governance, Sage, London.2011.

2.2 HRM reforms in a new governance context

For a long time, personnel administration happened in some form or another. HRM functions such as of hiring, training, compensation, and discipline/termination were not performed by HR specialists or HR departments. In fact, traditional HRM was rather HR administration and a technical duty within organisations. HR administration was subordinated to "the emergence of the doctrine and practice of scientific management (SM). The first professional/scientific writings on business organisation and management appeared in the early 1880s in the United States, authored primarily by engineers. The engineers sought to use principles of science to increase the efficiency of business production systems. Inevitably they were led to consider the 'people' side of production, including methods of employee selection, job assignment, supervision, work pace, and compensation. This new approach found its most influential and strategic formulation in the writings of Frederick Taylor, particularly his book *Principles of Scientific Management (1911)*"[44]. Personnel administration was about recruiting people, paying people, sanctioning, controlling and dismissing people. However, gradually, the notion and importance of HR administration changed with the birth of HRM (the Hawthorne Experiments[45]) and—later on—the further elaboration of motivation theories and the birth of performance management. From now on, HRM grew in complexity but it remains doubtful whether it also grew in acceptance, at least outside the field of HRM.

The study of HRM in central public administration has long concentrated on the bureaucratic state as a sovereign authority and dedicated personnel with specific working conditions and ethical requirements. The notion of the sovereign state and the need for a specific category of public employees arose gradually and contingently during the Renaissance and Reformation in Europe. The emerging modern concept of bureaucracy and civil service was by nature a "republican" concept that was designed as a rational counter concept to the traditional and charismatic power structure of the monarchist and medieval times[46].

---

44 Bruce E. Kaufman.: The Development of HRM in Historical and International Perspective. In: Peter Boxall/John Purcell/Patrick Wright.: The Oxford Handbook of Human Resource Management, Oxford Press, Oxford.2007.

45 Chan Su Jung & Soo Young Lee.: The Hawthorne Experiments Studies Revisited, Evidence from the US Federal Workforce. *Administration & Society*, Vol. 47.2015, pp. 507–551.

46 Christoph Demmke/Timo Moilanen.: Government Transformation and the Future of Public Employment, Peter Lang. Frankfurt/M. et al.2013., p. 1.

During the 19th century, central government employment was increasingly linked to the rule of law doctrine, to the principle of legality and (later on) the principle of merit. To this were added specific organisational features and working conditions in order to achieve fairness and equity, to implement the merit principle and to protect public employees against arbitrary administrative decisions.

In most OECD countries, hierarchical organisational structures, clear and rigid career paths, lifetime tenure, full-time employment, the application of the seniority principle, specific pension systems for civil servants, standardized remuneration systems and the prohibition to go on strike were introduced in order to reduce as far as possible the risk of excessive political influence, corruption, misconduct, the exercise of private interests and instability of government: "Traditionally, a hierarchical and formalized organisational structure, clear and rigid career paths, lifetime tenure, full-time employment, seniority, advantageous pension systems and rigid remuneration systems were introduced in order to reduce as far as possible the risk of too much political influence, corruption, misconduct, the exercise of private interests and instability of government. Consequently, the traditional argument for a specific organisational structure was to produce a certain ethical status for state employees who should be committed to the public good, neutrality, impartiality and to observing confidentiality and displaying expertise. In many OECD countries, public employees on central administration level were therefore working in hierarchical organisations, had very specific recruitment procedures, specific ethical obligations, little mobility, varying working conditions and specific social security systems"[47].

For a long time, experts were convinced that these specific organisational structures and employment conditions would indeed "produce" a certain public service ethos, individual performance and "public service motivation" for civil servants who—in exchange for many privileges—would be committed to the public good, neutrality, impartiality and to observing confidentiality and displaying expertise. Yet, bureaucracy was not only supposed to be a new form of rational power, it was also believed to be more efficient and more ethical than any other organisational form until the 19th century. Max Weber was convinced that the classical bureaucratic model would outperform all other existing organisational models. In fact, until today, central public employees are requested to do more than merely fulfilling functions in the field of exercising state powers and

47 Ibid.

safeguarding the general interest of the state. In fact, they should exercise their role with a certain sense of integrity—a public service ethos.

Within this bureaucratic structure, central public administrations were also closed off and separated from society and citizens. In other words, central public employees were seen as a protected category of staff and public administration was supposed to be separated from the political system. Because of their specific treatment, public perceptions arose of civil servants having different personalities, being motivated by different incentives, working less hard than employees in the private sector, being more security-minded, more rule-oriented and not very innovative.

Moreover, public HR administration was increasingly criticized for its bureaucratic features, high levels of red tape, little decision-making discretion of line managers and its technical and standardised focus in HR policies such recruitment, selection, pay, performance management and promotion.

Evidence was also growing that specific public working conditions and organisational structures do not necessarily produce less corruption and a specific public service ethos. In their seminal paper "The Merit of Meritocratization: Politics, Bureaucracy, and the Institutional Deterrents of Corruption", Dahlström et al. concluded that "The empirical results show that first, some bureaucratic factors (most notably the meritocratic recruitment of public employees) exert a significant influence on curbing corruption even when controlling for the impact of most standard political variables. We believe that these variables capture the effect of the bureaucratic professionalism. Second, the results also indicate that another set of bureaucratic characteristics that constitutes the backbone of what the literature defines as 'closed' bureaucratic structure (career stability and formal exams for bureaucrats) do not have any relevant effect. The second finding is surprising since 'closed' bureaucratic structures have previously been praised as key deterrents of corruption"[48].

Another criticism concerned the fact that traditional employment features (such as the principle of seniority) are expensive because of mechanisms such as automatic pay progression and career development linked to experience and length of service. For example, many OECD countries link holiday entitlements to the principle of seniority. In Belgium holiday entitlements increase by one day

48 Carl Dahlström/Victor Lapuente/Jan Teorell.: The Merit of Meritocratization: Politics, Bureaucracy, and the Institutional Deterrents of Corruption. *Political Research Quarterly*, Vol. 65(3). 2012, p. 665. See also: James Rauch &Peter Evans.: Bureaucratic Structure and Bureaucratic Performance in Less Developed Countries. *Journal of Public Economics, Vol.* 75.2000, pp. 49–71.

between the age of 45 to 49 and then up to additional six days after 64 years. In Korea, holiday entitlements vary between three days after three to six months of service to 21 days after six years (and more) of service.

Thus, public HR administration and classical HR features got into trouble, both theoretically and practically. Its core claims and professional self-image have become entwined with ethical, financial, budgetary and managerial narratives[49].

Overall, human resource management in the public sector was considered as an isolated, costly policy which is very complex, technical and dominated by legalistic approaches. As regards HRM, the discipline has come under attack particularly because of its focus on HR issues such as recruitment, selection, payroll, benefits, employee relations, performance management, industrial relations, legal issues and its limited role in achieving business objectives (Ulrich, 1998). Although many of these critics were well founded, positive features and developments were (often) neglected: positive features of stability, increasing levels of participation, formalized social dialogue, good working conditions, clear career paths, enhanced possibilities to combine professional and personal life.

With the emergence of management by objective doctrines and, later on, New Public Management in the 1990s, the influence of rational choice theories became stronger in central public administration[50] and the call for cost savings, accountability and output orientation ever-more dominant. Parallel to this trend, New Public Management also supported the individualisation of HRM, team work, coordination, decentralisation of responsibilities and a renewed focus on leadership. In this perspective, HRM was not only seen as a (cost) constraint and HR management as a subordinate function of managerial and economic issues. In fact, some core claims of the Human Resource Management movement were also accepted by NPM doctrines. For example, the importance of ethics, decentralisation, responsibilisation and job autonomy.

Still, the HR function remained among the least influential in most organisations, and competitive strategies have not typically been based on the skills, capabilities and behaviours of employees. Moreover, formalised social dialogue and employee participation deteriorated in many western European countries and was replaced by various forms of employee voice. Ever new performance management and performance assessment instruments were increasingly criticized

---

49 Paul Thompson.: The Trouble with HRM. *Human Resource Management Journal*, Vol. 21, No. 4.2011, p. 363.

50 David A. Spencer.: Barbarians at the gate: a critical appraisal of the influence of economics on the field and practice of HRM. *Human Resource Management Journal*, Vol. 23, No. 4.201,3 pp. 346–359.

because they also brought new forms of performance measurement and accountability bureaucracy.

Consequently, despite new trends towards strategic management and performance management, HRM continued to be considered a soft issue and not related to business strategies. Literature on public management reform emphasized the importance of leadership but downplayed the importance of HRM for a long time, and "silo-thinking" dominated in both disciplines. In many cases, this is still the case. Public management theory is discussing the reform of HRM as a symptom of resource scarcity and efficiency. From the HRM perspective, this focus on managerial, economic and administrative issues has come under severe criticism as all organisations are dealing with people-oriented issues which inevitably require sophisticated HR interventions[51]. On the other hand, HRM literature was dominated by discussing the reform of HR as a contingency for public employees, focusing on HR policies and practices and failing to pay sufficient attention to the bigger picture, such as the importance of political, organisational and economical contexts for the way HR reforms are implemented, the impact of leadership skills and different leadership styles on individual and organisational performance, the link between HRM, work systems and learning organisations and the effects of public management reforms on HR reform outcomes as such[52]. The low importance of HRM in the public management discourse can also be explained by the grand tradition of the concept of "administrative neutrality" and the dominance of legal approaches. Consequently, the role and importance of emotions at the workplace is still widely under-researched and, sometimes, not even recognised in the public sector[53]. This is surprising as changing behaviours and attitudes is more than difficult and cannot be accomplished by a simple introduction of new rules, standards and HR policies.

As a consequence, Ulrich et al. (2012) claimed that "the bar has been raised for HR; HR must create and deliver value in real business terms"[54]. Did HR deliver? Is the public workforce more effective, efficient, innovative and motivated than decades ago?

---

51 Kusum Sahdev, Susan Vinnicombe and Shaun Tyson.: Downsizing and the changing role of HR. *The International Journal of Human Resource Management*.1999, p. 909.

52 Todd Jordan/R.Paul Battaglio.: Are we there yet? The state of Public Human Resource Management Research. *Public Personnel Management*, Vol. 43 (1).2014, pp. 25–57.

53 Russel Cropanzano/Jorgan H. Stein/Thierry Nadisc.: Social justice and the experience of emotion. Routledge, New York.2011.

54 Dave Ulrich/Jon Younger/Wayne Brockbank/Mike Ulrich.: HR from the Outside in, McGraw Hill. 2012, p. 9.

Especially saving policies provide a significant example of the importance of achieving vertical integration between business, management, leadership, organisational reform and human resource strategies[55]. Literature points to the importance of line managers to the efficacy of HR practice and as a driver of organisational performance. However, during times of budgetary crisis, managers are required to serve organisational targets and have little understanding of why trust levels in leadership decline and HR experts are calling for the introduction of soft-instruments and point to the importance of intrinsic motivators.

Despite all these limitations and "silo-thinking" within the different disciplines, there are at least four core claims to which most public management scholars, organisational experts and HRM professionals subscribe.

- First, budgetary pressures have placed additional performance pressure on organisations to become more strategic in their management of employees. While some sector differentiation is made, it is through employees that enhanced efficiency and performance levels can best be developed[56]. For example, literature on job engagement is almost unanimous on the positive link between employee engagement and organisational performance[57].
- Second, there has been a shift away from traditional Taylorist management practices that involve the attempt to control employees towards those which seek to win employee commitment and generate motivation. The essence of this argument is that Taylorist labour management practices, with their emphasis on mechanistic work systems and a focus on controlling employees, simply do not work in an environment where organisations must develop the competences, skills and motivation of their workforces[58].
- Third, both workers and managers can increasingly be beneficiaries of the new approaches to work and employment. This is because in an environment where employee skills and commitment are central to organisational success, it is precisely by motivating and involving employees more that organisations will gain more. Increasingly, HRM is based explicitly or implicitly on a pluralist perspective of competing, but containable interests amongst the different

55 Adrian Thornhill/Mark N.K.: The meanings, consequences and implications of the management of downsizing and redundancy: a review. *Saunders Personnel Review*, Vol. 27 No. 4. 1998, p. 291.

56 Paul Thompson & Bill Harley.: HRM and the Worker, in: Peter Boxall/John Purcell/ Patrick Wright. In: Oxford Handbook of Human Resource Management, Oxford. 2007, p. 148.

57 Sahdev/Vinnicombe/Tyson, Downsizing and the changing role of HR, op cit, p. 909.

58 Thompson/Harley, HRM and the Worker, op cit, p. 148.

actors. Successful strategies therefore rely on the "principle of aligning employer and employee interests"[59].

- Fourth, in many OECD countries, innovation and renewal of work systems have tended to be overlooked by the dominant innovation literature which has focused on technology studies. In the meantime, there is an increased interest in linking theories on learning organisations and innovative work systems with the renewal of HRM.

The four claims implicitly assume that—at least in theory—there has been a move from classical hierarchical control structures to commitment as "command and control": coercion and rules are displaced by values, trust and self-direction as a means of coordination.

Another implicit assumption is that, despite budgetary pressures and the need to consolidate public finances, it is possible to increase efficiency, effectiveness, innovation and productivity by the way of changing work systems and employment practices.

In the following, we will discuss whether these claims can be confirmed by empirical findings in the central public administrations in OECD countries.

2.3 Linking organisational- and HR reforms with reform effects

Organisations change with time and differ from county to country and from sector to sector and organisation. Gouldner claimed in the 1950s that there is not only *one* "bureaucracy" but a plurality of bureaucratic systems[60].

At the same time, HRM—as an academic discipline—has grown in complexity[61]. This concerns the development of motivation theory and the expansion of leadership theories, the link between HRM and organisational performance[62]

---

59 Thompson/Harley, HRM and the Worker, op cit, p. 149.

60 Giuseppe Bonazzi.: Geschichte des organisatorischen Denkens (Veronika Tacke (Editor), 2nd edition, Springer VS, Wiesbaden. 2014.

61 Paul Boselie/Graham Dietz/Corine Boon.: Commonalities and contradictions in research on human resource management and performance. *Human Resource Management Journal*, Vol. 15, Issue 3.2005, pp. 67–94.

62 Meera Alagaraja.: HRD and HRM Perspectives on Organisational Performance: A Review of Literature. *Human Resource Development Review*, Vol. 12 (2).2012, pp. 117–143; Richard A. Posthuma/Michael C. Campion/Malika Masimova/Michal A. Campion.:, A High Performance Work Practices Taxonomy: Integrating the Literature and Directing Future Research. *Journal of Management*, Vol. 39, No. 5, July 2013, pp. 1184–1220.

and new evidence in the field of social dialogue, participation and voice[63]. Currently, HRM tries to distance itself from its stuffy and traditional welfare image and confirms its significance for corporate profitability, performance and innovation[64] while balancing different employee and employer interests with the need for change, discipline and stability. Today, HRM is the preserve of scholars from management, organisational theory and the behavioural sciences with an interest in leadership, organisational justice, psychological, motivation, engagement, performance and social aspects of human interaction and organisational behaviour.

Therefore, at least in theory, HRM is no longer a purely technical issue because of its traditional focus on HR issues such as recruitment, selection, payroll, benefits, employee relations, performance management, industrial relations and legal issues. Instead it has become an integral part of management, organisational theory and the behavioural sciences with an interest in leadership, organisational justice, motivation, engagement, performance and social aspects of human interaction and organisational behaviour.

Nowadays, it is widely accepted that the design of work systems is closely linked to organisational learning and individual performance. Still, one of the main challenges in the field of organisational theory and HRM is to develop and measure OECD-wide aggregate measures that can be used to measure the relation between work systems, HRM, organisational learning and innovation[65]. So far, empirical work on these links has only been carried out by the European Foundation for the Improvement of Living and Working Conditions (and to a lesser extent by the OECD). Basically, Eurofound has come to the conclusion that where work is organized to support high levels of discretion, team working, learning levels and job complexity, in solving complex problems, organisations tend to be better performing and more active in terms of innovation. For example, Eurofound distinguishes between discretionary learning forms,

---

63 John Godard.: The psychologisation of employment relations?. *Human Resource Management Journal*, Vol. 24.2014, pp. 1–18.

64 Ashly Pinnington/Rob Maqcklin/Tom Campbell.: Introduction: Ethical human resource management, in: Ashly Pinnington/Rob Maqcklin/Tom Campbell (eds.), Human Resource Management, Ethics and Employment, op cit, p. 1.

65 Pierre, J. Richard/Timothy M. Devinney/George S. Yip/Gerry Jonson.: Measuring Organisational Performance: Methodological Best Practice. *Journal of Management*, Vol. XX, No. X.2009, pp. 1–86; Wes Martz.: Evaluating Organizational Performance: Rational, Natural, and Open System Models. *American Journal of Evaluation*, Vol. 34 (3). 2013, pp. 385–401.

lean production models, Taylorist models and traditional forms of organisation and analyses a number of work variables (such as the degree of job discretion at work)[66].

Table 1: Work organisation variables across the classes (in % of employees)

		Work organisation classes				*Total*
		Discretionary learning	Lean production	Taylorist	Traditional or simple	
Autonomy in work	Methods of work	88,9	65,5	10,5	43	60,1
	Speed or rate of work	88,1	65,1	21,6	51,5	63,2
	Order of tasks	79,8	60,7	14,6	43	56,2
Cognitive dimensions of work	Learning new things	86,7	90,2	38,1	27,7	68,5
	Problem-solving activities	95,8	94	53,6	45,7	78,9
	Complexity of tasks	78,5	85,5	34,9	16,8	61,7
Quality	Self-assessment	80,1	92,1	58	24,1	69,7
	Quality norms	75,7	96,6	91,6	36,8	77,8
Task rotation		40,9	79,1	42,4	26,3	48,6
Teamwork	With control over task division	33,8	47,3	14,4	16,4	30,6
	Without control over task division	23,8	42,2	45,5	18,5	31,9
Monotony of tasks		23,8	59,2	75,4	36,9	45,1
Repetitiveness of tasks		11,6	39,1	41,2	16,7	25,3

66 European Foundation for the Improvement of Living and Working Conditions (Eurofound).: Working Conditions in the European Union: Work Organisation, Dublin. 2009.

		Work organisation classes				*Total*
		Discretionary learning	Lean production	Taylorist	Traditional or simple	
Work pace cons-traints	Automatic	4,1	46,6	60,6	5,7	26,3
	Norm-based	41,1	76,3	73,9	15,7	52,4
	Hierarchical	25,7	67	69,4	30,9	45,7
	Horizontal	36	85	64,9	25	52,4
Demand-driven without direct customer contact (or almost never)		15,2	24,2	25,9	11,4	19
Assis-tance	From colleagues	74,2	81,6	62,4	62,4	71,9
	From hierarchy	66,4	63,9	48,4	49,7	59,5
Sample		38,4	25,7	19,5	16,4	100

Note: Weighted proportions of employees in each work organisation class and in total population, in percent. For example, "88.9% of the employees grouped in the discretionary learning class of work organisation experienced autonomy in word methods, compared with only 60.1% of employed population as a whole".
Source: Eurofound (2009), Working Conditions in the European Union: Work Organisation, Dublin, p. 13

Overall, Eurofound concludes that work organisations differ considerably according to countries, sectors and employment categories.

Table 2: Distribution of work organisation classes, by country (%)

		Work organisation classes				**Total**
		Discretionary learning	**Lean production**	**Taylorist**	**Traditional or simple**	
Continental countries	AT	47,3	22,4	18,3	12	100
	BE	43,3	24,6	16,3	15,8	100
	DE	44,3	19,9	18,4	17,4	100
	FR	47,7	23,8	17,5	11	100
	LU	42,7	29,6	13,9	13,8	100

		Work organisation classes				Total
		Discretionary learning	Lean production	Taylorist	Traditional or simple	
Eastern countries	BG	20,6	27,2	32,7	19,5	100
	CZ	28	26,7	22,5	22,9	100
	EE	40,7	33,4	11,2	14,7	100
	HU	38,3	18,2	23,4	20,1	100
	LT	23,5	31,1	22	23,4	100
	LV	33,4	34,5	17,1	15	100
	PL	33,3	32,6	18,9	15,2	100
	RO	24	33,4	27,6	14,9	100
	SI	34,9	32,1	16,7	16,3	100
	SK	27,2	21	33,8	18,1	100
Nordic countries and the Netherlands	DK	55,2	27,1	8,5	9,2	100
	FI	44,9	29,9	12,6	12,7	100
	NL	51,6	24,3	11,4	12,7	100
	SE	67,5	16	6,9	9,6	100
Northwest countries	IE	39	29,2	11,3	20,5	100
	UK	31,7	32,4	17,7	18,2	100
Southern countries	CY	26,4	27	21,2	25,4	100
	EL	24	29,1	22,6	24,3	100
	ES	20,6	24,6	27,5	27,3	100
	IT	36,8	24,1	24,6	14,6	100
	MT	45,6	34,2	12,1	8,2	100
	PT	24,9	30,3	32,5	12,3	100
EU27		38,4	25,7	19,5	16,4	100

Source: European Foundation for the Improvement of Living and Working Conditions (2009), Working Conditions in the European Union: Work Organisation, Dublin, p. 22

There is no space here to discuss these findings. Suffice it to say that it is of great importance to continue this type of work in the field of central public administration. Unfortunately, to our knowledge, there is no existing study which has ever analysed the impact of the different work system variables in central public administrations. Instead, most studies focus on the effects of individual HR policies and employment practices.

What is known is that central public administrations in OECD countries focus on different work system variables which lead to different individual and organisational engagement, motivation and performance levels.

Work systems have also to do with the way the organisational aspects of work and the way work itself is organised (*e.g.* Taylorised jobs, supervised group work, self-managing teams, hierarchical and bureaucratic jobs, highly autonomous professional jobs etc.).

In order to improve the level of analysis as regards the development of work organisations and the link between innovation and organisational learning Eurofound constructed 20 variables that cover different variables of work organisation.

Table 3: Variables for work organisation: EWCS 2010[67]

Variables		**% of employees**
Learning new things in work		69.4
Problem solving activities		81.6
Complexity of tasks		55.2
Using one's own idea		52.1
Monotony of tasks		44.2
Team work	Members decide on division of tasks	32.9
	Members do not decide on division of tasks	27.3
Horizontal constraints on work pace		40.3
Hierarchical constraints on work pace		36.9
Numerical constraints on work pace		34.4
Demand-based constraints on work pace		72.0
Meet quality standards		70.6

67 European Foundation for the Improvement of Living and Working Conditions.: Fifth Working Conditions Survey, Dublin. 2012.

Variables	% of employees
Responsibility for quality control	70.8
Discretion in fixing work methods	64.1
Discretion in setting order of tasks	63.0
Help from colleges	69.2
Help from manager	58.5
Management holds meetings	56.6
Consulted on work targets	43.5
Consulted on choice of partners	19.9
Involved in improving work processes	43.0
Number of observations	*22736*

Source: Fifth Working Conditions survey, European Foundation for the Improvement of Living and Working Conditions Coverage: Service sector; weighted data.

As an example, the first four indicators analyse the degree of organisational learning within work organisations. Provision of autonomy, using one's own ideas, problem solving capacities and discretion in how employees perform their work appear to have prominent places in explaining impact across a number of innovations[68].

However, in many central public administrations, these indicators are rarely supported. For example, the variable "using one's own ideas" was not applied as much public administration function according to hierarchical and bureaucratic principles. On the other hand, horizontal and vertical constraints on work pace and job content were common.

Only recently, a growing awareness of both organisational and managerial aspects of work systems and employment practices has influenced the abilities (A), motivations (M) and opportunities (O) of individual employees (the so-called "AMO" model)[69].

---

68 Eurofound (2012), Work organisation and Innovation, op cit., p. 48.

69 Peter Boxall & Keith Macky, Research and theory on high-performance work systems: progressing the high involvement stream. *Human Resource Management Journal*, Vol. 19, No. 1, 2, January 2009, pp. 3–23.

> "In other words, every HR system works through its impacts on the skills and knowledge of individual employees, their willingness to exert effort, and their opportunities to express their talents in their work. However, HR systems also affect a range of variables on a more collective level, helping to build organisational capabilities, and influencing the organisational culture, and social and psychological climate in which individuals are embedded (*e.g.* Snell, 1999; Evans and Davis, 2005). How management deals with employee voice, including attitudes to employee unions or other forms of representation, forms part of this collective level (Wood and Wall, 2007). HR systems which help to enhance trust in management and/or among peers improve an organisation's 'social capital', the quality of relationships within and across groups (Leana and Van Buren, 1999). The individual and collective levels are inextricably linked because the performance opportunities of individuals and their motivations are influenced by the quality of resources, collaboration and trust in their working environment"[70].

The AMO model[71] underlines the need to influence at least three variables positively:

a) Employee ability to perform (they have the right skills, knowledge and aptitudes),
b) Employee motivation to perform (they will do the job because they are incentivized) and
c) Employee opportunity to perform (the work structure, processes, values and culture provide the necessary support).

Current budgetary constraints and HR reforms influence individual ability (A), motivation (M), and the opportunity to perform (O).

Although nobody knows the precise relationship between these three variables, it is clear that measures taken in the context of the financial crisis (such as reducing budgets for skill development, dismissals, reducing job protection, longer working hours, etc.) may have significant side effects on these variables. Thus, the ideal HR model in the context of the budgetary crisis would be one that delivers on the basis of the AMO model and combines these with the need for more efficiency, innovation and organisational learning.

---

70 Boxall/Macky, Research and theory on high-performance work systems, op cit, pp. 3–23.

71 See for a good introduction: Peter Boxall and John Purcell.: Strategy and Human Resource Management, 3rd edition, Palgrave MacMillan. 2011, pp. 5.

Nowadays, human resource management theories are increasingly linked with organisational and work system theories as well as with employer and employee interests[72]. Researchers and practitioners have found that organisational performance is substantially improved by organisational systems that leverage the above mentioned AMO variables while supporting organisational interests.

These systems are often called "high-performance work *systems*" (HPWSs). Numerous studies have demonstrated that organisations adopting HPWSs will have better operational and financial performance through enhanced intermediate outcomes such as increased job satisfaction and productivity and also reduced turnover and less absenteeism[73]. "HPWSs can be viewed as coordinated bundles of High Performance Work Practices (HPWPs) that create synergistic effects in which certain practices reinforce one another to increase organisational efficiency and effectiveness".[74]

In the meantime, an established body of literature suggests that high-performing work organisations require integrated business and HR strategies, considerable job discretion, problem-solving activity, job engagement, involvement in decision-making, communication and the ability to develop skills on the part of employees.

Figure 1: The link between HRM, Strategy and Performance

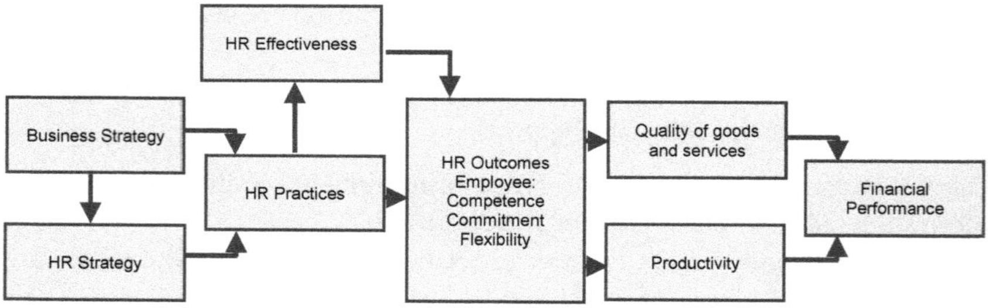

Source: Guest D., Michie J., Sheehan M., Conway N. and Metochi M.: Effective People Management: Initial findings of the Future of Work study. London, CPID. 2005, p. 5.

72 See for example: Randell Schuler/Susan E. Jackson.: Human Resource management and organisational effectiveness: yesterday and today. *Journal of Organisational Effectiveness, People and Perf*ormance, Vol. 1, No. 2.2014, pp. 35–55.

73 Richard A. Posthuma/ Michael C. Campion/ Malika Masimova/ Michael A. Campion.: A High Performance Work Practices Taxonomy: Integrating the Literature and Directing Future. *Research Journal of Management,* Vol. 39 No. 5, July 2013, p. 1184/1185.

74 Ibid.

If evidence can be hardened about the relationship between HRM, innovative work systems, leadership styles and organisational performance, this could also have significant implications for the future design of work systems and HR policies in the national central public administrations in OECD countries. It could also be a way to better combine organisational and HR reforms with the need to consolidate public finances.

Figure 2: Innovations, work systems and outcomes

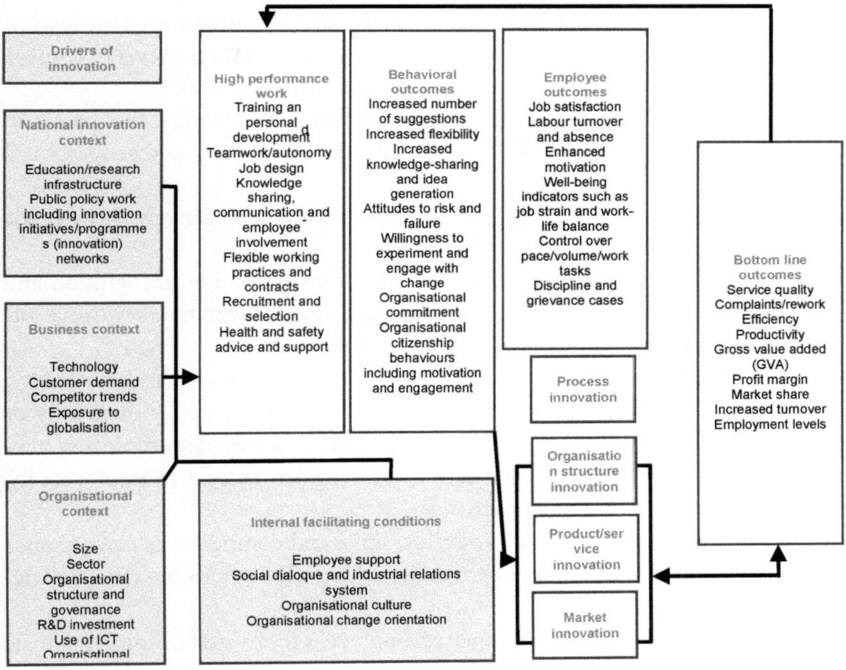

Source: European Foundation for the Improvement of Living and Working Conditions (2012), Work Organisation and Innovation, Dublin, p. 13

Thus, the way OECD countries organise work systems and design employment practices at the central public administration level has a strong impact on organisational outcomes. Still, more work should be carried out as regards the identification of variables and measurement of indicators for high-performance, high-innovatiom and creative workplaces[75]. This again suggests the need for an integrative approach.

One way of doing this could be by analysing organisational and job characteristics and linking these to outcomes such as job satisfaction, job commitment, job engagement, learning opportunities, innovation capacity, etc.

- *Degree of responsibility/scope of tasks.* What is the level of tasks and responsibilities exercised by an employee and how does this relate to work motivation, job satisfaction and job commitment?
- *Job control.* What is the degree of control, the level of autonomy or the level of discretion over operational aspects of work and how does the level of control, autonomy or discretion relate to motivation and satisfaction?
- *Flexibility/Stability.* What is the degree of flexibility/stability that exists in tasks and roles over time? What are the effects of functional and geographical job mobility?
- *Workload.* Workloads can be perceived positively or negatively. How is the workload and job intensity developing?
- *Communication, recognition and feedback.* Communication, recognition and feedback are considered as important motivational determinants within a job. Is the job combining one, two or all of these elements?
- *Participation, involvement and interdependence.* Performance and motivation levels vary according to whether tasks/roles are performed individually or are assigned to a group (or team) of employees and whether employees have the possibility to influence the decision-making processes. Are employees involved in decision-making processes?
- *Development.* Opportunities to develop skills and competences can enhance individual and organisational performance levels. Do employees enjoy job development perspectives?
- *Intrinsic and extrinsic motivation.* Are employees motivated through intrinsic and/or extrinsic motivators? Is the internal reward system related to the type of motivators?

---

75 T. M. Amabile.: The social psychology of creativity. New York, NY: Springer-Verlag. 1983; M. Amabile.: A model of creativity and innovation in organisations.In: B. M. Staw & L. L. Cummings (Eds.), Research in organisational behaviour (Vol. 10, pp. 123–167), Greenwich, CT: JAI Press. 1998; T.M. Amabile.: Creativity in context. Oxford, UK: Westview Press. 1996; T. M. Amabile.: Motivating creativity in organisations: On doing what you love and loving what you do. *California Management Review*, 40(1). 1997, pp. 39–58; T. M. Amabile/E.A. Schatze/G.B. Moneta/S.J. Kramer.: Leader behaviours and the work environment for creativity. *Leadership Quarterly*, 15. 2004, pp. 5–32.

- *Leadership*. There is no good practice in leadership. In fact, effect leadership differs according to context and situation. However, there is no denying that good leadership (transformational, transactional, situational, ethical, etc.) is crucial. How is leadership affecting the job characteristic and employee performance?

This model is similar to Hackman and Oldham's (1976) job characteristics model (JCM) which explains how five sub-variables of work systems (skill variety, task identity, task significance, autonomy and feedback) contribute to different psychological states of mind and important effects on organisational performance. The model also underlines the importance of communication, problem-solving and learning as independent HR variables[76]. These components are more likely to be effective if they are supported by a particular organisational culture, varying leadership styles and fair HR policies concerning pay, training, career development and HR planning[77].

In the following, we will discuss how work systems and HR employment practices could be linked and, following this, analysed: "The analysis illustrates that the state of research on organisational theory and HRM is emerging into an era that requires researchers to challenge conventional wisdom about organisation structures, job design, organisation culture, employee expectations and motivation and the related HR systems and processes required to implement new ways of working (Flood *et al.*, 1996; Sparrow, 1998). HR practices, in this sense, provide the backbone upon which the relative success of significant organisational changes rests (Ulrich, 1998)"[78].

Today, most experts believe that trends in HRM are towards a move to non-Taylorist learning work organisation and agree upon the proposition that new forms of HR strategies and HR practices are associated with superior performance[79]. However, current changes take place in very different contexts and in many different forms. Because of the bureaucratic heritage and the still-existing specific features in central public administrations, many work systems still differ considerably from the discussed theoretical scenarios.

---

76 Hackman, J. R. and Oldham, G. R.: Motivation through the design of work: Test of a theory. *Organizational Behavior and Human Performance*, 16. 1976, pp. 250–279.

77 Eurofound, 2009, op cit.

78 Kusum Sahdev/ Susan Vinnicombe/Shaun Tyson, Downsizing and the changing role of HR, op cit, p. 908.

79 Eurofound, 2009, op cit, p. 153.

In fact, in OECD central public administrations, organisational differences range from lean, traditional, hierarchical, bureaucratic, Tayloristic and professional to highly-innovative and learning organisations.

Current research in organisational behaviour is interested in exploring how employees' perceptions of organisational structures, HR policies and leadership influence their work-related thoughts and behaviours and how transformational and transactional leadership supports organisational performance. Also, literature on engaging employees[80] has become popular and advocates the link between engagement levels and organisational performance. The latter is the more interesting as different engagement levels seem to correlate with individual performance, organisational performance and levels of innovation. There is also an emphasis on engagement that encourages and rewards learning and is positively linked to organisational performance. However, the level of engagement depends on many variables, such as the design of the work organisation, leadership, work environment, working conditions and the psychological contract between the employee and the employer.

Figure 3: Predictors that influence work engagement significantly

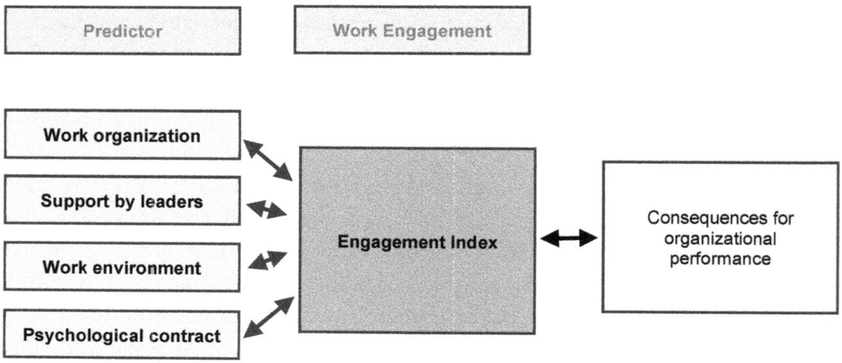

Source: German Federal Agency of Work

80 Jamie Gruman & Alan M. Saks.:, Performance Management and employee engagement. *Human Resource Management Review*, Vol. 21.2011, pp. 123–136; David MacLeod & Nita Clarke, Engaging for Success, Report to Government, no year.

Employees who rate their work organisation, the support of their leaders, the work environment and the psychological contract highly have significantly better results in work engagement as well.

Still, the literature on the importance of job engagement is far from conclusive and even sceptical, as the concept as such operates in "different worlds" (Guest, 2014) and is concerned either with employee well-being or with organisational performance[81]. Purcell (2014) argues that the concept lacks a contextual understanding and that the concept of engagement pictures a person "so engrossed in work that it can only ever apply to a minority of employees"[82]. This again leads to a negative view of employees who are not fully engaged and a psychologisation of employment relations where problems of motivation and "engagement" can easily be attributed to individual phenomena: "This is a dangerous reduction of work relations to individual attributes and failings"[83]. There is a clear danger that, increasingly, employees who are not fully engaged are described in negative terms implying this is their own fault…[84] Next, self-efficacy theory[85] explains why employees want to be engaged and committed. People with a strong sense of efficacy approach difficult tasks as challenges and are motivated through engagement. Consequently, employers want engaged employees, too. However, this "ideal combination" leads to a situation where, as Rosa states[86], employers exploit their "engaged" employees without exchanges: for example, as regards offering decent work conditions.

Thompson and Harley (2007)[87] suggest that the current trend is not towards one best-practice work system model but towards a hybridization of HR strategies and hybridization in work organisation. They argue that many discussions on *change* in the field of work organisation rests on a dichotomous distinction

81 David Guest.: Employee engagement: a sceptical analysis. *Journal of Organisational Effectiveness, People and Performance*, Vol. 1, No. 2.2014, pp. 141–156; see also: John Purcell (2014), Disengaging from engagement, in: Human Resource Management Journal, Vol. 24, No. 3, pp. 241–254.

82 Purcell: Disengaging from engagement, op cit, p. 242.

83 Purcell: Disengaging from engagement, op cit. p. 244.

84 Purcell: Disengaging from engagement, op cit, p. 245.

85 A. Bandura.: Self-efficacy: Towards a Unifying Theory of Behavioral Change. *Psychological Review*, No. 84.1977, pp. 191–215; A. Bandura.: Self-Efficacy: The exercise of control, New York. W.H. Freeman. 1997.

86 Hartmut Rosa.: Resonanz: Eine Soziologie der Weltbeziehung, Suhrkamp. Frankfurt/M.2016.

87 Paul Thompson/Bill Harley.: HRM and the Worker.In: Oxford Handbook of HRM, op cit, pp. 147.

between high-performance forms of work organisation[88] and a more traditional and hierarchical "bureaucratic", "lean production" and/or "Taylorist" form. This dichotomy is a reductionist reading of the organisational literature, which is rich in complex typologies[89]. In fact, many organisations on central public administration level combine many elements of high-performance work systems with established Tayloristic-, rule-bound, hierarchical and traditional bureaucratic models. Also, different types of employees work in different work systems. For example, whereas top civil servants increasingly enjoy modern work system contexts, this is not the case for lower-level employees. As regards different occupations, Eurofound concludes that there is no trend towards one best way management practice[90]. Moreover, the number of employees having access to work settings characterised by high levels of learning, complexity and discretion is relatively stable and differs enormously amongst sectors and countries[91]. This trend is alarming, as evidence is hardening about the link between innovative workplaces, learning organisations, high performance workplaces and organisational performance. One reason for these mediocre results can be that discretionary learning forms of work organisation are characterised by high levels of training, long-life learning, teamwork and learning cultures. Since learning and problem solving abilities are central to new innovative and learning organisations, it can be expected organisations adopting them will invest in training and skill development[92]. However, as we will see later on in the empirical part of this survey, investments in training are strongly decreasing, at least in many European countries.

Also, Arundel/Lorenz/Lundvall and Valeyre (2007) come to the conclusion that pure organisational types are unlikely to be found in the real world[93], and that "each form of work organisation tends to be associated with particular

88 See Bradley L. Kirkman/Kevin B. Lowe/Dianne P. Young.: High Performance Work Organizations, Center for Creative Leadership. 1999.

89 Other authors use different typologies such as learning community, professional organisation, lean service and traditional organisation and distinct 'cultures' of innovation which are associated with different sets of HR practices.

90 European Foundation for the Improvement of Living and Working Conditions.: Working Conditions in the European Union, Work Organisation, Dublin. 2009, p. 15.

91 European Foundation for the Improvement of Living and Working Conditions, Working Conditions in the European Union, Work Organisation, op cit, pp. 17–27.

92 European Foundation for the Improvement of Living and Working Conditions, Working Conditions in the European Union, Work Organisation, op cit, p. 27.

93 Arundel/Lorenz/Lundvall and Valeyre.: op cit, p. 10.

sectors and occupational categories"[94]. In Europe there are "wide differences in the importance of the four forms of work organisation across European nations. The discretionary learning forms of work organisation are most widely diffused in the Netherlands, the Nordic countries, and to a lesser extent, Germany and Austria, while they are little diffused in Ireland and the southern European nations. The lean model is most in evidence in the UK, Ireland, and Spain, and to a lesser extent, in France, while it is little developed in the Nordic countries or in Germany, Austria and the Netherlands. The Taylorism forms of work organisation show almost the reverse trend compared to the discretionary learning forms, being most frequent in the southern European nations and in Ireland and Italy. Finally, the traditional forms of work organisation are most in evidence in Greece and Italy, and to a lesser extent, in Germany, Sweden, Belgium, Spain and Portugal each form of work organisation tends to be associated with particular sectors and occupational categories. This raises the question of what part of the variation in the importance of these forms across EU nations can be accounted for by the nation's specific industrial and occupational structure, or by other unexplained national factor s that could influence the use of specific organisational forms".[95]

Cordery and Parker[96] distinguish between three existing grand archetypal work system configurations: a) "mechanistic" work systems, b) "motivational" work systems and c) "concertive" work systems.

The content of work activities within the mechanistic work system is typically characterized by high levels of job specialization, tight constraints on the manner in which work is performed (low discretion) and little variation in the tasks performed (low variability). For these reasons, jobs that arise within such configurations are frequently described using adjectives such as "simplified," "narrow," "deskilled," "fragmented" or "standardized". Furthermore, work activities are invariably organised with an individual (rather than a group) as the focus of task performance and accountability (low interdependence). Mechanistic work systems clearly have the primary objective of delivering efficiency-related outcomes.

In contrast to the mechanistic archetype, "motivational" work system configurations are founded upon prescriptions for work content that are seen as being

94 Arundel/Lorenz/Lundvall and Valeyre.: op cit, p. 13.

95 Ibid.

96 Cordery and Parker.: Work Organization. In: Peter Boxall/John Purcell/ Patrick Wright, Oxford Handbook of HRM, op cit, pp. 187.

intrinsically motivating or psychologically empowering for those performing the work—that is, the work involved satisfies innate psychological needs such as those for autonomy, competence and relatedness.

"Motivational" strategies

1. Arrange work in a way that allows the individual employee to influence his or her own working situation, work methods, and pace. Devise methods to eliminate or minimize pacing.

2. Where possible, combine interdependent tasks into a job.

3. Aim to group tasks into a meaningful job that allows for an overview and understanding of the work process as a whole. Employees should be able to perceive the end product or service as contributing to some part of the organisation's objectives.

4. Provide a sufficient variety of tasks within the job, and include tasks that offer some degree of employee responsibility and make use of the skills and knowledge valued by the individual.

5. Arrange work in a way that makes it possible for the individual employee to satisfy time claims from roles and obligations outside work (e.g. family commitments).

6. Provide opportunities for an employee to achieve outcomes that he or she perceives as

desirable (e.g. personal advancement in the form of increased salary, scope for development of expertise, improved status within a work group, and a more challenging job).

7. Ensure that employees get feedback on their performance, ideally from the task as well as from the supervisor. Provide internal and external customer feedback directly to employees.

8. Provide employees with the information they need to make decisions.

Source: Parker and Wall 1998: 20, in: Cordery and Parker, Work Organisation, in: Peter Boxall, John Purcell, and Patrick Wright, Oxford Handbook of HRM, op cit, p. 197

Concertive work systems are sometimes referred to as team-based or high-involvement models of work organisation. They form a part of the definition of High Performance Organisations[97]. The aim of the "concertive" work system is to put in place a participative model of working arrangements: "Overall, the mechanistic model is characterised by its focus on efficiency, simplicity, low levels in job discretion, variability, feedback, and interdependence"[98]. The motivational work system is focused on job motivation and job commitment with high job discretion, and the concertive work system emphasizes high levels of job engagement and team working.

Table 4: A taxonomy of work content characteristics associated with different work system archetypes[99]

Work System	Scope	Discretion	Variability	Demands	Inter-dependence	Feedback
Mechanistic	Low	Low	Low	Physical	Low	Low
Motivational	High	High	Moderate	Cognitive	Moderate	High
Concertive	High	High	High	Cognitive and affective	High	High

Source: Cordery/Parker, Work Organisation, Peter Boxall, John Purcell, and Patrick Wright, Oxford Handbook of HRM, op cit, p. 194.

2.3.1 Reform effects: The search for empirical evidence

So far, the empirical analysis of variables for work organisations has generated evidence to which employees in certain mechanistic models (which are characterised by an absence of autonomy, high degree of repetitive work, little job control and high internal and external constraints) express the greatest dissatisfaction with the work. On the other hand, variables such as job autonomy, teamwork, participation, involvement, communication, problem solving activities, ethical, transformational and transactional leadership seem to suggest that these variables produce higher levels of performance, job satisfaction and job commitment as distinct from the mechanistic model practices of traditional Taylorist systems of management[100].

---

97 See Bradley L. Kirkman/Kevin B. Lowe/Dianne P. Young.: op cit.

98 Cordery & Parker.: op cit.In: Boxall/Purcell/Wright, Oxford Handbook of HRM, p. 203.

99 Cordery & Parker.: In: Boxall/Purcell/Wright, Oxford Handbook of HRM, op cit, p. 194.

100 Eurofound.: Work organisation and Innovation.2012, op cit, p. 10.

We can only speculate that there is a great variety of work systems amongst countries and even within central public administration level. Consequently, it would be wrong to qualify one country as reform laggard and another country as best-practice country.

In reality, some organisations in some countries will correspond more to one model whereas others will correspond more to another. There is no clearly superior model, as each model is offering a distinctive value and advantages and disadvantages for individuals and organisations. Even the mechanistic work system may be more efficient and less stressful in some cases but offers few motivational incentives. The concertive approach may be motivating but is also more complex and bears the risk of more job intensity. Moreover, there is no automatism to which both the motivational and concertive approach offer more flexibility, innovation and performance outcomes, as their overall effect on organisational effectiveness has been less consistently demonstrated[101]. Therefore, Cordery and Parker (2007) conclude that "the effectiveness of any particular work system will be determined by the degree of consistency amongst its constituent elements. If team working or empowerment is not supported by appropriate changes to supervisory leadership, or the reward system continues to only reward individual performance, or if the technology either over determines the manner of task performance or generates few real opportunities for collective decision and action, then concertive configurations are obviously less likely to flourish"[102].

As regards concertive work systems, the literature focuses on the development of teams that are relatively autonomous and in which the members are heavily engaged and committed.

In fact, evidence suggest that many concertive work practices which include innovative work practices, autonomous teamwork, flexible job assignments, intensive communication and training achieve higher levels of productivity than more traditional approaches, including the mechanistic model[103]. The reason for this is basically that providing employees with the autonomy to control their own work is linked to psychological and physical health and, by extension, to increased productivity through lower absenteeism and sickness rates (Chandola,

101 Cordery & Parker.: In: Boxall/Purcell/Wright, Oxford Handbook of HRM, op cit., p. 203.

102 Cordery & Parker. In: Boxall/Purcell/Wright, Oxford Handbook of HRM, op cit., p. 202.

103 European Foundation for the Improvement of Living and Working Conditions.: Work organisation and Innovation, Dublin. 2012, p. 50.

2010; cited in Gallie, 2011)[104]. The intrinsic effects derived from concertive work systems such as teamwork and job complexity can also lead to higher levels of job motivation, engagement and satisfaction.

Concertive and cooperative styles of management are increasingly in vogue and also gaining ground in the design of performance management systems. At least in theory! This is in accordance with the main body of management literature which positively links engagement, participation and teamwork to motivation. However, this should not be interpreted in the sense of "the more participation the better" since participation and teamwork also have implications with regard to cost, time and power[105]. Still, other models seek to explain organisational performance by evaluating the levels of stress experienced by staff with reference to the level of job control. Here, control refers to how much discretion employees have over the tasks they perform and how they undertake them. However, it can also be that employees within the mechanistic system experience more job control, less stress and less job intensity than employees in the concertive work system.

Without going too much into detail, it is important to mention that the term High Performance Work Practice (HPWP) is linked to some aspects of the concertive work system (and including variables such as discretionary learning, autonomy and job control) whereas "lean production", the hierarchically structured Taylorist form and the "traditional" organisation are described as aspects from the mechanistic model based on a simple management.

Therefore, the definition of HPWP is useful but need further refinement of indicators[106]. Moreover, discussions of HPWP and concertive work systems require a more realistic approach, as reality is mostly a mix between the three models. To convince organisations of the benefits of specific types of work systems and HR bundles, it is essential to invest in more research on the impact of different sub-aspects of work systems on organisational performance[107].

---

104 European Foundation for the Improvement of Living and Working Conditions (2012), Work organisation, op cit, p. 32.

105 Christoph Demmke/Gerhard Hammerschmid/Renate Meyer.: The Impact of Individual assessments on organizational Performance in the Public Services of EU Member States, Luxemburg, Official Publications of the EU. 2007, p. 54.

106 Cordery & Parker. In: Boxall/Purcell/Wright, Oxford Handbook of HRM, op cit, p. 202.

107 Eurofound, Work organisation and Innovation, op cit, p. 50.

Terms like "teamwork", "participation", "social dialogue" or "involvement" also come with different meanings in different administrative cultures[108]. For example, whereas "participation" —especially in countries with a tradition of co-determination such as Austria and Germany—can be understood as a legal and formal concept, in other countries it is understood in the sense of "staff consultation". However, in most cases, participation is different than consultation, which normally implies that lower-level staff is simply asked to provide data, knowledge, information etc.

Thus, engagement, participation, staff involvement and communication cannot be implemented through top-down directives. Superiors have to believe in the benefits of engagement and participation and "live" it on a daily basis. In addition, they must be convinced that taking into account opinions from the staff will have positive effects. At the same time employees must show trust in their superiors' willingness to involve their subordinates—and not only because of formal obligations.

A study from Szabo (2007)[109] indicates that participative forms of management differ across cultures. According to this comparative study, Sweden has the highest degree of management participation followed by Germany, Austria and the Netherlands. On the individual level, it seems that older managers tend to be more participative than younger ones, and female managers more than male (although as regards to the latter, evidence is less clear). However, the degree of allowing participative forms of leadership also depends on the question how far managers want to avoid feelings of insecurity. The more the managers want to control things in order to avoid such feelings the more they will restrict staff involvement, communication and staff participation in setting and revising targets.

Despite such positive evidence, "the devil is in the details". While everybody seems to agree about the need for more and better communication, staff involvement, engagement and participation, the practical implementation of these concepts in daily administrative life at central administration level may be quite different. In fact, participation, engagement, involvement of staff and feedback, in many cases, seems to be more preached than practiced. In "Management by

---

108 See for example: Tony Boivard & Elke Löffler.: Public Management and Governance, Routledge, Cheltenham.2015; Berry Tholen.: Citizen Participation and bureaucratization: the participatory turn seen through a Weberian lens. *International Review of Administrative Sciences*, Vol. 81.2015, pp. 585–603.

109 Erna Szabo.: Participative management and culture, Peter Lang, Frankfurt/M. et al. 2007.

whose objectives?" Levinson[110] pointed out that "top management typically assumes that it alone has the prerogative to a) set the objectives, b) provides the rewards and targets, and c) drive anyone who works for the organisation"[111].

It somehow remains questionable whether top managers (are able and willing to) take enough time, communicate and involve their employees sufficiently in the decision-making process. In fact, it seems that top managers still prefer top-down approaches instead of participative approaches[112], sometimes also for understandable reasons: "The field of organisation development teaches that the best way to manage change is to encourage the maximum amount of participation by all affected parties. But, a rational cutback process will require that some people and programs be asked to take greater cuts than others. By encouraging participation, management also encourages protective behaviour by those most likely to be hurt the most. The participation paradox confronts management with a nearly insoluble problem: How does one single out units for large sacrifices who have people participating in the cut process? The usual answer is to avoid deadlocks or rancorous conflict and allocate cuts across-the-board"[113].

The concept of "communication" and "feedback to the staff" also causes considerable challenges[114]. Despite the positive meaning and the importance of communication and feedback in practice "people avoid feedback because they hate being criticised, plain and simple"[115]. In addition to this, many superiors are also afraid of bringing bad news in difficult times. Another problem is also obvious: particularly in times of financial constraints, downsizing and political turbulence, many employees regard concepts such as job engagement and motivation management rather cynical and as a call for working harder in a tough context.

All these difficulties and challenges clearly do not mean that attempts to introduce innovative work systems and more communication, job engagement, feedback and staff involvement should not be pursued. The critical experiences should only illustrate that reality occasionally looks different, however. Popular

---

110 Harry Levinson.: Management by whose objectives?, 1970, reprinted in *Harvard Business Review*, Harvard., January 2003, Vol. 81, Issue 1, pp. 107–116.

111 Levinson (2003), Management by whose objectives?, op cit, p.

112 Christoph Demmke/Gerhard Hammerschmid/Renate Meyer (2006), Decentralisation and Accountability as a Focus of Public Administration Modernisation, op cit.

113 Charles H. Levine.: More on Cutback Management: Hard Questions for Hard Times. *Public Administration Review*, Vol. 39, No. 2 (Mar. – Apr., 1979), p. 181.

114 Ibid.

115 Jay M. Jackman &Myra H. Strober.: Fear of Feedback. *Harvard Business Review*, April 2003, p. 31.

ideas of the developments towards more innovative work systems, teamwork, job engagement and participative approaches have to be freed first of all from all too naive and normative expectations.

Administrative reform should also be aware of trendy management advisers who often spin an unrealistic yarn about administration by giving the impression that hierarchic and bureaucratic administrative structures have long since ceased to exist. Despite a number of decentralisation trends, in reality, almost all administrative models continue to be based on the principle of "hierarchy" and bureaucracy[116].

An empirical study by Vie[117] comes to the conclusion that post-bureaucracy is "only a language construction that has little impact on everyday practice in organisations. Especially the proclamation of a general downfall of hierarchic structure in organisations stands in sharp contrast to the empirical reality"[118]. In fact, reported radical breaks from the past are exaggerated. In reality, new elements of work practices are gaining ground without replacing old ways[119]. Vie concludes that the work practices of top managers change faster than of middle managers who are still preoccupied with administrative routine and bureaucratic control.

Eurofound studies in the public and private sector confirm Europe-wide trends towards hybrid work organisations and no development towards one best-practice innovative learning model. Eurofound revealed that new forms of work organisation at least partly fail to enhance employee discretion and lead to enhanced managerial control and more work intensification. At the same time, many Taylorist approaches to work remain widespread (especially in the field of accountability and performance management) and new forms of work organisation have not necessarily displaced traditional approaches. Moreover, tough austerity measures have also shown that much of the above-mentioned theoretical assumptions only mask other trends towards traditional mechanisms of bureaucratic rationalization, work intensification and aspects of scientific management: "The rhetoric of devolved decision making and 'working smarter not harder' was countered by qualitative research showing work intensification and multi-tasking under modified traditional methods, dubbed variously democratic Taylorism or participative rationalization. To gain competitive advantage through interactive service work, companies frequently seek to generate high commitment and shared identity, but

---

116 Christoph Demmke/Gerhard Hammerschmid/Renate Meyer (2006), Decentralisation and Accountability as a Focus of Public Administration Modernisation, op cit.

117 Ola Edvin Vie.: Have post-bureaucratic changes occurred in managerial work?. *European Management Journal*, Vol. 28. 2010, pp. 182–194.

118 Vie.: Have post-bureaucratic changes occurred? op cit, p. 191.

119 Vie.: Have post-bureaucratic changes occurred?, op cit, p. 191.

these interventions are built on top of traditional controls"[120]. Thus, overall change seems to be towards the increased hybridity of control structures as environments and organisational structures become more complex[121].

These trends are confirmed by Demmke and Moilanen who measured the (non-) existence of traditional bureaucratic features (as described by Max Weber) in the national central public administrations in the EU Member States)[122]. Demmke and Moilanen used a set of fourteen indicators and measured whether HR policies and organisational structures can still be considered as bureaucratic systems. They concluded that the national central public administrations (civil services of the EU Member States) are a rather heterogeneous group of countries with different structural characteristics. Organisational structures range from (still very) bureaucratic features in Greece to post bureaucratic features in Sweden.

Figure 4: Traditional bureaucracy – post-bureaucracy continuum score by EU Member State

0% = traditional bureaucracy, 100% = post-bureaucracy (*) Non-career system country

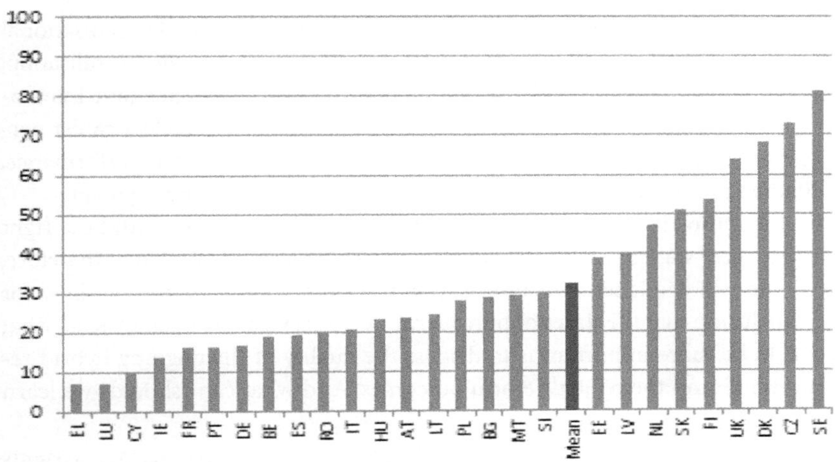

Source: Christoph Demmke & Timo Moilanen, Civil Services in the EU of 27, op. cit., pp. 187–188.

120 Thompson & Harley, HRM and the Worker, op cit, p. 153.

121 Thompson & Harley, HRM and the Worker, op cit, p. 154.

122 Christoph Demmke and Timo Moilanen.: Civil Services in the EU of 27, Peter Lang, Frankfurt/M. et al.2010; See also Carl Dahlström/Victor Lapuente/Jan Teorell.: Dimensions of Bureaucracy, A Cross-National Dataset on the Structure and Behavior of Public Administration. *Quality of Government Working Paper Series* 2010:13, University of Göteborg.

If the traditional bureaucracy is slowly disappearing, what will happen to the attitudes, values, motivation and performance levels bureaucrats and civil servants? The decline of classical bureaucratic systems and the changing values and societal norms reveal the urgency of a new discussion: how is public employment changing in times of government restructuring and changing into Governance? What are the effects of changing employment patterns on Public Service Motivation (PSM)? Do we still need civil servants with a specific public law status? Should there be fewer differences between public and private sector employment? If not, for whom and in which sectors should distinctions be upheld? Do we live the emergence of an entirely new public employment model?

In the 21st century, issues such as innovative and high-performing workplaces have become quasi-sacrosanct principles. Nothing seems more attractive than novelty and flexibility. This is a counter-reaction to the overly rigid, hierarchical and bureaucratic times until the end of the 20th century. However, in the meantime, awareness is growing that too much flexibility, decentralisation and innovation also have negative side-effects.

Thus, HR scholars aim at the right mix between flexibility and organisational stability, mobility and expertise, a strong public service ethos, decentralisation, outsourcing and professional coordination structures, coherence and integration. It has also been shown in many cases that job stability and clear career perspectives can have a strong and positive impact on organisational performance, individual motivation and the attractiveness of public sector employment.

In the future, it seems that the real challenge will indeed be to find the right mix between stability, security, rigidity, flexibility and adaptability. Therefore, Demmke and Moilanen conclude that current developments do not allow for the conclusion that the times of bureaucratic civil services are over. Instead, what seems to be more important is to discuss the quality of the ongoing hybrid reform trends and the related reform outcomes. And what can (should) we learn from this?[123]

Also Mayer-Sahling concluded in his analysis of the civil service systems in central- and eastern European states that there is "considerable variation"[124] Moreover, there is a difference between the existence of formal rules and an "implementation gap"[125]: "Clearly, the trends within the last two decades went clearly

123 Demmke and Moilanen, 2010, op cit.

124 Jan Mayer-Sahling.: The Sustainability of Civil Service Reform in Central and Eastern Europe Five Years after Accession. *SIGMA Paper* Nr 44. Paris: OECD Publications. 2009, p. 65.

125 Mayer-Sahling, 2009, The Sustainability of Civil Service Reform, op cit, *p. 68.*

into the direction of post-bureaucratic models"[126]. According to Mayer-Sahling, the large differences imply "that the CEE region can by no means be seen as one world of civil service governance. Instead, we can identify different groups of countries in CEE that share broad characteristics, levels of fit with European principles of administration and recent reform trajectories. This finding contradicts the expectation associated with the notion of the European Administrative Space, whereby administrative systems in the EU should converge on the basis of certain principles of administration"[127].

Mayer-Sahling concluded: "It remains to be seen whether the conditions for investment in civil service professionalization are currently improving or worsening. The current economic and financial crisis has hit the new CEE Member States particularly hard and has ambiguous consequences for the future of the civil service in these countries. On the one hand, it puts a further squeeze on public finances, which is bad news for civil service reformers, especially when taking into account the need for increased investment in civil service salary systems. For instance, several countries have already reduced salary levels and put off further salary reforms, which may be inevitable from a fiscal point of view but is unlikely to support the further professionalization of state personnel. On the other hand, it is conceivable that a new role for the state in the economy will affect the perception of the civil service by the public and by political actors. If a change in perception is accompanied by the recognition that the quality of the civil service can make a real difference, in terms of both the efficiency and effectiveness of the public sector and the intervention of the state in the market, then it is also conceivable that the conditions for reform of the civil service will improve in the years to come"[128].

2.3.2 Reconciling conflicting objectives

Thirty years ago, Levine wrote (Levine, 1979) "We know almost nothing about what works best under different kinds of cutback conditions. So, the first thing we need to develop is a baseline inventory of tools and techniques for managing cutbacks along with case studies of their application. With this information we can begin to sort out methods for scaling down public organisations and make some judgments about their appropriateness to solve cutback problems of different types and severity. Second, we need to find methods for solving the

126 Demmke /Moilanen, 2010, op cit.

127 Mayer-Sahling, 2009, The Sustainability of Civil Service Reform, op cit, p. 75/76.

128 Mayer-Sahling, 2009, The Sustainability of Civil Service Reform, op cit, p. 82.

credibility, civility, and consensus problems that plague organisations and governments during periods of large scale cutbacks. We need to invent and perfect democratic processes for allocating cuts which will make cuts effective yet equitable. Third, we need to devote a great deal of thought to the ethical dimensions of cutbacks. We need to ask, for example, what the ethical responsibility of an organisation is to its terminated employees and decoupled clients. No one to my knowledge has systematically struggled with this problem yet. Finally, we need to understand how cuts affect public expectations and support for government, i.e., whether expectations about government performance will be lowered and toleration for poor services will be increased"[129].

According to Levine, the reform of HRM in times of budgetary constraints is a symptom, a problem, and a contingency.

- It is a symptom of resource scarcity at a societal and even global level that is creating the necessity for governments to terminate or lower the activity level of some programs, confront trade-offs between new demands and old programs rather than to expand whenever a new public problem arises.
- It is a problem for managers who must communicate difficult reforms within prevailing structures that were designed under assumptions of better circumstances.
- It is a contingency for public employees and customers; employees must sustain their morale and productivity in the face of increasing control from above and shrinking opportunities for career development, pay increases and promotion while customers must find alternative sources for the services governments may no longer be able to provide[130].

Despite the importance of these issues, there is no existing comparative study world-wide that analyses how central public administrations organisations change (on the basis of commonly established indicators). Also this study is not looking into these issues. Therefore, we suggest that, in the future, more research should be invested in the analysis of work systems at central public administration level.

In large part, the consistent evidence of positive effects of new work systems and employment practices reflect the interdependence between work organisation, the choice of HR bundles and other contextual elements: "Aligning these

129 Levine, 1979, op cit, p. 183.

130 Charles H. Levine.: Organizational decline and cutback management. *Public Administration Review*, July/August 1978, p. 316.

subsystems to be coherent and internally consistent is difficult, especially when implementing motivational and concertive work systems that often require a quite radical departure from traditional mechanistic practices"[131].

So far, empirical evidence leads to the conclusion that many portrayed organisational and HR changes are also described as a caricature and many reforms do not entail a radical shift away from traditional models, but a more limited change to a different form of bureaucracy in which hierarchy, control and rules have been retained. In some cases, a form of bureaucracy-lite[132].

All existing empirical comparisons of how national HR systems on central administration levels adapt to the changing circumstances have so far produced a contrasting picture. Most of these comparisons are based on qualitative and literature research. Overall, there is very little factual and empirical evidence about reform outcomes in HR policies on the central public administration level which covers a vast array of activities and shows a huge range of variation across countries, sectors, organisations, work systems and HR policies.

In most countries, it becomes ever more difficult to identify differences between public and private sector employees.[133] Currently, job security is being reduced, recruitment procedures are being flexibilised, pay systems are individualised and linked to individual performance and career structures are modified and, in some cases, even abolished. As a consequence, civil service employment differs less from private sector employment than ever before. Moreover, the differences between civil service employment and public service employment are becoming less clear.

As an EU wide study on central public administration by Demmke and Moilanen (2013) shows, there is a trend towards the alignment of employment conditions between civil servants and other public (and also private sector) employees. Overall, differences between civil servants and public employees are getting less.

---

131 Cordery & Parker, Work Organisation. In: Boxall/Purcell/Wright, Oxford Handbook of HRM, op cit, p. 203.

132 Colin Hales.: Bureaucracy-lite' and Continuities in Managerial Work, in: British Journal of Management, Vol. 13, pp. 51–66.2002.

133 Celine Desmarais &Emmanuel Abord de Chatillon.: Are there Still Differences between the Roles of Private and Public Sector Managers. *Public Management Review*, Vol. 12:1.2010, pp. 127–149.

Table 5: Differences between civil service employment and public employment by policy issue and by EU Member State[134]

	Very much	Somewhat	Fairly little	Not at all	Cannot say
Pension system	25 (6) BE, CY, DE, DK, EE, ES	18 (5) EL, FR, IT, NL, SE	4 (1) PT	46 (11) BG, FI, HU, IE, LY, LV, LU, MT, PL, SI, SK	4 (1) EC
Job security	17 (4) BE, ES, FR, PL	50 (12) BG, DE, DK, EE, FI, HU, LV, MT, NL, PT, SE, SK	17 (4) CY, EL, LT, SI	13 (3) IE, IT, LU	4 (1) EC
Pay systems	20 (5) EE, FR, IT, LT, PT	36 (9) AT, BE, DE, EL, ES, MT, PL, SE, SK	16 (4) CY, HU, IE, NL	24 (6) BG, DK, FI, LU, LV, SI	4 (1) EC
Holiday arrangements	0 (0)	32 (8) BE, BG, EE, ES, IT, PT, SE, SI	24 (6) CY, DE, HU, IE, LT, PL	40 (10) AT, DK, EL, FI, FR, LU, LV, MT, NK, SK	4 (1) EC
Working time	4 (1) CY	20 (5) ES, HU, IT, PL, PT	28 (7) BE, EE, FI, IE, MT, SE, SK	44 (11) AT, BG, DE, DK, EL, FR, LT, LU, LV, NL, SI	4 (1) EC

134 It is important to note here that in Luxemburg the comparison concerns public law officials and labour law officials on the central level; in the Netherlands the comparison is between central public law officials and public sector employees with a labour law contract; in Germany state civil servants and public employees (all incl. federal employees) are compared; in Ireland established civil servants and unestablished civil servants are compared. Finally, in Finland the distinction is made between state employees with a public law status and central labour law employees.

	Very much	Somewhat	Fairly little	Not at all	Cannot say
Career development	32 (8) BE, CY, ES, FI, FR, IT, LT, PT	12 (3) BG, LV, MT	36 (9) DE, EE, EL, HU, IE, NL, SE, SI, SK	16 (4) AT, DK, LU, PL	4 (1) EC
Health insurance	4 (1) BG	20 (5) AT, BE, CY, DE, ES	16 (4) FR, MT, NL, SE	48 (12) DK, EE, EL, FI, HU, LT, LU, LV, PL, PT, SI, SK	12 (3) EC, IE, IT
Right to strike	17 (4) BG, DE, DK, EE	29 (7) CY, ES, FI, HU, IT, NL, SI	25 (6) IE, LU, MT, PT, SE, SK	25 (6) BE, EL, FR, LT, LV, PL	4 (1) EC
Recruitment procedure	36 (9) BE, BG, CY, ES, FI, FR, LT, LU, LV,	32 (8) DE, EE, EL, MT, PT, SE, SI, SK	20 (5) DK, HU, IE, NL, PL	8 (2) AT, IT	4 (1) EC
Ethical obligations	12 (3) BG, EE, LT	32 (8) DE, HU, IT, LV, NL, PL, SE, SK	12 (3) BE, IT, MT	40 (10) AT, CY, DK, EL, ES, FI, FR, LU, PT, SI	4 (1) EC-

Frequencies in parenthesis; Source: Demmke and Moilanen, Governmental Transformation and the Future of Public Employment, Peter Lang, Frankfurt/M., 2013, pp. 68–70.

Still, in only two EU countries recruitment procedures are the same for civil servants and public employees, job security only in three countries and pay systems only in six countries. Thus, despite alignment trend, differences are also maintained. Also HR practices in the private sector are not necessarily seen as a role model for the public sector. Almost no EU Member State envisages a complete harmonisation of employment features amongst the different public employment categories. This finding is intriguing as most of the experts only focus on the so-called alignment trend but less on the reasons why certain differences prevail.

The case of the EU shows that HR policies in OECD countries are also very different and are being implemented in very different contexts. Still, all countries (although to a different degree) are confronted with budgetary pressures and the need to consolidate public finances. Therefore, in this study, we also claim that consolidation in the field of HRM can be done in many different ways. We distinguish between a soft-reform path, responsible restructuring as a second reform path and tough cost-cutting as a third reform path. All three reform paths are connected to different reform effects. We will argue that all countries, independently of what kind of financial pressures they experience, have the possibility to choose amongst a certain types of reform instruments, the design of work systems, organisational reforms and HR reform bundles. Like this, all countries can steer and manage the effects of HR reforms and avoid negative reform outcomes. Thus, the crisis also bears huge opportunities: the identification of innovative HR practices and smart strategies.

The current challenge is not to show that certain work systems and HR practices are related to organisational performance. The real challenge is to explain why these practices are not fully implemented and the identification of the main obstacles to achieve a better situation. These issues involve a set of related "path dependency" questions. For example, why should countries like France and Germany abolish their traditional civil services other than for budgetary reasons? In both countries, the civil service is a two-hundred-years-old constituent and a highly-performing part of the system of government.

Still, we also wish to warn of the need for precaution. Especially in times of tough austerity measures, reform of work systems, change, reform and alignment of employment conditions may have an adverse effect on—rather than improve—working conditions, performance and motivation. Also, the proponents in favour of innovation, change and alignment may view the civil service status as an obstacle to realising cutbacks in terms of personnel in the civil service. Especially given the current pressure on public expenditure, innovation, reform and "normalisation" could be seen as a way to achieve budgetary cutbacks.

3. Methodology

3.1 Linking HR bundles and (un-) intentional reform outcomes

In order to avoid making ideological or personal judgments as regards the effects of HR reforms, we start from a general point of view to which the outcomes of public management and HR reforms can be positive and/or negative, effective and/or ineffective. Hesse et al. have presented a useful matrix to assess various effects of public management reforms[135]. According to this model, reforms may also have an impact not only on the main goal but also on some other goals. In other words, they may have positive or negative side effects, paradoxical effects or they may not have any side effects at all. This suggests that also positively intended policies, such as good government policies, integrity, anti-discrimination and anti-corruption policies are creating side-effects such as reform paradoxes[136]. From these combinations it is possible to construct a nine-fold table describing nine different effect combinations (see table). Applying this analytic framework to the field of HRM may also help to encourage a more rational discourse.

Table 6: Effects of public sector reforms (Source: Hesse/Hood/Peters, 2003, op cit)

	Impact on other goals		
Impact on major goal	**None** (no side-effects)	**Positive side-effects**	**Negative side-effects**
Positively effective main goal achieved	(1) *Simple effectiveness* (operation according to plan)	(2) *Effectiveness with a bonus* (objective reached with reinforcement of other goals)	(3) *Effectiveness plus jeopardy* (objective reached with some sacrifice of other goals)
Ineffective no effect	(4) *Simple futility* (e.g. "all talk and no action" in reform programmes)	(5) *Futility but with a bonus* (main target untouched but positive side-effects)	(6) *Futility plus jeopardy* (main target untouched but negative side-effects)

135 Joachim Hesse/Christopher Hood/Guy Peters (Eds.).: Paradoxes in public sector reform: An international comparison, Duncker and Humblot, Berlin. 2003.

136 Mark Evans.: Beyond the Integrity Paradox – towards good enough governance?. *Policy Studies*, No. 33:1. 2012, pp. 97–113.

	Impact on other goals		
Impact on major goal	**None** (no side-effects)	**Positive side-effects**	**Negative side-effects**
Negatively effective reverse effects	(7) *Simple perversity* (outcome the very opposite of the aim)	(8) *Perversity but with a bonus* (perverse effects on target but positive effect elsewhere)	(9) *Perversity plus jeopardy* (perverse effect on target plus other negative effects)

Therefore, our main (general) hypothesis in this study is that the present reform trends in the field of HRM have a number of positive and negative effects, but they also a number of unintentional positive and/or negative side effects, such as more bureaucracy, higher stress levels, more job intensity, less job control, higher leadership skill expectations, more ethical challenges etc.

A case for unintentional side effects is the situation even if strong economic growth and advance towards a knowledge society, together with high investments in skill development, leadership and good governance policies, can be in conflict with the political and institutional underpinnings of the merit principle, the destabilization of the standard employment contract, the deterioration of working conditions, the polarization between skilled and unskilled workers and the drastic reform of classical HR principles and policies.

Another example concerns (the still missing) link between organisational justice and performance. So far, there are only few studies existing on the relationship between organisational fairness and performance. For example, it may very well be that HR reforms in the context of performance management enhance the unfairness of decision-making and structures and, consequently, lead to the deterioration of task performance.

As already mentioned, in the field of public management, the strongest impetus for change is usually argued to come from the social, economic, organizaional and technological developments, whereby such trends are often depicted as "universal" for all OECD countries and thereby implicating a preference for "universal" solutions. Moreover, effects of reforms do not only depend on the impact of budgetary constraints but also on many other micropolitics variables such as leadership, communication, teamwork, skills, perception of organisational justice, organisational culture, qualification, age, function, ranking, experience, personal situation etc.

Our survey clearly shows that public administration and HR modernisation in almost all OECD countries is strongly driven by economic and budgetary pressures and this even increased after the financial crisis in 2008. However, this does not suggest that reform pressures and reform priorities are the same in all OECD countries. For example, demographic developments are a huge change factor in some countries (for example in Japan), whereas they are not in others (for example in Brazil).

Still, in this survey, we will focus on one variable/reform pressure: the effects of budgetary constraints on the number of HR reforms, the effects of HR reforms on trust levels in leadership and in the own organisation, workplace behaviour, job commitment, engagement, ethics and fairness perceptions.

Obviously, the choice of level of analysis should be determined by the outcome. Therefore, if the outcome is higher budgetary pressures, then the level of analysis may be the degree of reduction of personnel costs. If the level of analysis is organisational performance, then the level of analysis should be that of an integrated high performance system, the existence of high performance work systems and fair HR policies. If the level of analysis is job motivation, then we will have to analyse the relation between the implementation of HR reforms/HR bundles and effects on job motivation. If the focus of interest is staff competence and skill developments, then an analysis of training policies may be appropriate. Finally, one could argue that reducing pay and public employment is necessary after long years of steady increases in pay and public employment. The results will be efficiency gains and even enhanced productivity in those cases where intelligent restructuring processes are implemented. On the other hand, reductions in public employment and in pay may have severe effects on job motivation and morale. Again, the choice of analysis determines the answer to the question. Finally, training may be helpful to ensure a highly competent workforce. But training and development may also influence motivation. Overall, job ability and the opportunity to apply its own skills as well as team working, communication, job design and leadership contribute potentially to skill development and motivation. This case only shows how difficult it is to analyse effects of HR reforms.

Because of the complexity at hands, our survey will serve a more modest objective. We are particularly intrigued by three aspects:

- First, the "manner" in which OECD countries have implemented HR practices in the context of budgetary pressures after the outbreak of the financial crisis in 2008.
- Second, what kind of reform effect has been experienced?
- Third, what kind of relationship exists between the choice of reform bundles and reform effects?

As already noted, there is very little knowledge as to the management of fewer resources. One reason for this may be because the public sector as a whole has continuously expanded over the last four decades. Not long ago, nobody would have imagined that government organisations are neither immortal nor unshrinkable[137].

Charles H. Levine, More on Cutback Management: Hard Questions for Hard Times, in: Public Administration Review, Vol. 39, No. 2 (Mar. – Apr., 1979), p. 181 and 182

"Behavioural scientists have demonstrated that change is most easily accomplished when the people affected have something to gain, but under conditions of austerity the acceptance of change will be unlikely because the rewards required to gain cooperation and build consensus will be unavailable. Second, public organisations are confronted with professional norms and civil service procedures and collective bargaining agreements which constrain the ability of management to manage budgetary constraints. Third, organisational contraction produces some serious morale and job satisfaction problems which make it difficult to increase productivity to make up for the cuts. Fourth, cutbacks reduce the enjoyment of working and managing in an organisation because nearly everyone is forced into a position of having to do with less. Under these conditions, creativity diminishes, innovation and risk taking decline, and the sense of excitement that comes from doing new things disappears. Next, when dealing with productivity, it takes money to save money. Productivity improvement requires upfront costs incurred by training and equipment expenses. Under conditions of austerity, it is very difficult to find and justify funds to invest in productivity improvement, especially if these funds can only be made available by laying off employees or failing to fill vacancies. Finally, „The Efficiency Paradox," is perhaps the most important and most troublesome to public managers. This paradox stems from two ironies of public management. First, it is one of the hard realities of cutback management that it is easier to cut inefficient and poorly managed organisations than those that are efficient and well run. Inefficiency creates slack and waste that can be easily identified for cuts. Efficiency, on the other hand, tends to enmesh slack resources in the organisation's core tasks by encouraging the commitment

137 Levine, 1978, op cit, p. 316.

of spare resources to long-term planning and capacity-building activities. When cuts are to be taken across-the-board, efficient organisations are likely to be penalized more than their poorly performing peers because they will be forced to make much tougher decisions about who, what, and how cuts will be distributed. Also, efficient organisations have a difficult search for more productivity gains because they are likely to have already exhausted most of the easy and obvious productivity improvement strategies. For poorly performing organisations the task is much simpler: to achieve higher performance, all they have to do is borrow the management practices and productivity ideas already employed by high performing agencies"[138].

In order to systematically evaluate the effects of the budgetary crisis on HRM reforms, we start by analysing whether OECD countries are introducing specific HR bundles in an effort to cope with recessionary times[139]. We are also interested to know whether alternative policies and practices are open to Governments as they seek to balance the negative effects of austerity measures on HRM and whether countries may adopt internally consistent bundles of HRM policies and practices to stave off the negative impact of the crisis[140].

HR bundles are a "distinctive coherent combination of practices built around an organisational logic"[141]. In our survey, we distinguish between bundles in the field of public employment, the management of salaries, training policies, saving measures in the field of HRM, changing working hours and working time, job security and status reforms.

Teague and Roche[142] distinguish between technical and behavioural HRM bundles:

- Technical HRM bundles are mostly aiming at cost control measures and reducing operational spending. These include the reduction of personal, pay reductions, recruitment freezes, savings in training policies, short-time working,

138 Levine, 1979, op cit, p. 181 and 182.

139 Paul Teague & William K. Roche.: Recessionary bundles: HR practices in the Irish economic crisis. *Human Resource Management Journal*, Vol. 24, no 2, 2014, pages 176.

140 Paul Teague, William K. Roche, op cit., p. 177.

141 David Guest/Neil Conway/Philipp Dewe.: Using sequential tree analysis to search for "bundles" of HR practices. *Human Resource Management*, Vol. 14. 2004, p. 81.

142 Paul Teague, William K. Roche, op cit.

temporary lay-offs, furloughs, incentivized sabbaticals and voluntary departures, reducing contract or agency employment and pension reforms etc.

- Behavioural HRM bundles are primarily intended to ensure that the motivation and commitment of employees are retained in otherwise difficult retrenchment programmers. Practices falling under behavioural HRM bundles include employee and union engagement measures, and competency development.

Thus, countries may either choose a "soft" approach or a "hard cost control", situational, contingent approach. The "soft" approach involves a focus upon behavioural instruments and fostering employee motivation, commitment and development. It is an approach that acknowledges the importance of HRM to the aims of the business, whilst reflecting attempts by management to create a work environment that emphasises employee development, through practices such as training, participation and communication, and the importance of having innovative, flexible, committed employees who are valued resources.

The "harder cost control" approach focuses on technical bundles and views HRM effectiveness as contingent upon cost minimisation measures rather than upon significant investment in human resources. A "harder" contingency-based approach to HRM is often seen as an essential part of a cost-minimisation strategy.

Often, pure downsizing and restructuring programmes concern themselves exclusively with technical bundles such as payroll cost reductions and reductions of personnel. No complementary measures are undertaken either to sustain motivation, morale or commitment. Studies carried out by Eurofound[143] also find that many of these reforms have been implemented without engaging unions, staff representatives and employees in problem solving.

We expect that most OECD governments seek to adjust their HR systems mostly by introducing technical bundles and by controlling compensation costs through pay cuts, pay freezes, pension reforms and downsizing policies, cutting training budgets and more rigorous performance assessment processes.

The effectiveness of these technical, cost-control HR bundles has been discussed and analysed in the literature. Most authors come to the conclusion that the focus on these measures (and especially on downsizing) produces a number of negative effects, such as low morale, less commitment, deskilling trends, limited productivity improvements and increased financial performance[144].

143 For example, European Foundation for the Improvement of Living and Working Conditions.: Working Conditions in Central Public Administration, Dublin. 2013.

144 Wayne F. Cascio.: Strategies for responsible restructuring. *Academy of Management Executive*, Vol. 19, No. 4 (Preprinted from 2002, Vol. 16. 2005, No. 3, p. 40.

Therefore, some countries may want to combine technical bundles with behavioural bundles. The latter instruments are primarily intended to ensure that the motivation and commitment of employees is retained through different employee and union engagement measures and measures that counteract the so-called survivor syndrome.

Teague and Roche[145] differentiate between organisations that follow different HR retrenchment paths:

a) Employment stabilisation paths,
b) Responsible restructuring and
c) Pure Restructuring paths.

According to Cascio, in the context of budgetary constraints, most organisations follow "pure downsizing" (Cascio, 2002) programmes that focus on cost reductions and downsizing.

Cameron[146] has defined downsizing as an intentional set of activities that usually involves three forms of downsizing:

a) Downsizing as a workforce reduction strategy,
b) Downsizing as a work redesign strategy and
c) Downsizing as a systemic strategy

These different strategies have different effects: "The firms that improved their performance were those that prepared for downsizing in advance. They invested time and resources in systematically analysing tasks, personnel skills, resource needs, time use, process redundancies, and inefficiencies (….). Increased communication and participation of employees in the downsizing process also were associated with improvement"[147]. In order to be successful, Cameron suggests 30 best-practice measures, and distinguishes between approach, preparation, involvement, leadership, communication, support, cost-cutting, measurement and implementation[148]. He concludes that the effective management of the human resource system is the most critical factor leading to successful downsizing, such as employee involvement, teamwork, communication, training and administrating downsizing in a trustworthy and fair manner.

---

145 Teague/Roche (2014), Recessionary bundles: HR practices in the Irish economic crisis, op cit, pp. 176–192.

146 Kim S. Cameron.: Strategies for Organisational Downsizing. *Human Resource Management*, Vol. 33, No. 2. 1994, p. 189–211.

147 Cameron (1994), Strategies for Organisational Downsizing, op cit, p. 201/202.

148 Cameron (1994), Strategies for Organisational Downsizing, op cit, p. 207–210.

The term responsible restructuring was invented by Cascio (2002/2005). Cascio differentiates between companies that see employees either as costs or as assets to be developed. He concludes that, often, the pure cost restructuring approach produces ten mistakes:

- Failure to be clear about long- and short term goals and the failure to consider alternative approaches to reducing costs
- Use of downsizing as a first resort, rather than as a last resort
- Use of non-selective downsizing
- Failure to change the ways work is done
- Failure to involve workers in the restructuring process
- Failure to communicate openly and honestly
- Inept handling of those who lose their jobs
- Failure to manage survivors effectively
- Ignoring the effects on other stakeholders
- Failure to evaluate the results of downsizing policies

Consequently, Cascio advocates responsible restructuring as an alternative to pure restructuring/downsizing. According to Cascio[149], responsible restructuring includes:

- "Carefully consider the rationale behind restructuring. Invest in analysis and consider the impact on those who stay, those who leave, and the ability of the organisation to serve its customers"[150]
- Consider the virtues of stability
- Before making decisions, managers should make their concerns known to the workforce
- Do not use downsizing as a "quick fix" to achieve short term goals,
- If dismissals are carried out, the process should be as fair as possible and be explained in a consistent manner,
- Regular communication is vital in the process,
- "Give survivors a reason to stay, and prospective new hires a reason to join"[151]
- Continue to train employees and managers in the new context
- Examine all HR policies in light of the changes taking place

149 Cascio, Strategies for responsible restructuring, op cit., p. 48 and page 49.
150 Cascio, Strategies for responsible restructuring, op cit, p. 48.
151 Cascio, Strategies for responsible restructuring, op cit, p. 48.

3.2 HR bundles and categorization of countries

Because of the difficulty of identifying "best practice" in public management reform, we are careful in making judgments because of the difficulty of finding methods for solving problems that plague organisations and governments in 32 OECD with different institutional systems and democratic systems. It is also difficult to invent solutions for all cases which will make austerity measures efficient, effective yet equitable and fair. Next, ideally one should also devote a great deal of thought to the ethical dimensions of budgetary constraints and cutbacks. Finally, we need to understand how cuts affect public expectations and support for government, i.e., whether expectations about government performance and leadership will be lowered and toleration for poor services and poor leadership will be increased[152].

As already discussed, this survey accepts the assumptions that performance in the field of HR is not possible without the right organisational context and the design of effective and fair work systems. On the other hand, organisational and individual performance is not possible without the right design of HR policies and instruments. As regards the latter, our survey rests on the theory of contextual work systems and HR bundles[153]. The latter theory claims that some combination of work systems and HR practices may have advantages above and beyond the implementation of general fashionable techniques[154]. Basically, the idea is that a particular bundle of HR practices has the potential to contribute improved employee attitudes and behaviours, lower levels of absenteeism and labour turnover, and higher levels of productivity, quality and customer service. This, it is argued, has the ultimate effect of generating higher levels of profitability. Since the HR practices that supposedly contribute to an improved bottom line performance are generally perceived as "good" for workers—for example, employment security, training and development, information and consultation, and higher levels of pay—this looks like an attractive scenario for employers and workers alike.

In order to systematically analyse the choice of HR bundles in the different countries, we have used a baseline inventory of different HR bundles and HR instruments for managing budgetary constraints. All OECD countries who have

152 Levine, 1979, op cit, p. 183.

153 Teague/Roche (2014), Recessionary bundles: HR practices in the Irish economic crisis, op cit, pp. 176–192.

154 Guest/Conway/Dewe, Using sequential tree analysis to search for 'bundles' of HR practices, op cit.

participated in the OECD survey have answered whether (or not) they have adopted these HR bundles and corresponding instruments. With this comparative database, it was possible to analyse and to compare the choice of HR bundles and the implementation of different instruments in the different countries.

Table 7: HR bundles – Indicators and Classification of countries

HR Bundles	Country
Changing Public Employment • Strong Decrease • Moderate Decrease • Stable • Increase Strong Increase	OECD country A, B, C, D ....
Changing public employment and use of instruments • Dismissals • Recruitment Freeze • Outsourcing • Annual Productivity targets • Non or partial replacement of retiring persons • Privatization • Decentralization of employment • Supporting of voluntary departures	
Changing salaries • Reforms implemented • Reduction of remuneration for top-level • Reduction of remuneration for all staff • Reduction or abolishment of allowances • Reduction of performance related pay • Pay freeze	
Changing Training Policies • Have training policies been affected • Reduction of budgets • Reduction of training days? • Measures introduced in order to increase efficiency • Assessment of training needs to ensure that it is only provided when necessary • Shift employee training to employment desk • Reduce travel costs to travel to events	

HR Bundles	Country
Cost Savings in the field of HRM • Use of furloughs • Reduce/cut hierarchical level of careers • Stop/put on hold promotion opportunities • Encouraging voluntary departures • Leaving allowances • Early retirement packages	
Changing Working hours/Working time • Reform of working hours • Increase of working hours • Reform of holiday entitlements • Decrease of number of vacation days • Decrease of number of public holidays • Change of calculation of paid leave • Less paid sick leave days • Measures to reduce absenteeism • Recommendation for preventive medical care • Limitation of paid sick days	
Job Security • Measures implemented in order to dismiss central workforce • In case of restructuring • In case of budgetary constraints • In case of shifting personnel • It has become easier to dismiss Civil Servants • Easier to dismiss public employees • Notice periods have been shortened	
Status reforms • Reforms of fixed-term employment • Substitution of Civil Servants because of cost reasons • Substitution because of shortages in employment • Substitution of civil servants because of recruitment freezes • Need for fixed-term employees in order to save resources • Employment of fixed-term because of budgetary constraints • Will budgetary constraints lead to abolishment of Civil Servants?	
Total Number of HR Bundles and reforms implemented	

The data allows us to analyse not only the choice of measures but also the focus on different instruments and the number of HR bundles and reforms that have been implemented.

By applying a similar methodology used by Teague and Roche (as discussed in this chapter), we are able to group the countries in three different groups:

a) Countries with a soft employee focused reform path,
b) Countries that follow a responsible restructuring reform path and
c) Countries with a tough cost control / downsizing path.

Table 8: Framework for recessionary bundles and reform trajectories in the field of HRM

Soft employee focused reform path	**Responsible restructuring**	**Tough cost control / downsizing path**
• No compulsory lay offs • Voluntary lay-offs • High use of communication/leadership to explain rational for HR bundles • Focus on efficiency, productivity, innovation and learning, skill training, reallocation and value management • Retention of staff • Abolishing seniority • Employees involved in developing options for responding to the recession • Further investments in skill, learning and innovation policies • Focus on Leadership • Introduced short-time working while maintaining pay	• Improved workforce planning • Relaxing Job Security • Reform of Civil Service Status • Flexibilisation of Working Time • Longer Working hours • Reform of Pension systems • Introduction of voluntary departures • Furloughs • Reform of holiday system • Active new health policies in order to reduce sickness rates • Reform of bonus system (cuts) • Dismissal for poor performance • Replacement of civil servants by more fixed-term employees • Increasing training efficiency • Reform of promotions • Professionalization of recruitment system, mobility policies • Maintenance of skill, learning and innovation and leadership policies • Introduced outsourcing after careful evaluation of added value • Set up new shared services after careful evaluation of added value	• Downsizing personal • Cut wages, reform pension system • Enhanced job security abolished • Working longer, reform of holiday system • Tightened discipline, time keeping and attendance requirements • Promotions and recruitments frozen • Reduction of civil servants • Abolishment of civil servant status • Enhanced outsourcing and introduction of new shared services • Staff performance managed more rigorously

Source: Adapted model of Paul Teague et al., Recessionary bundles: HR practices in the Irish economic crisis. *Human Resource Management Journal,* Vol. 24, no 2, 2014

We accept that, ideally, technical and behavioural measures should be combined and integrated. However, in reality, employee focused reform paths or responsible restructuring reform path strategies may only be implemented in countries where recessionary pressures are less acute and/or in organisations with high-commitment HRM policies, because these organisations are influenced by an HR philosophy treating staff as assets rather than costs.

We also expect that HR bundles will not necessarily be deployed in any systematic sense by countries. Thus, it is very well possible that countries without heavy consolidation pressures introduce heavy downsizing and cost-containment measures. It is also possible that a variety of adjustment routes are available to countries facing a different degree of difficulties and involving different bundles of HR practices as each combination of HR bundles has a different impact on employees, job satisfaction, moral, job commitment, trust levels etc.

Some studies on technical bundles suggest that these measures are likely to produce negative or even no effects if they are not supplemented by behavioural bundles that counteract what is commonly referred to as "survivor syndrome" —low morale and commitment among employees who escape the downsizing exercise. These measures may include complementary communication, engagement, HR development and culture change practices in downsizing programmes. In this way, the literature on downsizing recognizes the existence of behavioural complementarities: certain sets of HR practices, focused on motivation and commitment, are important complements to payroll-focused and work reorganisation practices as they enhance the effectiveness of such practices. In this vein, Casio advocates "responsible restructuring" based on the "3 Rs": redeployment, relocation and retraining (Cascio, 2009)[155].

Because of the complexity at hand in defining best – practices in choosing the most effective HR bundles, we have focused our work on a lower level: collecting and comparing the choice of instruments and the adoption of HR bundles in OECD countries during times of budgetary constraints.

It seems plausible to expect that our empirical research might lead us towards some kind of hypothesis and—then following—answer. For example, countries with high budgetary pressures that implement HR bundles and follow a tough cost control/downsizing path experience the most negative reform effects. On the other hand, countries with high budgetary pressures that follow a responsible restructuring path experience better reform effects. Or, alternatively, countries

155 Cascio.: Strategies for responsible restructuring, op cit, pp. 39.

with low budgetary pressures that follow a tough cost control / downsizing path also experience negative reform effects.

Thus, we are particularly intrigued by trying to link budgetary constraints, the choice of HR bundles and the evidence on effects of reforms. More specifically, we are interested in finding out whether OECD countries with different budgetary pressures implement different HR bundles and—consequently—experience different reform effects.

- H 1: Our main hypothesis is that countries with higher consolidation requirements and higher budgetary pressures (group one countries) will implement more HR measures (HR bundles) (Hypothesis 1). Overall, these countries will also introduce tougher cuts in operational measures, including a freeze of salaries and training budgets etc.
- H 2: Our second hypothesis is that any of these "tough" reforms will have an overall negative effect on the workforce (Hypothesis 2).
- H 3: Our third hypothesis is that countries with lower consolidation requirements introduce fewer HR measures (HR bundles) that may have either positive, negative, unintentional or mixed effects on the workforce (Hypothesis 3).
- H 4: We also expect that countries are introducing HR bundles that differ according to the national economic, political, cultural and organisational context. The choice of HR bundles may be similar for some countries or very different. OECD countries seek to adjust their HR systems in one way or another in order to ease budgetary pressures. For example, many countries may implement pay freezes and cuts, and also changes as regards wage structures, allowances and performance related pay. Other countries will focus on the introduction pension reforms and do little in the field of reform of wage structures. As regards downsizing, some countries may focus on the reduction of public employment by using dismissals and others by the outsourcing of personnel, incentives for voluntary departures, freezing of recruitment or non-replacing retiring staff. The choice of instruments is strongly determined by constitutional and legal requirement, the status of personal and "path dependency". Again, choices for the implementation of HR bundles differ and depend on the national context (Hypothesis 4).
- More concretely, we expect that countries which continue to invest in training despite budgetary pressures, and continuously develop high skills and competence, have a high level of job ability and job motivation and offer better opportunities to contribute to organisational performance.

- H 5: On the other hand, reducing training budgets and "axing" training policies have negative side effects on skill developments of staff and individual motivation. In order to perform well, employees must also have high fairness and justice perceptions, trust in the organisation and in the existence of professional and trustful leadership. Contrary to this, dismissals and unequal reductions of pay levels have negative consequences. Moreover, stopping promotion opportunities, relaxing job protection and threatening "job survival" also have many negative effects on job satisfaction, job commitment, trust in leadership and trust in organisations as such. Most countries with high budgetary pressures and very high consolidation efforts follow a tough cost control and downsizing path which include the above mentioned measures. Without the complementary introduction of behavioural HR bundles, mostly, no complementary measures are undertaken either to sustain motivation, morale or commitment. Following this, reform effects on personnel are negative as people are naturally attentive to the justice of events and situations in their everyday lives across a variety of contexts.[156]. This scenario strongly influences the individual behaviour and exerts a negative impact on individual and organisational performance[157] (Hypothesis 5).
- H 6: We assume that all countries have a certain degree of flexibility as regards the choice of reform measures and the choice of reform instruments. Still, we expect that countries with high budgetary pressures are guided by that "tough cost-control path" and by a focus on cost-minimisation whereas countries with fewer constraints are opting either for a restructuring approach or for a "soft" approach. The more difficult the economic situation, the harder the chosen approach (Hypothesis 6).
- H 7: We expect that only a minority of countries have implemented a soft employee focused reform path (which basically means no implementation of severe cuts in employment levels, pay, no cuts in training and no changes as regards job security etc.) Hypothesis 7).
- H 8: More common are responsible restructuring paths that combine technical and behavioural HR bundles and a pure downsizing path (Hypothesis 8).

156 Mark J. Martinko/Michael Gundlach/Scott Douglas.: Towards an integrative theory of counterproductive workplace behavior: A casual reasoning perspective. *International Journal of Selection and Assessment*, No. 1–2/2002, pp. 36–50.

157 A. de Schrijver/K. Delbeke/J. Maesschalck/S. Pleysier.: Fairness perceptions and organisational misbehaviour: An empirical study, *The American Review of Public Administration*, Vol. 40, No. 6/2010, pp. 691–703.

3.3 Shortcomings and further suggestions

In order to get more evidence on reform effects and reform outcomes, the OECD survey asked countries whether they carry out employee surveys and if so, in which policy field. Countries were also asked about evidence of reform effects as regards job intensity, job quality, sickness levels, trust levels, job satisfaction, job commitment, development of perceptions of unfairness etc. Still, the existing database is very thin and does not allow for important conclusions as regards the link between reform measures taken and reform effects. Also here, further research should aim at improving the existing data as regards the effects of reforms.

Another shortcoming concerns the bundle theory: whether or how countries' HR adjustment programmes during the recession involve technical and behavioural bundling and complementarities remains largely a black box[158]. We expect that OECD countries seek to adjust their internal employment systems in one way or another to survive. Most OECD countries try to consolidate public budgets via the introduction of downsizing measures, freezing of recruitment policies, non-replacement of retired employees, pay roll cost adjustment, which usually involves pay freezes and cuts, reforms of compensation systems and pension system reforms. We also expect that consolidation measures lead to more rigorous performance management and measurement processes, tighter controls of sickness policies, reduction of training budgets, changes in work organisation and higher job intensity and stress levels.

Overall, a full analysis of the situation is a complicated undertaking and requires additional work in the future. The bundle approach suggests that the synergies are achievable only with the adoption of all these practices, and that if one is missing the whole effect will be lost. For example, if one organisation implements new forms of job engagement and teamwork while maintaining individual approaches to performance related pay, effects will most likely be disappointing. Consequently, it is assumed that contradictions between HR practices will undermine the package as a whole[159]. Organisational justice theory has demonstrated how employees notice unfair and inconsistent HR practices. Inconsistencies between different HR practices are likely to be even more apparent in situations where employees experience different forms of organisational injustice.

158 Paul Teague/William K. Roche (2014), Recessionary bundles, op cit.

159 Mick Marchington & Adrian Wilkinson.: Human Resource Management at Work, Chartered Institute of Personnel & Development, 3rd edition. 2005, pp. 82.

The concept of bundles suggests that a particular set of HR policies (HR bundles) combined with a certain organisational context have the potential to bring about improved organisational performance. However, we also acknowledge some weaknesses of this approach[160]. One of the problems with survey research is that, while it may be possible to demonstrate links between work organisation, the choice of HR bundles and performance, it is unable to explain in any detail why this might happen. For example, it is as much likely that the use of a HR bundle which is composed of high commitment HR practices leads to improved performance as that high commitment HRM is made possible by high levels of organisational performance. Another weakness is what kind of HR bundles should be included. For example, whereas Pfeiffer includes job security, other authors do not. Also, the OECD survey only includes a restricted number of HR bundles. Other problems concern the different types of performance measurement that are used. For example, should organisational performance be measured as an objective or subjective criterion? Should profitability be applied or workers' productivity?

Bundles can also be "additive". Generally speaking, the more practices that are in place the better. In other words, it may be possible to adopt a large number of high commitment HR practices and ignore others, but still gain from the interactive effects of those that are in place. Questions then arise as to how many practices are needed to make a difference, from what areas of HRM these are to be drawn and whether certain practices are fundamental to make the synergies work[161].

Finally, it is assumed that organisations are free to choose which HR practices they wish to employ without considering any forces beyond their own organisational boundaries. However, central public administrations are rarely free to determine their own HR bundles, as many HR practices are determined by legal instruments, organisational culture or standardised practices.

Although the principle of bundling together HR practices may appear sound, what happens if the achievement of one of these practices contradicts with or undermines (some of) the others? For example, employers invest in training but make employment security conditional on the budgetary situation. Of course, there are many more possible cases and trade-offs amongst HR bundles.

160 Marchington/Wilkinson, Human Resource Management at Work, op cit., p. 91.
161 Marchington/Wilkinson, Human Resource Management at Work, op cit., p. 82.

3.4 Budgetary constraints and reform trajectories

As already discussed, the current crisis and the subsequent government responses have by now been extensively studied by international organisations and scholars from a political and economic perspective. Adding to this, public management, organisational theory, administrative sciences and HRM researchers are well-positioned to contribute to research on the crisis by bringing in the dimensions of cutback decision-making, the management of implementation of austerity measures and ultimately the impact of the crisis on public administration and public personnel itself. Still, the connection between budgetary constraints and administrative and HR reform is a complex one. On the one hand, budgetary constraints make it more difficult to reform because of the lack of financial resources. On the other hand, budgetary constraints make it easier to implement unpopular and radical options. Finally, it is important to add that major reforms occur within financial difficulties.

In the OECD survey, it was decided not to discuss other major HR reforms such as diversity policies, anti-discrimination challenges, combining private and professional life, promotion policies and pension policies. In all of these fields, major reforms have also been implemented because of many reform pressures and reform priorities.

Another point is that while everybody agrees that savings need to be made because of the financial crisis starting in 2008, for many governments, rising costs for personnel have also become a major concern and a subject of a new reform discourse. Compensation of employees in general government varies across member countries, and it is comparatively lower in Japan and Korea—around 6–7% of GDP in 2009—than in the Nordic countries— above 14% of GDP in 2009[162].

162 OECD.: Restoring Public Finances, 2012 Update, OECD: Paris.2012.

Figure 5: General government compensation of employees (2007–11)[163]

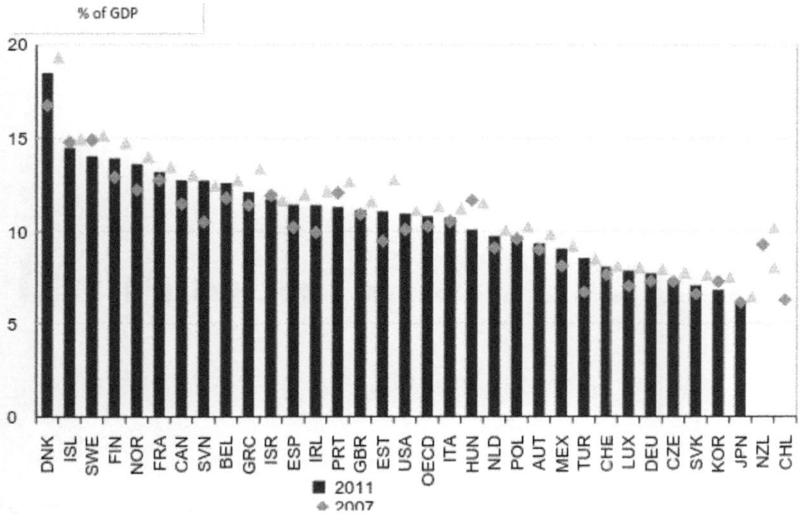

Notes: Data for Australia are not available. The 2011 data for Chile and New Zealand are not available and these countries are not included in the OECD average. Data for 2010 instead of 2011 were used for Canada, Israel, Japan, Korea, Mexico, Switzerland, Turkey and the United States. The statistical data for Israel are supplied by and under the responsibility of the relevant Israeli authorities. The use of such data by the OECD is without prejudice to the status of the Golan Heights, East Jerusalem and Israeli settlements in the West Bank under the terms of international law.
Source: OECD National Accounts Statistics. StatLink *http://dx.doi.org/10.1787/888932696970*

During the last years, compensation costs have also been linked to consolidation requirements. Almost all OECD countries try to consolidate national budgets via the reform HRM, operational costs and other budgets. Thus, HRM has become a direct target in the framework of national consolidation programmes. Still, OECD countries are facing different budgetary pressures and constraints, decide upon different reform priorities, face different consolidation needs and are responding differently to them.

163 Ibid.

Figure 6: Consolidation requirements to reduce government debt to 60 per cent of GDP

Change in the underlying primary balance, percentage points of GDP

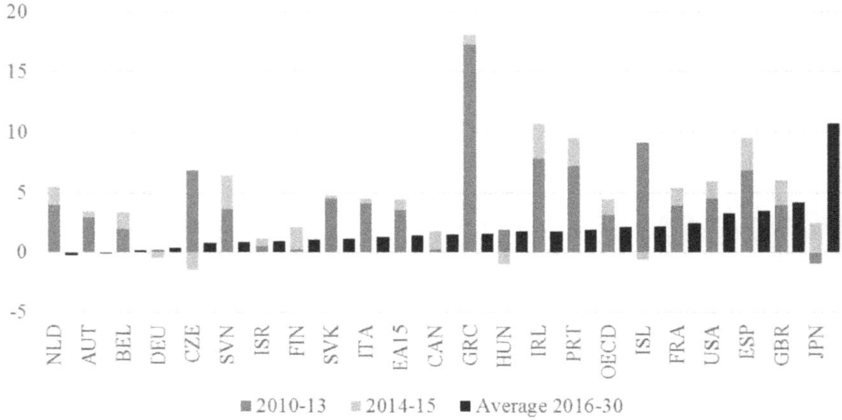

Note: The average measure of consolidation is the difference between the underlying primary balance in 2015 and the average underlying primary balance between 2016 and 2030, except for those countries for which the debt target is only achieved after 2030, in which case the average is calculated up until the year that debt target is achieved.
Source: OECD Economic Outlook 95 long-term database.

One hypothesis is that countries with higher consolidation requirements will also implement more radical HR reforms and cut operational measures more drastically than other countries with lower consolidation requirements.

Still, there are many ways to implement savings: the so-called egalitarian "cheese slicing", "doing more with less", "doing less with less", "decentralised priority setting", "centralised target setting" etc. The existing scholarly research has provided multiple insights about the implications and impact of the 2008 financial crisis on public administration. The crisis has been treated as both a dependent and an independent variable in theoretical and empirical works addressing different policy areas and aspects of public administration[164].

Until today, government responses to the crisis have been diverse; there have been "as many responses as countries" (Peters 2011, 76), and in many cases the responses have been diverging. (…). Although the number of publications in the fields of public administration and political science addressing the recent crisis

164 Walter Kickert & Tiina Randma-Liiv Riin.: Fiscal Consolidation in Europe: A Comparative analysis, COCOPS Trend Report. 2013, p. 3.

has been vastly growing during the past couple of years, there is still a lack of comparative studies based on common methodology[165].

So far, there is wide disagreement on the impact of consolidation policies on HRM. Current discussions can be grouped in three opposing opinions:

The first group criticises the negative effects of restructuring and downsizing policies on service delivery, job satisfaction, job commitment, trust levels and morale. According to this group, operational measures such as wage cuts, recruitment freezes and staff reductions have a negative impact on organisational performance and on the performance of the workforce. Another point of criticism concerns the fact that HRM is seen as a cost factor and the contradictions in the official discourse, although it is often suggested that the mantra that traditional sources of competitive advantage such as access to capital and advanced technologies must be supplemented by the ability to innovate, adapt, learn and develop new skills and that people are our most valuable asset has largely been a rhetorical one in most organisations[166]: "In fact, the harsh reality is that labour is often viewed merely as a cost to be minimized, particularly in tough times"[167].

The second group believes that cuts in operational expenditure are unavoidable, given the fact that government compensation costs continue to rise. Moreover, fiscal consolidation depends largely on spending restraint. Past experience shows that consolidation based on cuts is more likely to lead to long-term growth than relying on higher taxes and raising revenue (OECD, 2011, p. 30). Efficiency gains can also be achieved through intelligent restructuring, reorganisation policies, redeployment, outsourcing, privatisation and the introduction of shared services in order to render overly costly public administrations more efficient. Often this group is also arguing that public employment systems are over-regulated, not effective, risk averse and not innovative. Advocates believe that "doing more with less" is possible.

The third group believes that the present crisis bears risks and opportunities in order to make HR systems more innovative and productive. As regards risks, observers believe that reductions in operational expenditure have a positive impact on the short-term budgetary aims of government, "they may also act to the detriment of government's long-term capacity for service delivery"

165 Kickert/Randma-Liiv/Savi, Fiscal Consolidation in Europe, op cit, p. 4.

166 Ibid.

167 Adrian Wilkinson/Tom Redman/Scott A.Snell/Nicolas Bacon.: Field of Human Resource Management. In: Adrian Wilkinson/Tom Redman/Scott A.Snell/Nicolas Bacon (Eds.).: The SAGE Handbook of Human Resource Management, SAGE, London/Thousand Oaks/New Delhi/Singapore. 2010, p. 3.

(OECD, 2011, p. 51). On the other hand, opportunities exist by supporting concepts of learning organisations, innovative workplaces, responsible restructuring, context-embedded reforms and the creation of high performance work places. Accordingly, if HRM is managed professionally, it is also likely that it contributes significantly to organisational performance, organisational learning and innovation. Adherents of this group suggest that it is long established that professional HRM practices have a positive impact on motivation, knowledge, skills and behaviours of employees and contribute to better organisational and financial outcomes[168].

In the literature on cutback management, a number of categorisations of the cutback approaches have been put forth. In most cases, the usual economic classification of consolidation measures (see e.g. OECD 2011, 2012) into (operational and programme) expenditure and revenue measures has been followed. As regards consolidation measures, the OECD distinguishes between operational and programme measures.

The first category, operational measures, can be broadly defined as expenditure reductions of governments' running costs. These measures include wage or staff reductions, government reorganisation, and across-the-board efficiency reductions in the administration.

The second category, programme measures, reflects expenditures by functional classification in the *OECD National Accounts*. This classification includes health care, social benefit systems, old-age pensions, capital infrastructure, official development assistance and transfers to sub-national government.

In most countries, programme expenditure measures contribute more to consolidation than operational measures. However, many countries have also implemented important operational expenditures for savings such as wage cuts and staff reductions.

We have grouped the OECD countries in different budgetary constraint categories and classified the countries according to different budgetary pressures. This is not evident, as budgetary pressures vary enormously and are continuously changing. In principle, Governments can choose to spend their financial resources on a variety of goods and services. As of 2010, social protection, including social welfare, is the largest category of spending and is on an increasing trend when compared with 2007. The second-largest share of total expenditures

168 Saba Colakoglu/Ying Hong/David P. Lepak.: Models of Strategic Management, in: The SAGE Handbook of HRM, op cit, p. 31.

is spent on health, followed by education, which are both on a slightly decreasing trend from 2007.

In order to classify OECD countries into different budgetary constraint groups we have applied as a starting base a methodology which groups OECD countries according to (fiscal) consolidation requirements (OECD, 2012, p. 38; OECD, 2014, p. 239)[169]. The background for grouping countries in budgetary constraint typologies is changing constantly and it is not easy to group countries into different groups. During the last years, Greece, Ireland and Portugal have agreed upon a formal and ongoing programme with the International Monetary Fund, the European Central Bank, and/or the European Commission. These countries have formally committed to introducing substantial consolidation measures and wide-ranging structural reforms. In the meantime, Portugal and Ireland have been released from these commitments. As of 2007, Latvia and Estonia had started to implement similar harsh national austerity measures, but not in an international binding context. Other countries such as Spain, Italy, or the United Kingdom have started to implement similar measures or are continuously adopting new measures.

It should also be highlighted that for countries with a consolidation plan, the nature, content and size of the plan vary significantly depending on the country's fiscal position, the political and administrative context and the time frame of the consolidation plan. Thus, consolidation requirements may be translated differently depending on the specific national context. Moreover, fiscal requirements do not sufficiently reflect budgetary constraints. Hungary and Slovenia face similar consolidation requirement data than Austria and New Zealand (see OECD, 2014, p. 239).

Japan faces the toughest consolidation requirements of all OECD (OECD, 2014, p. 239). However, consolidation requirements and efforts were very low until 2013 (OECD, 2014, p. 239). On the other hand, fiscal consolidation requirements are relatively low for Belgium despite its very high public debts levels and the (already) implemented ambitious operational consolidation efforts which have a direct impact on HRM policies.

We decided to group the countries into different country groups. Still, any such scoring exercise has obvious limitations, both because of sudden changes in market perceptions of vulnerability and because countries may quickly move from low vulnerability to high vulnerability or vice versa.

---

169 OECD Economic Outlook.: OECD. Paris, 2014, pp. 239 and 240, see also: OECD, Restoring Public Finances, 2012 Update, p. 38.

The listing of countries does not necessarily imply that countries in group 3 or group 4 (see below) do not implement tough consolidation measures in the field of HRM because consolidation requirements and efforts are lower than for countries in category 1 or category 2. Finally, we have considered the situation in countries which have implemented tough consolidation measures in 2007 (in order to better accommodate countries such as Latvia and Estonia in our groupings).

As we will argue later on in this chapter, the purpose of this survey is not limited to the effects of economic pressures on HR reforms in central public administration. In fact, it is important to include political and administrative parameters and indicators when analysing the link between budgetary constraints and HR reforms.

Therefore, given the specific features of this survey we have slightly deviated from a pure economical focus (by taking into consideration the above-mentioned consolidation requirements and a number of additional indicators such as the development of economic growth rates between 2008–2013 (OECD, 2014, p. 224)[170] and the development of Government debt as a share of GDP (OECD, 2014)[171]). Consequently, we have included—as qualitative indicators in the field of HRM in central public administration—political reform trends and the actual implementation of HR reforms in central public administration as consequence of economic pressures. As regards the latter, we have examined the work carried out by Eurofound on the reform of working conditions in central public administration (Eurofound, 2013)[172]. Moreover, we have analysed the responses of all countries to this survey as regards the implementation of political and administrative reform trends. To this end, countries were invited on a number of open questions (such as, for example, answers of countries to question 4c in the OECD survey).

170 OECD Economic Outlook (2014), Volume 2014/1, 2014, p. 224.

171 OECD Economic Outlook (2014), Government debt, No. 95, Paris, 2014.

172 European Foundation for the Improvement of Living and Working Conditions.: Impact of the Crisis on Working Conditions, Dublin. 2013; European Foundation for the Improvement of Living and Working Conditions.: Central Public Administration: Working conditions and industrial relations, Dublin. 2013.

Analysing the effects of Budgetary Constraints on HR reforms – Indicators
1. OECD statistics on consolidation requirements in order to reduce governmental debt
2. OECD statistics on economic growth rates
3. OECD statistics on public deficit as percentage of GDP
4. Analysis of comparative data on political, administrative and HR reforms implemented in EU countries as a consequence of budgetary constraints
5. Analysis of country responses to open questions in this survey on political and administrative reforms implemented in OECD and non-OECD countries

Understanding the forces at work – linking economical with political, managerial and administrative indicators

The need for a more complex analysis as regards the link between budgetary and HR reforms in central public management is important because of the inter-disciplinary (economics/politics/administrative/HRM) and sectoral (exclusively central public administration) interest in this survey.

This survey is at the "middle" level of analysis between economic pressures and governmental reforms, with a focus on HR reforms in central public administrations.

It does not address directly economic and financial reforms and neither the broader reasons for reforms at central public administration level. Thus, a comprehensive analysis of the causal links between budgetary constraints and government reforms is beyond the scope of this survey. Still, it is important to consider all forces at work (Pollitt/Bouckaert, 2011). In fact, pressures for reforms are manifold but must always be taken into consideration when linking the impact of budgetary constraints on HR reforms.

Figure 7: The context of public management reforms – forces at work

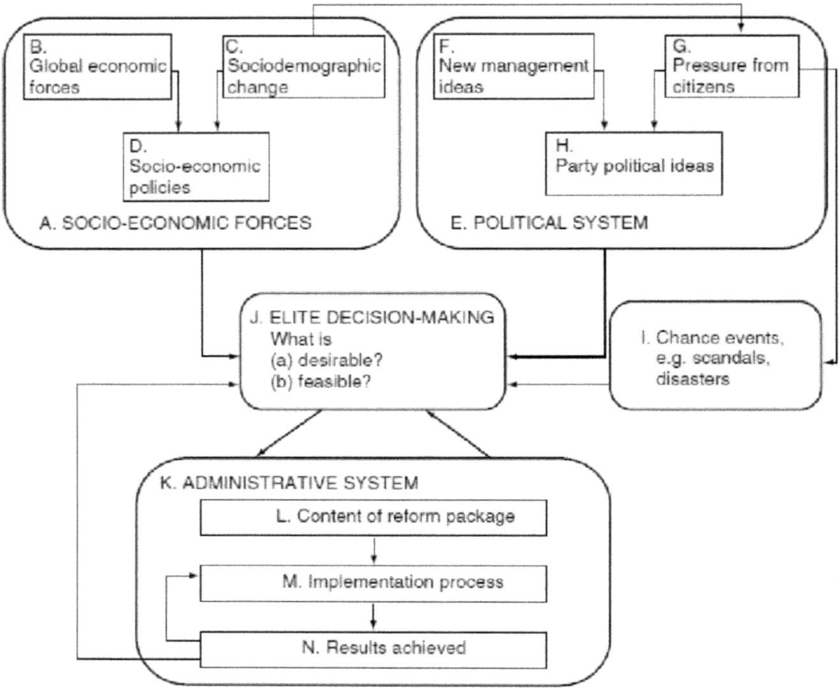

Source: Pollitt/Bouckaert, 2011, 33

The term "reform" is used to describe the range of processes and induced changes in different systems (such as the political system, the administrative system, the socio-economic system etc.) that produce positive, negative and other reform (un-) intentional effects in the relationship between central public administrations, HR management and public employees.

Thus, even if the focus in this survey is on the link between budgetary constraints and HR reforms in central public administration, it is not enough to focus only on the direct link between economy, finances and HR reforms. Such an approach would only lead to a very narrow understanding of causal links and reform effects and distort the overall analysis. Moreover, existing economic and financial indicators only relate to the public sector and/or to government but rarely to central public administration and to HR policies. Existing OECD statistics on consolidation requirements and public debts are too broad in order to allow for conclusions as regards on the effects on central public administration level and, in the field of HRM. We have therefore decided to include political and administrative reform measures as additional indicators. In order to do so, we have monitored recent reform trends and used the data set of the European Foundation for the Improvement of Living and Working Conditions which has carried out a vast analysis and comparison of Governmental and HR reforms at central public administration[173]. Moreover, in order to generate additional data on reform trends in OECD and non-OECD countries, we have analysed the country responses in the OECD survey as regards the most important (political, administrative and HR) reform trends that had an effect on HR reform outcomes.

The answers from the 32 countries have resulted in the following classification of countries in four categories as regards the effects of budgetary constraints and HR reforms.

- Category 1. These countries experience serious financial, economic and budgetary challenges and have committed to introducing substantial and very tough consolidation measures. In parallel these countries have introduced a number of wide-ranging political, administrative and (mostly technical) HR reforms (mostly as a direct response to economic and financial pressures).
- Category 2. These countries experience high financial, economic and budgetary challenges and have committed to introducing substantial consolidation measures. In parallel these countries have introduced a number of wide-ranging political, administrative and (technical and behavioural) HR reforms (mostly as a direct response to economic and financial pressures).
- Category 3. These countries face less financial, economic and budgetary challenges and have committed to introducing moderate consolidation measures. These countries have also introduced a number of political, administrative and technical and behavioural HR reforms which may also be linked to budgetary constraints.
- Category 4. These countries face low financial, economic and budgetary challenges and have committed to introducing limited consolidation measures. As a consequence, these countries have introduced a number of political, administrative, technical and behavioural HR reforms which are not directly linked to budgetary pressures.

173 http://www.eurofound.europa.eu/observatories/eurwork/comparative-information/working-conditions-in-central-public-administration.

To capture such complexity and heterogeneity, this report classifies countries into four groups.

Table 9: OECD countries according to budgetary pressures 2008–2013

Group 1	Greece, Ireland, Portugal, Czech Republic, Spain
Group 2	Slovakia, USA, Italy, Great Britain, France, Australia, Slovenia, Belgium, Hungary, Estonia.
Group 3	Austria, Korea, Poland, New Zealand, Mexico
Group 4	Germany, Finland, Canada, Sweden, Norway, Chile, Switzerland, Japan

Not listed/no data: non OECD countries (Costa Rica, Brazil, Latvia, and Colombia).
Source: OECD, Own classification.

This method allowed for more concrete evidence on the effects of budgetary constraints on HR reforms in the national central public administrations. Take the case of the Czech Republic: although the Czech Republic has very high consolidation requirements in order to reduce government debts (which are only comparable to those of Greece, Spain, Portugal and Ireland), its public debts in percentage of GDP are considerably lower than those of Greece, Italy, Portugal and Spain (although increasing much faster than those of the other countries). Growth rates in the Czech Republic have been much better than in Greece, Portugal, Spain, Italy and even Germany, The Netherlands etc. Thus, from a purely economic point of view, it may be difficult to classify the Czech Republic in the same group as Greece, Portugal, Ireland etc.

However, the Czech case clearly shows that the financial context must always been seen in the political and administrative context. In the case of the Czech Republic, the Czech survey response to this survey noted that in 2010, the Nečas government ordered 10 % savings across all state authorities. Moreover, the Nečas government decided for austerity measures that were later on criticized both from the European Commission as well as the OECD as too strict and having negative effects on the Czech economy. In fact, the measures introduced can only be compared to those which were also implemented in Greece, Portugal, Ireland and in Spain. One reason for these tough austerity measures are, again, of economical nature. During the last years, the Czech Republic has experienced soaring public debts and almost a doubling of public debts from 2007 to 2014. According to Eurofound data (Eurofound, 2013), "statistics on remuneration, benefits and working time, working conditions in the Public Administration sector appear to be more favourable than those in other sectors of the Czech economy. However, those public employees who are directly dependent on the national budget were hit by the economic crisis to a more considerable degree than the majority of other employees. In addition to austerity measures introduced in the context of the economic slowdown, workers in the CPA sector have been subject to more profound changes related to the general reform of Central Public Administration involving a reduction in the number of employment positions and the modification of CPA remuneration systems"[174].

As a consequence, we have decided to group the Czech Republic in category 1 together with countries like Greece, Portugal, Spain and Ireland.

3.5 Human Resource Management reforms – towards best practices or best fit?

Currently, research on HR reforms and work organisation is focusing on the characteristics and prevalence of high performance work systems (HPWS) that are applicable in both the public and in the private sector. Much of this literature assumes that HPWS constitute "best practices" and universal applicable management, although a distinction can be drawn between those arguing for a contextual best-fit approach and those arguing for a more best-practice approach, which believes in the more universal advantages of HPWS. The best-practice approach believes HRM is capable of being used in any organisation, irrespective of product market situation, industry, or workforce[175]. For example, Huselid (1995,) states that "all else being equal, the use of High Performance Work Practices and good internal fit should lead to positive outcomes for all types of firms"[176].

For example, Pfeffer (1998)[177], suggest that the application of seven HR components will increase the possibility to enhancing organisational performance in all types of organisations.

174 Eurofound, Czech Republic: Working conditions in central public administration, http://www.eurofound.europa.eu/observatories/eurwork/comparative-information/national-contributions/czech-republic/czech-republic-working-conditions-in-central-public-administration.

175 Eurofound.: Working Conditions in the European Union: Work Organisation. 2009, op cit.

176 Mark H. Huselid.: The Impact of Human Resource Management Practices on Turnover, Productivity, and Corporate Financial Performance. *The Academy of Management Journal*, Vol. 38, No. 3, Jun., 1995, p. 644.

177 J. Pfeffer.: The Human Equation: Building profits by putting people first. Boston, Harvard Business School Press. 1998.

Components of Best-Practice/High Commitment HRM

- Employment security and internal labour markets
- Selective hiring and sophisticated selection
- Extensive training, learning and development
- Employee involvement, information sharing and worker voice
- Self-managed teams/team working
- High compensation contingent on performance
- Reduction of status differentials/harmonisation

Neo-institutionalists have indeed shown how much organisations can change due to the influence of coercive mechanisms, mimetic forces and normative pressures. DiMaggio and Powell[178] described these trends because of these factors:

- Coercive isomorphism (changes across institutions because of pressures from other external sources),
- Mimetic isomorphism (changes because of new managerial fashions or other external forces which lead to a shift in culture and
- Normative isomorphism (changes because of the adoption of new reforms because of claims that new models are superior).

The best-practice school agrees on the importance of contingency factors but advocates that all organisations can improve performance if they identify and implement best practices. In the meantime, there is indeed much universal agreement on what constitutes bad practices; for example, subjective personnel assessments, unprofessional performance measurement or unstructured selection interviews. Consequently, many authors have published books about best-practices as the search for benchmarks is becoming ever more popular. Many authors have also attempted to define macro models of best practices. For example, recommendations how to achieve highly innovative workplaces, high-performance work systems or high-involvement HR systems. We will discuss these concepts later in this survey.

While many OECD countries are influenced by international reform change processes and the implementation of comparable formal or explicit strategic management plans and goal statements, these developments masks a more

178 P.J. DiMaggio &W.Powell.:The iron cage revisited: Institutional isomorphism and collective rationality in organisational fields. *American Sociological Review*, No. 48. 1983, pp. 147–160.

context- and institution-based, ad-hoc and pragmatic reality[179]. The financial crisis has clearly supported the latter. Our survey does not assume that a best-practice model exists for all types of organisations and culture. We are also sceptical as to developments towards convergence trends towards a universal best-practice model of work organisation. Rather, we start from the premise that institutional differences—notably the levels of labour markets, education and training systems and the collective organisation of employers and employees—mediate the impact of converging processes. Thus this study draws theoretical inspiration from various literature sources developing the idea that "institutions matter".

As such, the use of institutional and organisational models and clusters is ambiguous: "Not only is it difficult to know what the exact reference is about, but the word 'model' is often used with an everyday language connotation… One of the most typical uses of this kind of concepts of models is illustrated by the recurring temptation to look at so-called best practices in public management. Comparing experiences can be very fruitful if it is done according to a carefully designed programme, but it usually ends up at best in misunderstandings, at worst in used-car salesmen attitudes…"[180].

One example is the so-called Napoleonic and Weberian (Prussian) bureaucratic model of public administration. Although both models are often seen as comparable, there are nonetheless a number of important differences. For example, Weber focuses a lot of attention on the importance of rules, but had little interest in the role of courts, corps and local administration.

Another example is the distinction between the Rechtsstaat model and the Anglo-Saxon notion of the "public interest." Most comparative studies list very few systems that fall between these two models, which appear to be inherently inconsistent and irreconcilable[181]. In fact, at the beginning of the 21st century this distinction is no longer very helpful, seeing as it is obviously very broad and too general.

Another possibility is to classify central public administration systems as Weberian or neo-Weberian systems, career or position systems, new public service systems or postmodern public administrations. For some time, the OECD and others classified the national public services into career system countries, position system countries or hybrid countries. This classification resulted from the

179 Peter Boxall.: The Goals of HRM. In: Peter Boxall, John Purcell, and Patrick M. Wright (eds.).: The Oxford Handbook of Human Resource Management.2008, op cit, p. 48.

180 Jacques Ziller.: European Models of Government – Towards a Patchwork with Missing Pieces.: *Parliamentary Affairs*, No. 54, 2001, p. 102.

181 Guy Peters & Jon Pierre (eds.).: Handbook of Public Administration, 1st edition, Sage Publisher. 1995, p. 8.

fact that—as a result of a broad range of other reforms in most public administrations over the last decade—there is no longer a civil service model that could be described as a "classical bureaucratic career model". This statement is obviously correct. However, this also means that the term position system includes all institutional settings that do not correspond to the traditional bureaucratic model. And this again can include many different institutional settings.

Demmke and Moilanen (2010) came to the conclusion that pure models no longer exist. Instead of clear-cut categories, there seems to be a global trend towards hybrid systems that combine elements of more traditional Weberian and mixed public-private systems. At the same time, there are considerable differences between work systems and HR systems in the various countries.

Still, it seems, universal typologies are popular and even useful in research, but they rely on the assumption that countries, organisations, structures and individuals have stable attitudes and a stable identity, assumptions that are now increasingly questioned. Indeed, changes are a common feature of today's HR policies, and central public administrations are not resistant to change. In reality, they have been subject to multiple reforms, and stability has become an old-fashioned word. The good old times of long-enduring leading role models (such as at the time of the Napoleonic or Prussian model and later on the bureaucratic model) are definitely over. Also the concept of "national typology", implying coherence and homogeneity within countries, and geographical typologies, is therefore increasingly being put in question. National public services increasingly vary across sectors (civil service, public service, public administration, services of General interests), organisations and staff categories (civil servant, public employees etc.) as deeply as they differ between central public administration, regional administration and local administration, at least in many countries.

Thus, any administrative typology of central public administration faces the criticism of a potential danger of methodological inflexibility, and standardisation.

In fact, the current trend is moving away from classical bureaucratic features. However, new developments are rather towards the testing of new organisational models and work systems that fit into the national context. Best-fit schools are associated with this contingency approach and argue that organisations must adapt their HR strategies and implement reforms to the specific local strategy and to its environment. Thus, the answer to the question what is the best HR strategy always depends on the specific context.

According to Baron and Krep (1999)[182], reforms should consider the impact of five forces on HR policy choices:

- the external environment (social, political, legal, economical),
- the workforce of the organisation (size, diversity, skills, competences
- the organisational culture (values, norms, trust)
- the technological dimension and
- the organisation of work (leadership style, hierarchical levels, communication, accountability).

Baron and Kreps argue for a contingent understanding of HR strategies and the need for a societal, sectoral and organisational fit of reforms[183]. Others like Cordery and Parker[184] agree that it is difficult to identify a superior best-practice organisation model and work system. In fact, the effectiveness of any particular work system will be determined by the degree of consistency amongst its constituent elements and the way they fit into the organisation, HR policies, culture and leadership styles: "If team working or empowerment is not supported by appropriate changes to supervisory leadership, or the reward system continues to only reward individual performance, or if the technology either over determines the manner of task performance or generates few real opportunities for collective decision and action, then concertive configurations are obviously less likely to flourish"[185].

Different budgetary pressures also suggest that reforms in the field of HRM do not suggest a single direction of travel as OECD countries differ markedly in their vulnerability to different pressures as well as key pressures such as demographic and political pressures. Moreover, different administrative cultures and leadership styles as well as different HR systems have a considerable impact on public management modernisation paths and on the outcomes of HR reforms. The relevance of context and diversity in public administrations also has critical implications for the concept of mutual learning and the possibility to "import" so-called best practices from one country to another. This makes it also difficult to make judgments about national government performance.

---

182 James Baron & David M. Kreps (Eds.).: Strategic Human Resources: Frameworks for General Managers, John Wiley and Sons. 1999.

183 Ibid.

184 Cordery & Parker, Work Organization, in: Oxford Handbook of HRM, op cit., pp. 187–209.

185 Cordery & Parker, Work Organization, in: Oxford Handbook of HRM, op cit, p. 202.

In this survey, we agree about the importance of the socio-political-institutional context and the need for a best-fit approach. On the other hand, we think there is also scope to identify some general principles in HRM that help organisations to improve performance levels and to align their interests with those of employees.

In fact, a good performance HR system is always about whether multiple and conflicting goals could be managed. We expect that, also in the future, HRM strategies will be not associated with any particular philosophy or style of management. Therefore, working conditions and work organisations continue to differ from traditional Taylorist models to high-involvement or high-job autonomy models with low hierarchies and high levels of job autonomy. Also, the role of employees varies from very paternalistic to very communicative and partnership oriented forms of social dialogue. Consequently, there will be multiple forms of organisations in use within different governmental organisations and even within the same organisations. The same is true as regards important variations in the spread of learning forms of work organisation across countries. A deep respect for context also implies an understanding for the fact that motives and objectives of national HRM policies are multiple, subject to tensions and related to national political and institutional structures. Hofstede illustrated in Culture's Consequences (2001)[186] how values and organisational norms vary across countries. He distinguished countries by measuring five cultural elements: power distance, uncertainty avoidance, individualism versus collectivism, masculinity versus femininity and long-term versus short-term orientation. Today, awareness is growing that value changes are taking place everywhere but also remain different.

Therefore, the study contrasts time and again with "the belief in the early 1990s that the worldwide trend of public management reforms in the Western administrations would tend to converge to one single, common, universal "new public management" pattern". Pollitt claims that public management convergence has occurred much more as a result of replication of rhetoric, fashion and symbolism than the "grim dictates of the world economy or the functional necessity for increased efficiency"[187].

---

186 Geert Hofstede.: Culture's consequences – comparing values, behaviors, institutions and organizations across nations, second edition, Thousand Oaks, London, New Delhi. 2001.

187 Christopher Pollitt.: Convergence: The useful myth?, *Public Administration,* Vol. 79 No. 4, 2001, p. 934.

In his paper on clarifying convergence, Pollitt[188] proposes a distinction between:

- Discursive convergence – more and more people are talking about the same concepts
- Decisional convergence – the authorities decide to adopt a particular form, policy or technique
- Practical convergence – public sector organisations begin to work in similar ways
- Results convergence – reforms produce similar or identical results and effects

Research about these different stages is obviously more difficult in relation to *practical convergence* and *results convergence.* In addition, convergence at one stage does not necessarily mean convergence at the next stage—far from it[189]. According to Pollitt, the "hypothesis proposed is that the extent of convergence declines rapidly as one moves through the four stages"[190]. Within the OECD countries there is considerable evidence of discursive convergence and also some form of decisional convergence. There is, however, limited information on practice or results convergence.

Thus, in this survey benchmarking and best practices are considered to be possible as long as naïve assumptions are avoided to which the adoption of best-practices—one by one—is only possible and lead to success if best-fit approaches are considered.

3.6 Empirical analysis and survey methodology

This survey aims to assess the impact of budgetary constraints on HR Management policies in national central public administrations, after 2008. It is based on the analysis of the OECD dataset on managing budgetary constraints: implications for HRM and Employment in Central Public Administration, Paris (OECD, 2015). The OECD dataset was generated in cooperation with the Public Employment and Management Network (PEM) which is a network composed of top-officials from Governments of all OECD-countries, accession and candidate countries. This dataset provides completely new quantitative data regarding

188 Christopher Pollitt.: Clarifying convergence, Striking Similarities and durable differences in public management reform. *Public Management Review*, No. 4, Issue 1. 2002 p. 478.

189 Christopher Pollitt, Clarifying convergence, op cit, p. 478.

190 Ibid.

the implementation of HR reforms in the context of budgetary constraints since 2008.

This study analyses the OECD data set and explores trends and reform outcomes at central public administration level. The research is comparative and evidence-based, drawing on the above mentioned OECD dataset, as well as on previous OECD surveys and a review of the existing academic studies in the field of public management and HRM.

As one of the largest comparative public management research projects at the intersection of public management and HRM, this study therefore intends to provide a comprehensive picture of the challenges facing public administrations in a turbulent financial context.

It compares the measures taken, analyses reform effects and discusses possible future trends.

The objectives of this survey are:

- To gain insight into the impact of HR reforms and the effects on efficiency, effectiveness, workplace behaviour, trust levels, job satisfaction, employment levels and HR policies in general.
- To compare the reforms and the type of HR bundles implemented
- To measure the perceived impact of reforms on HR policies
- To link budgetary constraints with the type of HR reforms and reform effects

3.6.1 Main steps in survey implementation

The OECD data set (OECD, 2015) was the result of a joint effort of the OECD secretariat and the partners in the PEM network.

Within the OECD secretariat, a core survey group was created in GOV (RPS) which worked intensively on the survey design. After each feedback discussion, the draft survey was adjusted accordingly. The guiding principles of the design process were to achieve reliable, accurate, relevant and comparable results by applying established theoretical and methodological standards.

Given the scope of the survey, the conceptual phases focused on three main challenges:

a) Clarifying concepts and definitions in order to allow for OECD countries to answer to comparable concepts
b) Designing a questionnaire fitting to the goals of the research project, the various interests of the stakeholders while taking into account the different national administrative context worldwide

During the period from February to April 2014 a questionnaire was drafted by the OECD secretariat, containing a number of open-ended and closed questions. The research topic was proposed and elaborated by the OECD secretariat and then discussed during the PEM meeting on 8 April 2014.

During this meeting, the PEM network endorsed the topic and requested the OECD to carry out an empirical survey. After approval on 8 April 2014 during the PEM meeting, the result of the design phase was a 13-page survey with 46 core questions, which was distributed in April/May 2014 to the PEM network electronically and to all OECD member countries, accession countries and candidate countries.

National experts were given a validation code in order to guarantee that only the official national respondents could submit their response to the OECD.

After validation of the survey during the PEM meeting in April 2014, the survey was conducted by means of personal email.

The questionnaire was shaped by the following factors/considerations:

a) Building the survey on a theory-driven basis, integrating different research disciplines and interests: the content of the questionnaire therefore links with central research concepts in different disciplines such as public administration, HR management, ethics, organisation theory, management theory and psychology.
b) Allowing for analysis of different levels/perspectives: the survey combines questions at macro-level (central public administration) and policy level (Public Management, HRM).
c) Based on the overall research goals a restricted set of key HR issues was developed (e.g. public sector employment, use of instrument in managing employment levels, job security, working time, leave policies, status reforms, remuneration policies etc.).
d) Analysis of reform effects by asking questions about the existence of data as such (are surveys carried out? If yes, in which fields, what is being done with the surveys? etc.), open questions on effects of reforms on sickness levels, work quality, job intensity, stress levels and reform outcomes (trust levels in leader and in the organisation, job satisfaction, job commitment, development of unethical behaviour and level of corruption etc.).
e) Focusing on current management practice rather than on past reforms and placing less emphasis on normative assessments (for example: How it should be?) and views on the future of the public sector, including positive effects of reforms.

f) With some exceptions as regards the effects of reforms, avoiding questions asking directly for a specific impact of certain management practices on particular outcomes, as well as questions on causalities (to avoid putting pressure on respondents, but also to avoid producing subjective, hard to verify replies).
g) Describing management practices and outcomes generically, simply and clearly, avoiding public management jargon, to ensure a clear understanding of the concepts used in the survey by the respondents targeted.
h) Referring to a standard period since 2008 as reference date of six years throughout the entire survey when time periods are mentioned in the questions.
i) Employing scales for answers. Starting from the examples of other public OECD surveys the survey team considered that a five-point scale would allow for sufficient variation in responses, while not burdening respondents with irrelevant scale values.
j) Allowing respondents to add comments but, as far as possible, refraining from open questions, to avoid interpretation issues during the data validation and analysis phase.
k) Use multi-item variables, reflecting the complex research dimensions of the survey.

Overall, 32 countries (including 28 OECD countries) responded to this survey which demonstrates a huge interest in this study. After completion of the questionnaire, the research team started with the data cleaning process, analysed and filtered all answers and identified those which were either still missing or unclear. In those cases, the respective countries were contacted on a bilateral basis in a "third round".

In order to cross-check, validate and discuss the national answers and the survey, another discussion with representatives from all Member States was organised during the PEM meeting in early 2015. Finally, the data set was used by the OECD in several publications (for example in OECD, Governance at a Glance, 2015).

3.6.2 Data collection and challenges

The OECD data set was released to the public in 2015. While studying and exploring the data, we came across a number of difficulties and challenges.

In particular, when comparing OECD countries and analysing HR reforms, challenges stem from the question as to whether different reform concepts and reform instruments mean the same thing and whether the comparison is really comparing the same issues and topics. In the OECD data set, this concerns the definition of central public administration, the definition of civil service but also instruments such as remuneration and performance related pay.

While carrying out this survey, we are aware of the fact that the discussion around the reform of central public administration in the context of budgetary constraints is also related to many other issues which are seen as political, sensitive, confidential or even secret. Therefore, some countries were reluctant to release sensitive data which is becoming a subject of comparative research.

One should also note that 18 of the participating 28 OECD countries are members of the European Union. Thus, almost 65% of all responding countries are EU-Member States. Here, it is important to note that 13 out of 15 countries with the highest budgetary constraints are also members of the European Union. We will see later on in the empirical analysis that EU countries are particularly affected by budgetary constraints and reform effects are often worse in Europe than in other parts of the world.

Figure 8: Budgetary constraints in Europe

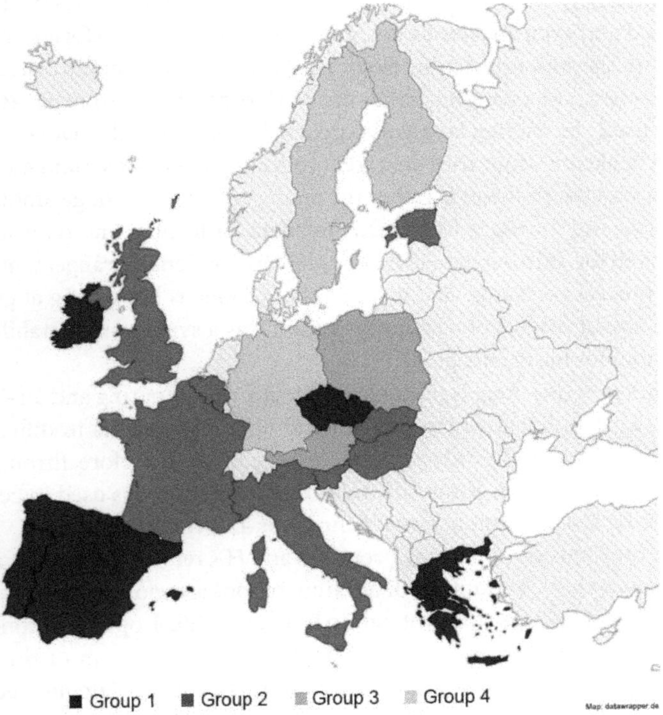

Moreover, there is a clear north-south divide in Europe as such, as most countries with highest budgetary constraints are coming from the southern part of Europe.

In analysing the raw data, it also became evident that there can be too little or too much attention on theoretical issues, too little or too much focus on historical explanations, or a too general analysis without taking into consideration the many existing specific features of the national systems, avoidance of different linguistic meanings and definitions etc.

Also in the above mentioned OECD data set (OECD, 2015), the availability and reliability of data were sore points in the development of our comparative work. This mainly concerned open questions on the development of work quality, stress levels and the effects of HRM reforms on workplace behaviour. Overall, as regards these issues, comparative data is scarce and it is also vulnerable to change and manipulation as it is difficult to define the term work quality. Moreover, many countries have only begun to collect data on the development of work quality, mostly through employee perception studies.

Other developments look brighter. Compared to the situation in the past, the quality of the data—not only in the above mentioned OECD dataset—has greatly advanced and even enables us to compare definitions, HR reforms and reform effects. With the support of technology, countries are increasingly collecting data to gain a better understanding about the workforce. Still, in some areas like special leave used, disabilities, languages spoken, harassment, effectiveness of HRM, unethical behaviour, countries are rarely collecting data in a systematic way.

Thus, today, the problem is rather the management of the huge amount of the existing data and the usage for the existing data for feeding into reform processes. Moreover, the existing data is fragmented and national arrangements are in a constant process of change and it seems that change is happening at ever faster speeds. If, decades ago, public administration was a synonym for stability, today it is a symbol for hasty change.

In addition to this there is the added difficulty of comparing and analysing the different (legal, political, organisational and HR) instruments in different legal and administrative traditions and in many languages. Therefore, throughout the work on this publication, a considerable amount of time was used in comparing and analysing the different national definitions and concepts.

Due to the focus on structures, processes and HR reforms, this study never intended to assess which countries or administrations are more successful or better than others. Instead, this study intends to initiate a critical, open and constructive dialogue on positive and negative developments in the reform of the national HR policies on central public administration level. Such a dialogue necessitates the ability to address difficult issues such as fairness, trust, competence and professionalism and the courage to express openly dissenting opinions. We believe that the interest in contributing to this study and its findings—several are very promising and others are surprising in that they contradict some common sense doctrines of public management reform—can be interpreted as an indicator of the increasing level of awareness, as well as the growing care and diligence devoted to the implementation and handling of HR reforms, and of the willingness to engage in such a dialogue.

The OECD survey (OECD, 2015) followed only partly the tradition of elite studies although our respondents are (top-) officials who are supposed to provide official data that does not reflect personal opinions. In many cases, the delivered data was discussed internally and coordinated with a number of other persons, stakeholders, agencies and ministries.

Parallel to this, we have also closely evaluated existing studies which have been carried out on the basis of employee-level data. In most cases, these studies were carried out by the European Foundation for the Improvement of Living and Working Conditions in Dublin.

Of course, both approaches present certain advantages and disadvantages.

In administrative elite studies, top officials are considered to be members of Organisations with expected higher reliability, institutional knowledge and experience. Putting forward questions to politicians or lower-level civil servants would increase the risk of receiving less "representative" information.

On the other hand, experience shows that official responses to empirical surveys differ according to the choice of the target groups. For example, leader respond differently than technical staff and official sources differ from academic sources. Generally, government responses are often more positive than individual responses by public employees. Thus, we are aware of the fact that the respondents in the OECD data set represented official governmental sources and that answers to the survey necessarily differed depending on the collected samples and the type of respondent.

Therefore, when analysing the dataset, we acknowledge the danger of significant sources of bias because we base most of our conclusions by examining the answers from higher ranking officials who provided official data. These officials may have had an interest in reporting favourable outcomes in order to present a positive and successful image on the international scene.

On the other hand, we acknowledge that, in this type of comparative surveys, independent datasets do not exist. As such we depend on the data as presented to us.

Other key methodological concerns considered were:

Regardless of the chosen access strategy, a web – version of the OECD survey was set up in English for each participating country. The link to the survey was included in the invitations sent, so that only the addressed respondents had the possibility to visit the webpage and fill in the questionnaire online. Each country was invited to follow the same concepts and definitions.

Once the OECD survey was launched, the OECD secretariat received access to the survey, allowing checking the response rates and to clean the data and to contact the countries on issues/answers which were missing, not clear or contradictory, but not allowing them to intervene in the survey implementation. To avoid any inconsistencies or technical problems, the OECD secretariat also managed the survey infrastructure and covered all technical difficulties.

This process took place from June 2014 to August 2014 until the first data were presented during an OECD meeting in early 2015. Afterwards the data were uploaded on the OECD website. Following this, this survey was carried out until the beginning of 2016.

4. Empirical Part

4.1 Introduction

Central public administrations are undergoing processes of profound reform and transformation in most OECD countries. While some of these changes can be associated to the current economic and financial crisis, overall, pressures for reforms come from various other sources. Consequently, important reforms are also implemented in those countries which were not seriously concerned by the crisis, e.g. in Switzerland, Finland and Sweden. We should also highlight at this point that many drastic reforms also concern HR policies which are not the subject of this survey, such as pension reforms and changes in the national social dialogue.

Thus, when analysing change processes, progress and successes in the field of HR management, one should take into consideration the fact that reform pressures and reform priorities vary considerably. Also, reform objectives are diverse such as the need to further improve the quality of HR services, decentralise responsibilities, enhance organisational performance, but also maintain the application of the rule of law, enhance anti-discrimination, support citizen orientation and increase efficiency and productivity.

Still, budgetary constraints have a very strong impact on HR reforms. The latter does not only concern the (higher) number of implemented reforms but also the quality of the reforms which were implemented. As we will see, almost every reform of each HR bundle and each HR instrument is influenced by budgetary constraints.

In all cases, budgetary constraints have supported views to which the most important reform objectives are saving resources, increasing organisational performance and enhancing flexibility. These opinions claim—as Woodrow Wilson did in 1887—that public administration is a field of business. Consequently, we are wondering whether the concept of HRM as such is in crisis because of the dominance of economic thinking in the HR discipline[191].

From a more positive point of view: Despite the existing differences amongst the 32 examined countries, all national central public administrations have shown a tremendous ability to react to changes. Public perceptions frequently suggest that central public administrations are reform-resistant and suffering

191 Spencer.: Barbarians at the gate, op cit.

from reform inertia. Instead, "long-standing taken for granted assumptions and orthodoxies no longer hold"[192]. The reform and innovation process as such is doing well and is alive.

4.2 Discussion and descriptive evidence

As regards the available data (OECD, 2015), we propose to distinguish between seven HR bundles which include approximately 40 different HR policies and HR instruments in 32 countries (amongst 28 OECD countries). Three HR bundles show an enormous amount of reform activity in three HR bundles:

a) Reform of public employment
b) Reform of salary systems
c) Reform of training systems

Before analysing the data, it is important to comment on the data as such.

Unfortunately, the data does not allow for a detailed evaluation of behavioural HR bundles, as most questions in the OECD survey deal with technical HR bundles. Therefore, we recommend to continue this type of research and focus on behavioural HR bundles (for example in the field of intrinsic and non-financial motivators, the analysis of indicators on work systems, the implementation of engagement policies, changes in the field of leadership, ethics etc.).

It is also important to note that the comparability of national answers and data was not always an easy undertaking. For example, in some cases countries reported that public employment is slightly increasing. This definition of "slightly increasing" is as such a subject of controversial discussions.

Also qualitative data is easily misleading. For example, as regards the HR bundle training. In this field, Greece has reported that it did not cut budgets in the field of training because most funds are financed by the EU and not from national budgets.

This example shows that all statistics need to be treated with some reservations and carefully.

192 Ewan Ferlie/Lawrence Lynn/Christopher Pollitt.: Introductory Remarks. In: Ferlie et al., The Oxford Handbook of Public Management, op cit, p. 1.

*Table SEQ Table * ARABIC 10: Overview*

	Australia	Austria	Belgium	Canada	Chile	Corea	Czech	Estonia	Finland	France	Germany	Greece	Hungary	Ireland	Italy	Japan	Mexico	New Zealand	Norway	Poland	Portugal	Slovakia	Slovenia	Spain	Sweden	Switzerland	United Kingdom	United States	Columbia	Latvia	Costa Rica	Brazil
Budgetary constraints categorisation	2	3	2	4	4	3	1	2	4	2	4	1	2	1	2	4	3	3	4	3	1	2	2	1	4	4	2	2				
Changing public employment and use of instruments																																
Privatisation			●			●	●		●							●		●				a			●		●					
Decentralisation of employment	●		●				●	●	●	●							●			●		a										
Supporting voluntary departures					●				●	●		●	●	●	●	●	●	●			●	a					●	●				
Dismissals	●			●	●		●	●	●			●	●				●			●	●	a	●	●	●	●	●					
Annual productivity targets		●	●			●	●		●	●		●	●	●			●	●			●	a	●		●	●	●					
Outsourcing		●	●		●	●	●		●	●		●		●	●	●	●	●		●	●	a		●	●		●	●				
Recruitment freeze	●		●	●		●	●	●	●	●		●	●	●	●	●	●	●		●	●	a	●	●	●	●	●	●				
Non or partial replacement of retiring persons	●	●	●	●	●		●		●	●		●	●	●	●	●	●	●		●	●	a	●	●	●	●	●	●				
Numbers of Reforms	4	3	6	3	4	4	7	3	8	6	0	6	5	5	4	5	7	6	0	5	6		4	4	6	4	7	4	3	5	4	5
Changing Salaries																																
Reduction of remuneration for top-level												●	●	●	●		●															
Reduction of remuneration for all staff										●		●		●							●		●	●								
Reduction or abolishment of allowances				●				●				●	●	●							●		●	●								
Reduction of Performance Related Pay								●					●	●	●					●	●		●				●					
Pay freeze						●	●	●		●		●	●	●	●		●			●	●		●	●			●					
Reforms implemented	●	●	●	●		●	●	●		●	●	●	●	●	●	●	●	●		●	●		●	●	●		●					
Numbers of Reforms	1	1	1	2	0	2	2	4	0	3	1	5	5	6	4	1	3	1	0	3	5	0	5	4	1	0	3	0	1	4	1	2
Changing Skill and Training Policies																																
Reduction of budgets		●	●					●	●				●	●							●		●	●			●					
Reduce travel costs to travel to events	●	●		●				●	●			●		●			●				●							●				
Assessment of training needs to ensure that it is only provided when necessary	●		●									●	●	●			●			●	●	●				●	●	●				
Reduction of budgets		●	●				●	●	●					●	●		●	a		●	●	●	●	●		●	●	●				
Shift employee training to employment desk	●	●	●	●		●		●	●			●	●				●		●	●	●	●	●	●		●	●	●				
Have training policies been affected?	●	●	●				●	●	●			b	●	●	●		●	a		●	●	●	●	●	●	●	●	●				
Measures introduced to increase efficiency?	●	●	●	●		●		●	●	●		●	●	●			●		●	●	●	●	●	●		●	●	●				
Numbers of Reforms	5	6	6	3	0	2	2	6	6	1	0	4	5	6	2	0	6	0	2	5	7	5	5	5	1	5	6	6	3	5	3	3
Cost-saving in the field of HRM																																
Use of furloughs								●														●										
Leaving allowances					●				●	●			●																			
Stop/put on hold promotion opportunities			●									●		●	●						●		●									
Reduce/cut hierarchical level of careers			●			●		●							●						●							●				
Early retirement packages									●			●	●	●	●	●											●	●				
Cost-saving in the field of HRM	●		●	●		●		●	●			●		●	●	●	●				●	●	●			●	●	●				
Numbers of Reforms	1	0	3	1	1	2	0	3	3	1	0	3	2	3	4	2	1	0	0	0	3	2	2	0	0	1	2	3	1	3	2	0

	Australia	Austria	Belgium	Canada	Chile	Corea	Czech	Estonia	Finland	France	Germany	Greece	Hungary	Ireland	Italy	Japan	Mexico	New Zealand	Norway	Poland	Portugal	Slovakia	Slovenia	Spain	Sweden	Switzerland	United Kingdom	United States	Columbia	Latvia	Costa Rica	Brazil
Budgetary constraints categorisation	2	3	2	4	4	3	1	2	4	2	4	1	2	1	2	4	3	3	4	3	1	2	2	1	4	4	2	2				
Changing working hours/Working time																																
Decrease of number of public holidays																		●			●		●									
Change of calculation of paid leave													●								●											
Increase of working hours												●		●				a			●						●					
Recommendation for preventive medical care									●	●	●															●						
Reform of working hours												●		●		●					●						●					
Decrease of number of vacation days														●							●		●	●			●					
Less paid sick leave days								●						●							●			●			●					
Reform of holiday entitlements	●							●					●	●				●			●	●	●	●			●					
Limitation of paid sick days							●		●			●		●	●	●					●			●								
Measures to reduce absenteeism	●	●	●				●		●	●	●			●	●	●		●	●		●			●		●						
Number of Reforms	**2**	**1**	**1**	**0**	**0**	**0**	**2**	**2**	**3**	**2**	**2**	**3**	**2**	**7**	**2**	**3**	**0**	**3**	**1**	**0**	**9**	**1**	**3**	**5**	**0**	**2**	**5**	**0**	**0**	**2**	**2**	**0**
Job Security																																
Measures implemented in order to dismiss central workforce																						●				●						
In case of restructuring								●	●								●															
In case of budgetary constraints			●									●	●													●						
In case of shifting personnel			●									●									●			●		●						
It has become easier to dismiss Civil Servants								●	●												●			●	●	●						
Easier to dismiss public employees				●				●	●				●				●									●	●					
Notice periods have been shortened				●				●	●			●	●			●	●	●		●	●			●	●	●	●					
Numbers of Reforms	**0**	**0**	**2**	**2**	**0**	**0**	**0**	**4**	**4**	**0**	**0**	**3**	**3**	**0**	**0**	**1**	**3**	**1**	**0**	**1**	**3**	**1**	**0**	**3**	**2**	**6**	**2**	**0**	**0**	**3**	**0**	**0**
Status reforms																																
Substitution of Civil Servants because of cost reasons			●																								●					
Substitution because of shortages in employment			●									●															●					
Substitution of civil servants because of recruitment freezes			●									●															●					
Reforms of fixed-term employment								●	●	●		●		●	●						●	●	●									
Employment of fixed-term because of budgetary constraints	●	●	●				●					●			●			●					●		●							
Need for fixed-term employees in order to save resources	●		●		●					●		●					●	●			●		●		●	●		●				
Will budgetary constraints lead to abolishment of Civil Servants?	●		●	●		●		●				●	●				●			●			●	●			●					
Numbers of Reforms	**3**	**1**	**6**	**1**	**1**	**1**	**1**	**2**	**1**	**2**	**0**	**6**	**1**	**1**	**2**	**0**	**2**	**2**	**0**	**1**	**2**	**1**	**4**	**1**	**2**	**1**	**4**	**1**	**0**	**1**	**1**	**0**
Total numbers of reforms	**16**	**12**	**25**	**12**	**6**	**11**	**14**	**24**	**25**	**15**	**3**	**30**	**23**	**28**	**18**	**12**	**22**	**13**	**3**	**15**	**35**	**10**	**23**	**22**	**12**	**19**	**29**	**14**	**8**	**23**	**13**	**10**

Note: ● Reform; a: no data available, b: The fact that Greece has not implemented reforms in the area is due to the fact that most training budgets are coming from the European Social Funds

Our survey confirms that there is a correlation between budgetary pressures and reform activity. Overall, countries with the highest budgetary pressures have implemented more reforms than countries with less budgetary pressures. Portugal, Greece, the United Kingdom and Ireland have implemented the highest number of HR reforms since 2008. This again confirms our hypothesis to which economic pressures are an important trigger for reforms and lead to many reforms. Still, it is important to mention a number of exceptions. For example, countries with low budgetary pressures implemented many reforms after 2008 and the Czech Republic with high budgetary pressures also implemented a relatively low number of reforms. Another example is Belgium which implemented the highest numbers of reforms in the HR bundle status reforms. These cases suggest that socio-economic variables cannot be the only explanatory variable. In fact, in some cases, specific historical and institutional reform "paths" play ever-bigger roles. The latter is well-illustrated by neo-institutional theories.

Figure 9: Total Numbers of reforms and budgetary constraint groups

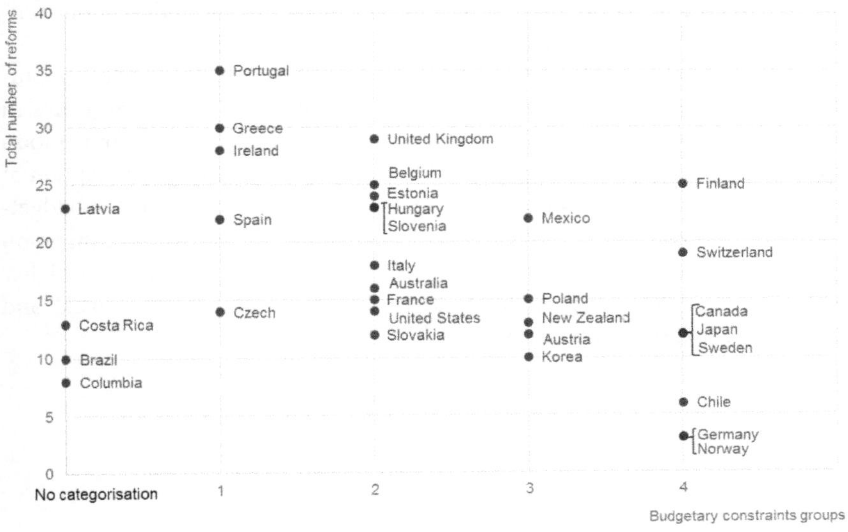

On the other hand, countries with modest budgetary pressures such as Germany, Norway, Sweden and Japan have implemented fewer HR reforms.

The fact that Finland and Switzerland have also implemented a high number of reforms can be explained by the fact that other factors (such as, first of all, political motives) play an important role in the reform process. Thus, budgetary pressures are important triggers for reforms. However, this is not the only reform pressure. For example, Pollitt and Bouckaert[193] discuss the important role of administrative elites and political interests in the reform process. In some cases, other international, national, sectoral contexts and the social dialogue also play important roles.

The answers of the countries confirm our hypothesis to which there is also a correlation between budgetary pressures and the implementation of technical downsizing and cost-control HR bundles: the more budgetary pressures, the more reform measures are focused on cost-control measures.

Countries with the highest budgetary pressures have adopted almost the whole menu of technical instruments (technical HR bundles). Countries like Greece and Portugal have implemented almost all existing reforms, as mentioned in the overview.

Together with a number of other countries (such as, for example, the United Kingdom, Finland, Belgium and Estonia) countries with the highest budgetary pressures are also implementing tough downsizing measures (including the dismissal of public employees, cutting of salaries, freezing of promotion opportunities and cutting training budgets).

As regards salaries, there is a clear connection between the budgetary situation of a country and the implementation of tough cost-control measures in the field of remuneration (the latter often means the reduction of remuneration for all categories of public employees). On the other hand, with the exception of Finland and Switzerland, countries belonging to the category 4 (modest budgetary pressures) have implemented fewer reforms and less drastic remuneration reforms than countries belonging to category 1. In fact, countries with higher budgetary pressures are particularly active in HR bundles where "quick" and clear cost saving measures can be achieved.

193 Pollitt & Bouckaert.: Public Management Reform, op cit.

Figure 10: Changing Salaries and budgetary constraint groups

The same relationship can be seen as regards working time. The higher the budgetary constraints, the more reform activity can be observed. More precisely, there is a correlation between budgetary constraints and the number of reforms in this field, amongst others the increase of working time.

Thus, cost-control reforms are deployed in a systematic sense by countries with highest budgetary pressures but not by other countries with lower budgetary pressures.

Figure 11: Changing working hours/time and budgetary constraint groups

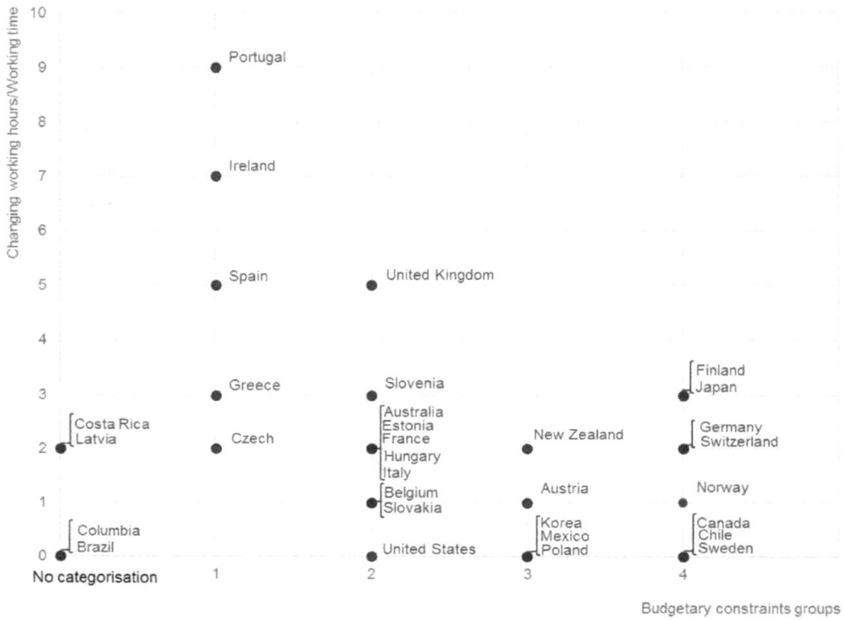

As already mentioned, the answers of some OECD countries also illustrate a relationship between context and reform activity. For example, there is no clear relationship between budgetary constraints and reform activity in the field of status reforms. As regards the latter, reforms in this field are rather depending on the national political and legal context and less on budgetary issues. As already mentioned, Belgium is particularly active in reforming the status of civil servants because the Belgium system still provide for important differences between public law civil servants and labour law public employees. In other countries, such as Finland or Sweden, this is not the case. Consequently, these countries have fewer reasons to reform in this area.

Figure 12: Status reforms and budgetary constraint groups

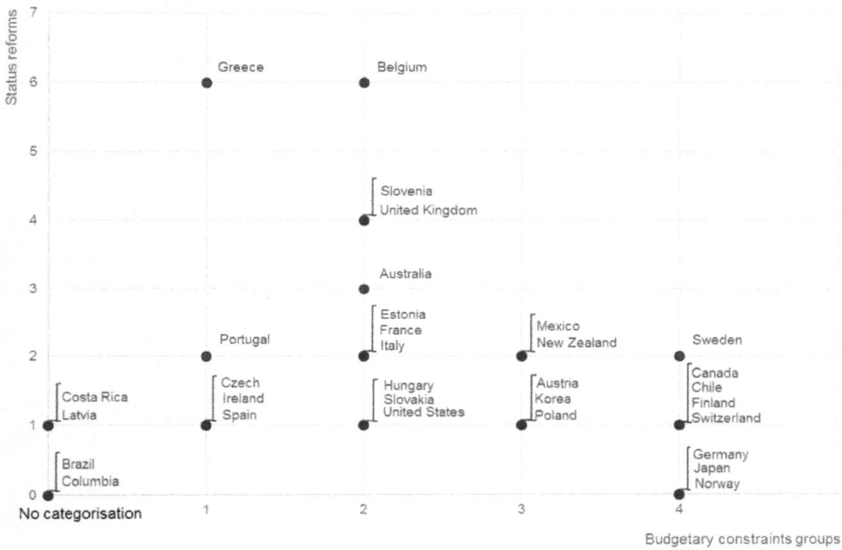

These cases confirm that many reforms are also linked to the national constitutional, legal, political, administrative and cultural context. Consequently, reforms which are not directly linked to cost-control measures are also not deployed in a systematic sense by countries.

Still, some reforms in some HR bundles are carried out systematically by almost all countries. For example, as regards the HR bundle "Changes in Public Employment". Although countries with highest budgetary pressures (category 1 countries) are strongly reducing public employment, this can also be the case for other countries with modest budgetary pressures. Here, an important case is Switzerland which has introduced heavy downsizing and cost-containment measures in the years 2005–5007, together with various cost-reducing programs before and afterwards. As a result, a substantial decrease could be observed already before the financial crisis. The moderate increase that has taken place in the meantime is essentially due to new tasks. Now, the number of posts is being stabilized on the lower level of 2004 (answer from Switzerland to this survey)[194].

194 Some answers to this questionnaire (e.g. personnel surveys) refer therefore not to the period around 2010–2013, but to the period 2005 and onwards.

A similar case is Germany which has reduced public employment continuously from 1990 to 2012 (and has stabilized employment levels since then).

Figure 13: Changing public employment and budgetary constraint groups

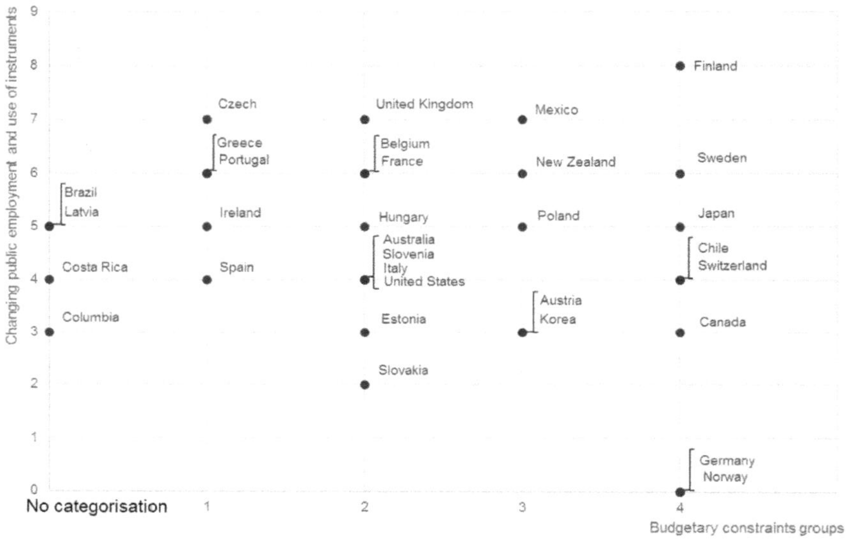

In the field of "Cost Saving Measures in the field of HRM", there is no correlation between budgetary pressures and reform activities. This can be explained by the fact that the term "Cost saving Measures in the field of HRM" is obviously too broad and allows all countries to reply positively. Moreover, the OECD survey provided only for a very limited number of cost saving issues. This again made it almost impossible to distinguish amongst a high number of instruments.

Figure 14: Cost-saving and budgetary constraint groups

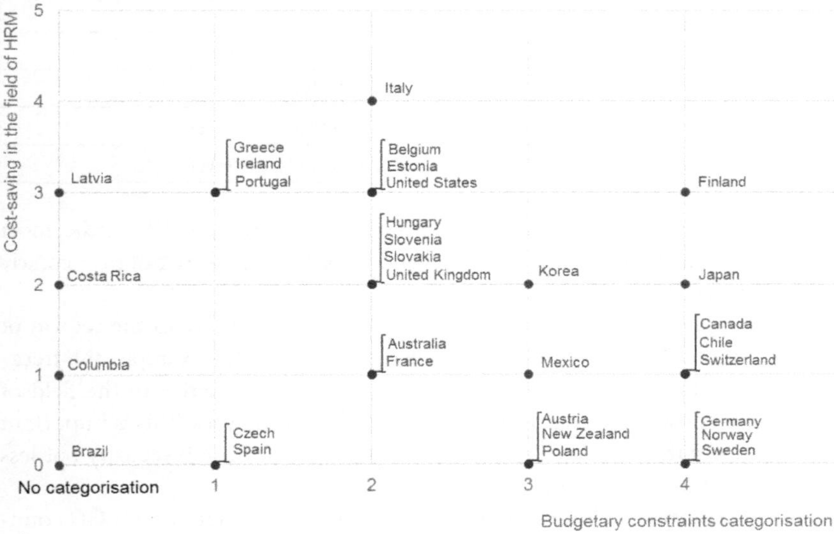

4.3 The reform of HR bundles and HR policies – comparative observations

If we continue with our quantitative analysis, we can conclude that, between 2008 and 2013, OECD countries were most active in the following HR bundles: reform of public employment, restructuring of the workforce, remuneration reforms, training policies and the reform of sickness policies.

Countries were less active in the field of employment security and, with the exception of some countries, were very reluctant to reform working time and holiday policies.

Table 11: HR Bundles and reform activity

HR Bundles	Reform activity
Reduction of Public Employment	Strong Activity
Remuneration Reforms	Strong activity
Reform of training policies and systems	Strong activity
Policies to reduce sickness	Activity

HR Bundles	Reform activity
Status Reforms	Activity
Fixed-term employment	Strong Activity
Job Security	Activity
Working Time	Low activity level
Holidays	Low activity level

When going into the details, we can observe that within each HR bundle, most countries focused on some instruments and priorities and were not particularly active in other HR bundles.

For example, whereas all OECD countries were very active in the reform of the HR bundle "Reduction of Public Employment" and, for example, the freezing of recruitments into the public sector, they were less active in the field of employment protection and the dismissal of public employees. This is important as it illustrates that most countries are reluctant to reform job security but less reluctant to introduce recruitment freezes, etc.

Similar features can be seen in other HR bundles. For example, OECD countries were very active in the HR bundle "Remuneration reforms". However, differences exist between the freezing of salaries (which took place in many countries) and the reduction of performance-related pay (which was implemented in a high number of countries, yet not in as many countries). On the other hand, the HR bundle "Working time" was the subject of relatively few reforms, at least compared to other HR bundles. On the other hand, changes as regards sickness days were implemented more frequently.

Table 12: Reduction of Public Employment

Non or partial replacing of retiring staff	Strong activity
Recruitment freezes	Strong Activity
Annual productivity targets	Activity
Outsourcing	Activity
Dismissal (sometimes easing of job protection)	Activity, strong link to national context
Dismissal of fixed-term people	Activity

Table 13: Pay reforms

Reduction of PRP	Activity
Pay freeze	Strong activity
Reduction of allowances	Activity
Reduction of remuneration for all	Activity
Outsourcing	Activity

Table 14: Training reforms

Reduction of training budgets	Strong activity
Reduction of training days	Activity
Shift employees training to employee desks (avoid travelling, saving time)	Strong Activity
Use training needs assessments to ensure that training is provided only when necessary	Strong Activity
Reduce travel costs to training events	Activity

Table 15: Policies to reduce sickness

Reduction of paid sick days (even with doctor's prescription) are limited	Activity

Table 16: Supporting Voluntary departures

Offering leaving allowances	Activity
Offering early retirement packages	Activity

Table 17: Sanctioning fixed-term employees

Reforming fixed-term employees (9)	Strong activity
Decreasing the number of fixed-term employees	Strong Activity

Table 18: Reforming civil service status

Substituting Civil servants with fixed-term employees for cost saving measures	Activity
More flexible employment in order to save resources	Activity
Replacing Civil servants as a consequence of budgetary constraints/austerity measures	Activity
Budgetary as an extra impetus to abolishing employment as civil servants	Strong activity

Table 19: Job security

Dismissing central public employees	Activity, strong relation to context
Dismissal as results of restructuring	Activity
Dismissal in case of budgetary constraints	Activity
Trend – easier to dismiss central public employees	Low activity

Table 20: Reform of working time

Reform of Working hours with few exceptions	Low Activity
Reform of holidays with few exceptions	Low Activity
Reform of public Holidays with few exceptions	Low Activity
Calculation of paid leave	Low Activity

4.4 Reforming HRM and HR policies

4.4.1 Restructuring public employment

Our data reveals that from 2008–2013, important downsizing trends took place in most OECD countries. As such, this reform trend in the field of public employment is the most important reform trend in most countries. Because of this, we will discuss this reform trend more in detail.

However, when looking into the details, differences are huge as regards employment developments in different sectors (and organisations), the choice of instruments and the importance of measures.

For example, whereas almost 60% of countries with very high budgetary pressures (category 1) decreased public employment drastically, only 14 % of category 4 countries (including Finland, Canada, Norway, Chile, Germany, Switzerland, Sweden, Japan) decreased public employment drastically. 57% of this category even increased employment.

However, strong reductions in public employment are also implemented by countries from other categories.

When looking at these trends from a geographic point of view, we can observe that almost all EU countries are in a process of reducing public employment. In the European Union, only Sweden has increased public employment. Germany and the Czech Republic have stabilised public employment (in the case of Germany after long years of reductions in the field of public employment). In Europe, only Norway reported high increases in public employment.

In most cases, reductions in public employment were modest to drastic:

In Belgium, the reductions were minus 7,05% over a period of 7 years (2006–2013), although there's an acceleration during the last few years: (in comparison to 2006):-7, 05 (2013); – 5, 26 (2012); – 2, 83 (2011. This diminution in the workforce is due to 2 factors: (1) the strategic workforce planning based on a selective substitution policy and (2) the ageing of the staff. However, it is difficult to separate those two factors. On the 4.591 staff supposedly to have left the federal civil service in 2011, 2.257 or 49% left on retirement. On the other hand, Greece decreased employment in central public administration by 19% since 2010. Until 12/2015 Greece is obliged to reduce public employment (of General Government) by at least 150.000 compared to 2010. Ireland reduced public service staffing levels from 2008 to Q1 2014 by 10%. Portugal reduced central public employment between 31 December 2011 and March 2014 by 8, 9%.

Not surprisingly, 18 countries reported that personnel reductions are taking place in order to restructure the internal workforce. This is also in accordance with other statistics in this survey which show that restructuring is closely connected with downsizing strategies.

Figure 15: Changes in public employment

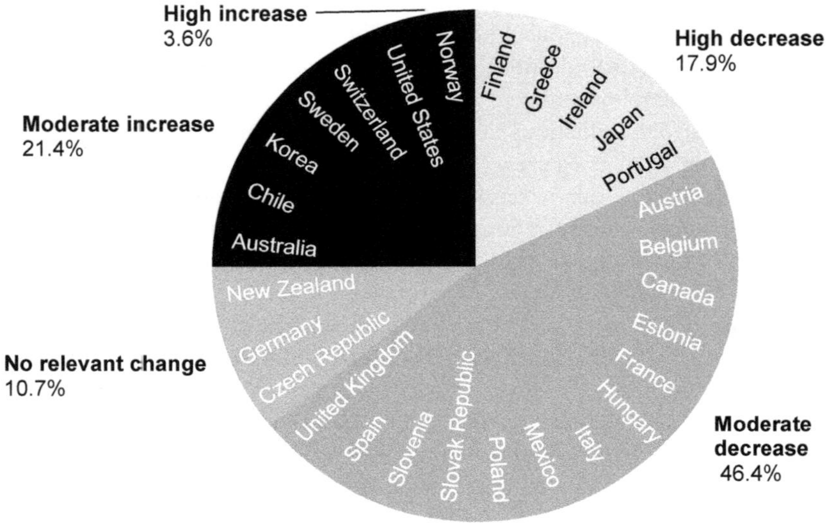

It is also important to distinguish the *timing* of public sector adjustments. Some reforms started well before the crisis and have merely been continued in recent years without much influence from the crisis, as in Sweden and Germany. Given the covered time span in this survey, one can also conclude that the reduction of public sector employees was carried out rapidly in Greece, Spain, the UK, Portugal, and Ireland and—to a lesser extent—Belgium.

As regards sectorial developments, one can observe a clear relationship between budgetary constraints and the reduction of personnel at all levels and in all sectors at the central administration level.

Most striking is the fact that this is not the case in countries with less budgetary constraints (countries of category 3 and 4). Take the case of central ministries/central departments. Whereas countries with high budgetary constraints decrease public employment at this level, this is not necessarily the case in countries with lower budgetary constraints (categories 3 and 4).

Figure 16: Have the following sectors been subject to personnel changes in the central public administration? Central Ministries/Departments

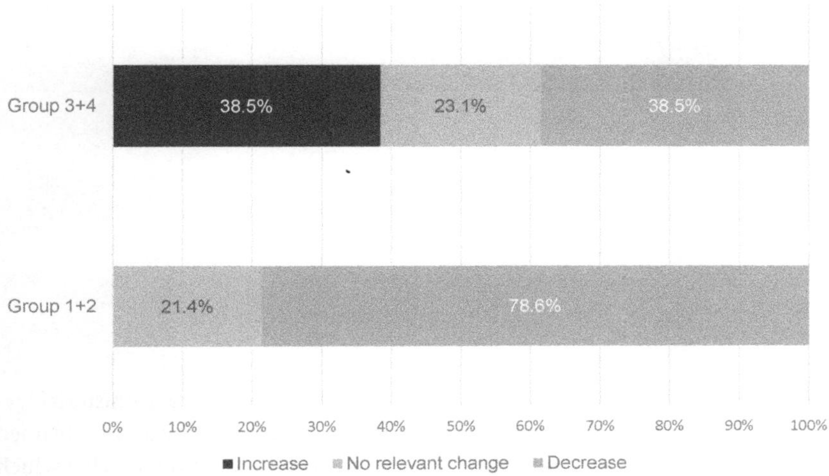

However, it can also be observed that overall reductions in public employment focus on the central ministries/departments and can go hand in hand with occasional increases in other agencies or sectors on the central level. As it seems, countries with lower budgetary constraints are much more selective and strategic as regards sectorial employment levels whereas countries with higher budgetary constraints try to reduce at all levels (and at any price), even if there is a need for an increase in employment.

However, we can also note a number of exceptions: For example, in Switzerland, Sweden, Brazil, New Zealand and Chile, there is a slight increase in public employment at ministerial level but not necessarily in other sectors such as in the field of education.

Figure 17: Have the following sectors been subject to personnel changes in the central public administration? Education sector

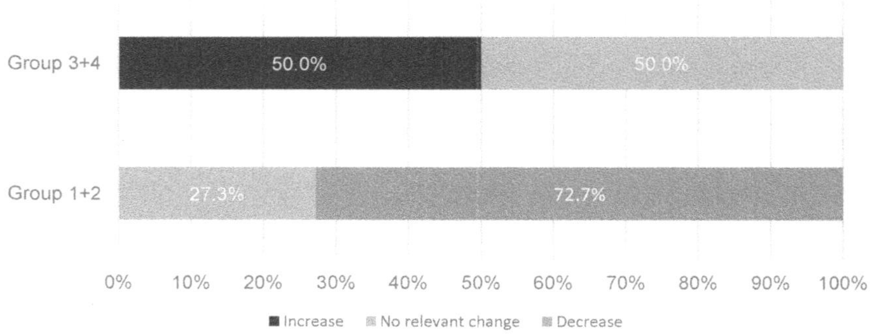

However, overall OECD countries reduce employment on central ministerial level more strongly than in the field of education and health. This can be explained by the fact that downsizing is more difficult in sectors and policy fields which have become politically more important in recent years. Moreover, the health sector is becoming more important in the context of demographic changes. On the other hand, some countries are in a process of shifting employment on the ministerial level to central government agencies.

Still, the fact that downsizing takes place almost everywhere illustrates that public employment levels do not only revolve around the economic and fiscal situation of a country. In fact, in some cases, countries reform public employment in the context of demographic challenges, restructuring measures, governance reforms, decentralisation of public employment or the change of work systems.

Downsizing in the OECD – a complex issue

Downsizing has been defined as a deliberate organisational decision to reduce the workforce that is intended to improve organisational performance[195]. In popular usage, "downsizing"" is frequently used as a synonym for redundancy and used interchangeably with a range of other terms such as "restructuring"",

195 Adrian Thornhill & Mark N.K Saunders.: The meanings, consequences and implications of the management of downsizing and redundancy: a review. *Saunders Personnel Review*, Vol. 27 No. 4. 1998, p. 273.

"reorganisation" and "rightsizing", to name but a few[196]. As we will see later on, our data indeed suggest a strong relationship between restructuring and downsizing. However, both measures are not the same.

Downsizing is also not the same as organisational decline. The fact that some countries decrease employment levels but still increase employment levels in some sectors shows that downsizing can be used as an intentional, proactive management strategy and be part of a management strategy for adjusting the workforce, competences and skills.

However, in other countries, downsizing is related to organisational decline in a crisis situation[197] if downsizing is exclusively used for cost-cutting and produces many negative side-effects (as will be discussed later on).

Downsizing also differs from restructuring in the sense that downsizing may only be one part of a restructuring strategy. In our survey, six countries have reported that downsizing is directly related to restructuring measures.

Downsizing is about the reduction of personnel and restructuring is about the strategic reorientation of personnel, including downsizing, workforce planning and other issues. Still, despite differences, "organisational downsizing and restructuring are common responses to changed economic circumstances and other environmental influences, with organisations implementing these strategies in order to improve their effectiveness." The reasons why, and how, organisations downsize and restructure have a major influence on perceived outcomes. Our data shows that there is a positive correlation between high budgetary constraints and downsizing and low budgetary constraints and restructuring.

Of course, clear distinctions are difficult, as almost countries define public employees in terms of compensation costs. Overall, OECD countries that decide to eliminate redundant employees do so by using four broad strategies: recruitment freezes, across-the-board cuts, outsourcing, compulsory termination, attrition and voluntary termination[198].

The extent of downsizing policies is also associated with the legal protection of public employees. For example, in Germany civil servants enjoy lifetime tenure and can, as a principle, only be dismissed for disciplinary reasons. On the other hand, many public employees have fixed-term contracts and can be dismissed.

---

196 Ibid.

197 Wayne C. Cascio.: Downsizing and Redundancy. In: Adrian Wilkinson/Nicolas Bacon/Tom Redman/Scott Snell (eds.).: The SAGE Handbook of HRM, Los Angeles/London/New Delhi/Singapore/Washington D.C., 2010: p. 336.

198 Wayne F. Cascio.: Employment Downsizing and Its Alternatives: Strategies for Long-Term Success, SHRM Foundation. 2009, p. 10.

Consequently, our data shows that Germany has focused on recruitment freezes and natural attrition as the main downsizing methods. Of course, civil servants were not dismissed.

Thus, certain downsizing methods such as compulsory redundancy can be very difficult or easier, depending on the legal and contractual status, not only in the German case. However, in many OECD countries the trend is towards the relaxation of job security, also for civil servants and at least in Europe and in the United States[199]. This process also confirms that jobs in the national central public administrations are not anymore "havens of security" (Demmke/Moilanen, 2010) as more countries allow for the termination of civil service employment in more cases and situations (for example, in cases of poor performance).

Table 21: Reasons for dismissing civil servants at central public administration level in the EU

	A	*B*	*C*	*D*	*E*	*F*	*G*	*H*	
Germany	1	0	0	0	0	0	0	1	
Greece	1	0	0	0	0	0	0	1	
Luxembourg	1	0	0	0	0	0	0	1	
Belgium	1	1	0	0	0	0	0	2	A = Disciplinary reasons
Cyprus	1	0	0	0	0	0	1	2	B = Poor performance
Ireland	1	1	0	0	0	0	0	2	C = Restructuring
Italy	1	1	0	0	0	0	0	2	D = Downsizing
Portugal	1	1	0	0	0	0	0	2	E = Re-organisation
Spain	1	1	0	0	0	0	0	2	F = Economic difficulties
Austria	1	1	0	0	0	0	1	3	G = Other
Malta	1	0	1	1	0	0	0	3	H = Sum
Sweden	1	0	1	1	0	0	0	3	
Czech Republic	1	0	1	1	1	0	0	4	
Estonia	1	1	1	1	1	0	0	5	
France	1	1	1	1	1	0	0	5	

199 Demmke & Moilanen, 2010, op cit.

	A	*B*	*C*	*D*	*E*	*F*	*G*	*H*	
Hungary	1	0	1	1	1	1	0	5	
Lithuania	1	1	1	1	1	0	0	5	
United Kingdom	1	1	1	1	1	0	0	5	
Bulgaria	1	1	1	1	1	0	1	6	
Denmark	1	1	1	1	1	1	0	6	
Finland	1	1	1	1	1	1	0	6	
Latvia	1	1	1	1	1	1	0	6	
Netherlands	1	1	1	1	1	1	0	6	
Poland	1	1	1	1	1	1	0	6	
Slovakia	1	1	1	1	1	0	1	6	
Slovenia	1	1	1	1	1	1	0	6	
Romania	1	1	1	1	1	1	1	7	
Mean	*1,00*	*0,71*	*0,61*	*0,61*	*0,54*	*0,29*	*0,18*	*3,93*	

Source: Demmke/Moilanen, 2010, op cit., p. 178

However, the relaxation of job security does not mean that public employees are dismissed on a massive scale. In fact, this is only the case as regards few countries. Most countries are implementing other measures in order to downsize public employment. For example, most countries focus the non-replacement of retiring personnel and on recruitment freezes.

4.4.1.1 Reducing public employment – the use of instruments

As already discussed, downsizing can be related to restructuring policies and to strategic management issues. In order to gain more knowledge on the link between downsizing and strategic management, we asked countries the following question: "If personnel reductions are taking place, to which of the following strategic objectives are they related?

- Anticipate the decreasing number of new potential recruits on the labour market
- Enhance productivity
- Restructure public administration workforce

Overall, only four countries responded that downsizing is carried out in order to anticipate the decreasing number of new potential recruits on the labour market.

This is a surprisingly low number as many countries with very high demographic pressures find themselves in a tough competitive situation with the private sector in order to attract talent people from a smaller pool of candidates. Thus, this result creates doubts as to whether countries link downsizing to the process of demographic changes.

On the other hand, 14 countries replied that downsizing is linked with strategies to increase productivity although little is known how the two issues are linked in practice.

Data also shows that there is a strong relationship between restructuring and downsizing: often, restructuring is used as a synonym for downsizing the workforce. In more of 40% of the surveyed countries, restructuring measures were sometimes combined with dismissals of the workforce.

Figure 18: Dismissals happen in case of…

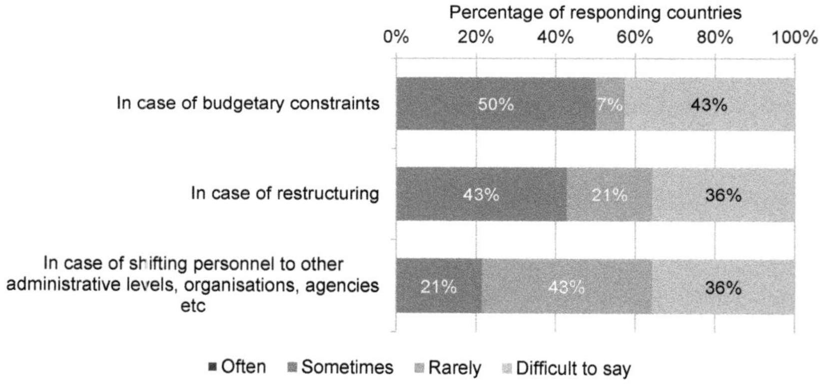

Overall, national replies to the OECD survey show important differences amongst the different country categories and mostly, amongst those with high budgetary pressures (group 1) and low budgetary pressures (group 4). Countries with the highest budgetary pressures have been active by using all discussed downsizing instruments. In most cases, they have not replaced retiring staff, set annual productivity targets and applied recruitment freezes. 40% of these countries have also frequently dismissed public employees. Countries with lower budgetary pressures have also been active in different ways. However, they focus less on instruments such as the decentralisation and shifting of employment, privatisation and outsourcing.

Figure 19: Managing public employment and use of Instruments

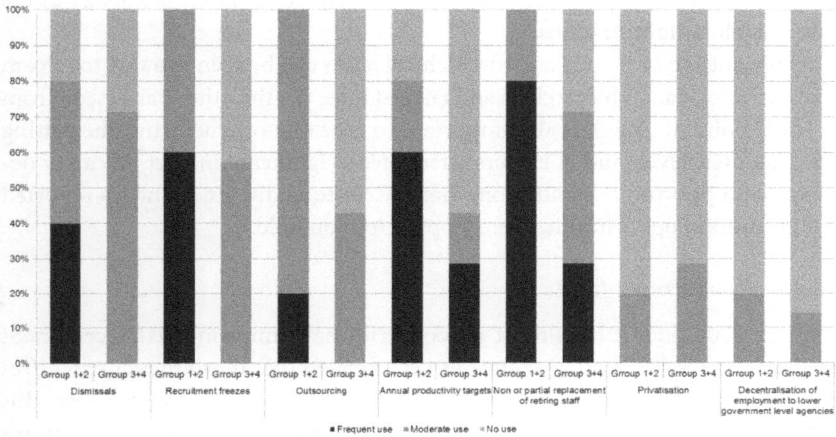

On the other hand, countries with lower budgetary constraints focus more on the non- or partial replacement of retiring staff.

Of course, size and features of such adjustments often depend on the structure of public sector employment in individual countries. Also, reform effects differ. For example, outsourcing, decentralising or, simply, shifting personnel to other administrative bodies may only disguise changes in workforce structure and developments towards the so-called shadow state: The term is designed to highlight "that many workers providing public services financed by the government are actually employed by the private or third sector"[200]. Moreover, many countries are in a process of outsourcing and/or establish so-called shared services. Almost all category 1 countries (countries with the highest budgetary pressures) are trying to reduce public employment levels by outsourcing public services.

One important side effect of this trend is that hierarchical, centralised and standardised structures are slowly being replaced by more decentralised and/or collaborative arrangements among public, semi-public and private organisations. Thus, new forms of governance emerge directly as a consequence of financial constraints.

Here, one should distinguish between external and internal reform trends. Often, new forms of governance emerge horizontally (amongst different administrative

200 Stephen Bach &Ian Kessler.: The Modernisation of the Public Services and Employee Relations, Palgrave, Hampshire.2012, p. 4.

bodies) and vertically (within the different organisations). As regards the latter, 8 countries reported that they had reduced/cut hierarchical levels or careers in the central public administrations.

Again, cutting of careers and hierarchical levels can be seen as a way to reform bureaucracies, flatten hierarchies and cut red tape. On the other hand, seen from an HRM point of view, it is also important to note that restructuring, the cutting of hierarchical levels and of careers often have a significant impact on career development opportunities and promotions. Consequently, six countries reported that promotion opportunities were stopped/put on hold.

4.4.1.2 Recruitment freeze

Between 2008 and 2013, almost all countries have implemented recruitment freeze measures. Ten OECD countries even replied that they are recurring "frequently" to the use of this instrument. 14 countries answered that they use this instrument to a "moderate degree". Countries with very high budgetary pressures either use this instrument "frequently" or to a "moderate" degree. On the other hand, three countries with modest budgetary pressures (category 4 countries) reported not to make use of this instrument at all.

Recruitment freeze – side effects

"A hiring freeze is a convenient short-run strategy to buy time and preserve options. In the short run it hurts no one already employed by the organisation because hiring freezes rely on "natural attrition" through resignations, retirements, and death to diminish the size of an organisation's work force. In the long run, however, hiring freezes are hardly the most equitable or efficient way to scale down organisational size (…). During a long hiring freeze an organisation may find itself short on some critically needed skills yet unable to hire people with these skills even though they may be available"[201] (…). "Also, without expansion, public organisations that are constrained by merit and career tenure systems are unable to attract and accommodate new young talent. Without an inflow of younger employees, the average age of employees is forced up, and the organisation's skill pool becomes frozen at the very time younger, more flexible, more mobile, less expensive and (some would argue) more creative employees are needed"[202]

201 Levine, 1978, op cit, p. 321.
202 Levine, 1978, op cit, p. 317.

4.4.1.3 Employee turnover and voluntary termination

Voluntary termination is connected to the field of employee turnover. As the data shows, this is a newly implemented instrument and connected to the field of turnover of staff. The latter notion can be defined as the rate at which employees enter and leave an organisation within a specific period. Voluntary termination is not only an important indicator for the attractiveness of an organisation. In fact, it can also be used as a strategical HR instrument in order to control costs. On the other hand, employee turnover but can also be a huge challenge for HR professionals because it is related to the workforce planning for the future and has direct implication on the remaining staff, cost developments, knowledge management and the productivity of the workforce.

For example, turnover has many side effects, such as lost productivity during the time when positions are vacant, diminished productivity and job satisfaction from those who remain at the organisation and must compensate for those who have left the organisation and who are required to take on additional duties. In other words, employee turnover can be very expensive and presents many HR challenges.

However, the fact that employees exit an organisation voluntarily may not only indicate that organisations are driving employees away. In fact, many organisations are also using the instrument of voluntary turnover to reduce public employment levels, increase efficiency and in order to control costs. Thus, voluntary termination may also include buy-out offers as another approach to downsizing a workforce.

Voluntary termination: Side effects

The challenge is that this process is not an exact science in that we are not able to accurately determine how many will accept the offers (answer from the United States to this survey).

Voluntary termination is a popular instrument because it gives employees a choice. It also seems to work in the sense that many employees accept these buy-out offers. Still, it is far from clear whether this instrument is effective and efficient. As regards our survey question "Did these policies produce efficiency gains in the central public administration?" only Ireland replied positively. Other countries were much more critical. Portugal answered that, as a consequence, the staff reduction led to increased workloads, the developments conflicts and demotivation on the side of those employees who stayed in the job. Also Greece answered that the moral of the remaining employees had been affected. Mexico and Ireland reported about a loss of talent and experience and a "significant loss of expertise and corporate memory and adverse impact on workforce planning". Thus, existing evidence seems to confirm that there is the clear danger that offers for voluntary departures are accepted by the brightest employees and those who are able to find other jobs. Thus, whereas in theory, HR planners are confident that voluntary termination is an opportunity to increase efficiency, the implementation of measures may in fact result in high performers leaving the organisation. Moreover, data seems to suggest that OECD countries have little evidence about reform effects in this policy area.

4.4.1.4 Early retirement policies

Early retirement policies are used if an organisation offers retirement benefits in return for an employee's decision to leave earlier in his/her career. 15 countries have reported to make frequent use of non or partial replacement of retiring staff and only five countries have reported to make no use at all.

Early retirement incentives: Side effects

From an organisational viewpoint, managers assume that early retirement opens up promotional opportunities for younger workers. On the other hand, early retirement schemes can be costly and be in conflict of ageing strategies and the need to keep older employees longer in jobs. Moreover, countries with demographic pressures must ensure that older employees remain active and not leave into retirement. Other forms of attrition, in which organisations do not replace a person who leaves, is the simplest method. With this approach, employees have the opportunity to exercise free choice in deciding whether to stay or leave, and thus the potential for conflict and feelings of powerlessness is minimized[203]. At the same time, however, attrition may pose serious problems for management, because it is unplanned and uncontrollable, especially in organisations which face "attractiveness" challenges on the labour market.

203 Ibid.

4.4.1.5 Dismissal and termination

Two countries have mentioned to use the instrument of "dismissals" frequently and 14 countries are using this instrument to a "moderate" degree. Thus, these numbers show that half of all analysed countries use this instrument. Again, these figures demonstrate that "job security" has become relative in the public sector. Whereas in the past it was possible to dismiss central public employees because of misbehaviour, the answers to our question "*Apart for reasons of misbehaviour, illegal conduct and poor performance, have measures been implemented in order to dismiss central public administration workforce since 2008*?" illustrate how much job security has been flexibilised. Fourteen countries have answered that measures have been implemented in order to dismiss central public administration workforce for other reasons than misbehaviour, illegal conduct and poor performance.

Still, this does not suggest that it has become easier to dismiss central public employees.

Interestingly, there is no clear link between the degree of budgetary pressures and compulsory termination. For example, Ireland did not refer to compulsory termination. However, Sweden applied this instrument to a moderate degree. Thus, the use of compulsory termination seems to be linked to other contextual variables, such as the national social dialogue, status issues and the degree of job protection. For example, in Sweden, civil servants can be dismissed, but still enjoy a high degree of job protection

Compulsory termination – side effects

Compulsory termination, in which employees are dismissed (for example, because of financial difficulties), is the final downsizing strategy. In the past, this instrument was almost never used as central public employees enjoyed life-time tenure or enhanced job security. However, in the meantime, more OECD countries have introduced possibilities to dismiss public employees for various reasons. These decisions are, of course, unappealing to employees but also to managers who make the decisions and often lead to costly lawsuits alleging discrimination. Because of its severe side effects, we will discuss this instrument more intensively in the following chapter.

4.4.1.6 Downsizing and cutting employment

Across-the-board cuts are centralised decisions to cut public employment on central public administration level, and/or in every ministry/department/ organisation by a given percentage. Overall, 17 countries have reported to use this instrument. For example, Germany has reduced public employment levels by cutting public employment levels by approx. 1, 5% per year since 1991.

The use of this instrument is linked to the budgetary situation. Eighty percent of all category 1 countries are using this instrument and only 20% reported not to make use of this instrument. On the other hand, 43% of the category 4 countries are applying this instrument and 57% do not.

Across the board cuts: side effects

These measures seem to be "fair" but are perhaps the least effective downsizing option. Such cuts emphasize standardized treatment of employees, but ignore the strategic importance of different organisations to the overall success *and* ignore different performance levels of organisations and employee levels "Sharing the pain of cuts by allocating them across-the-board to all units may minimize pain, help to maintain morale, and build a good team spirit in the organisation; but it is not responsible management. Not every unit in an organisation or every agency in a government contributes equally to the goals, purposes, and basic functions of that organisation or government… Targeting cuts is a difficult job that tends to be avoided by all but the most brave or foolhardy public officials. But, if things get bad enough, and the across-the-board strategy is no longer feasible, somewhere along the path of decline, top management will have to switch from across-the-board to targeted cut"[204].

"Even percentage cut -across-the-board are expedient be- because they transfer decision-making costs lower in the organisation, but they tend to be insensitive to the needs, production functions, and contributions of different units. The same percentage cut may call for hardly more than some mild belt tightening in some large unspecialized units but when translated into the elimination of one or two positions in a highly specialized, tightly integrated small unit, it may immobilize that unit. Criticizing productivity criteria is more difficult but

204 Levine, 1979, op cit., p. 182.

nevertheless appropriate, especially when the concept is applied to the practice of cutting low producing units and people based on their marginal product per increment of revenue. This method is insensitive to differences in clients served, unit capacity, effort, and need. A more appropriate criterion is one that cuts programs, organisation units, and employees so that the marginal utility for a decrement of resources is equal across units, individuals, and programs thereby providing for equal sacrifices based on the need for resources. However, this criterion assumes organisations are fully rational actors, an assumption easily dismissed. More likely, cuts will be distributed by a mix of analysis and political bargaining"[205].

4.4.2 Downsizing consequences

As could be seen, most OECD countries have been particularly active in reducing public employment and used a wide menu of downsizing instruments in achieving governmental objectives.

In many cases, countries have been active, in other cases, very reluctant, to dismiss central public employees. In total, between 2008 and 2013, 17 countries have dismissed public employees. Fourteen countries have reported that they have used the instrument of dismissals to a moderate degree. Three countries have used this instrument "frequently". Mostly, these cases took place in the context of restructuring and budgetary constraints.

Cutting back an organisation and dismissing employees involves making hard decisions about who will be let go; what measures, tasks and programmes will be scaled down or terminated; and what categories of employees will be asked to make sacrifices. These are tough problems.

Therefore, in no case, things are without complications, although downsizing by the way of dismissing people may have the strongest organisational and individual effects.

However, very little is known whether and how governments consider the direct and indirect effects of downsizing on organisational and individual performance: "As with most issues of public management involving the distribution of costs, the choice of decision rules to al locate cuts usually involves the trade-off between equity and efficiency." In most cases, something of value is sacrificed[206].

205 Levine (1978), op cit, p. 322.

206 Charles H. Levine/Irene S. Rubin and George G. Wolohojian.: Resource Scarcity and the Reform Model: The Management of Retrenchment in Cincinnati and Oakland. *Public Administration Review*, Vol. 41, No. 6 (Nov. – Dec., 1981), p. 627.

In this case, "equity" is meant to mean the distribution of cuts across the organisation with an equal probability of hurting all units and employees irrespective of impacts on the long term capacity of the organisation.

"Efficiency" is meant to mean the sorting, sifting, and assignment of cuts to those people and units in the organisation so that for a given budget decrement, cuts are allocated to minimize the long-term loss in total benefits to the organisation as a whole, irrespective of their distribution.

Making cuts on the basis of equity is easier for managers because it is socially acceptable, easier to justify, and involves few decision making costs. "Sharing the pain" is politically expedient because it appeals to common sense ideals of justice. Further, simple equity decision making avoids costs from sorting, selecting, and negotiating cuts. In contrast, efficiency cuts involve costly triage analysis because the distribution of pain and inconvenience requires that the value of people and subunits to the organisation have to be weighed in terms of their expected future contributions. In the public sector, of course, things are never quite this clear-cut because a host of constraints like career status, veteran's preference, bumping rights, entitlements, and mandated programs limit managers from selecting optimal rules for making cuts. Nevertheless, the values of equity and efficiency are central to allocative decision making and provide useful criteria for judging the appropriateness of cutback rules. By applying these criteria to five of the most commonly used or proposed cutback methods—seniority, hiring freezes, even percentage cuts across-the-board, productivity criteria, and zero-base budgeting—we are able to make assessments of their efficacy as managerial tools…"

Charles H. Levine, Organisational Decline and Cutback Management, in: Public Administration Review, Vol. 38, No. 4 (Jul. – Aug., 1978), pp. 321

Almost all OECD countries undertake downsizing with the expectation that they will achieve economic benefits, although academic research also indicates that downsizing is not always economically beneficial and brings a number of additional side-effects: "The impact of decisions made and processes undertaken in downsizing and restructuring organisations… influence retention of organisational knowledge, which in turn may have a significant impact on perceived organisational effectiveness"[207].

207 Helen Sitlington.: Do downsizing decisions affect organisational knowledge and performance? *Management Decision*, Vol. 49 No. 1.2011, p. 117.

The belief that there are two ways to raise efficiency—cutting costs or increasing —leads to this expectation (Cascio, 2005). Another reason for downsizing is the explosion of compensation costs and the understanding that future costs are more predictable than future revenues. Payroll expenses are fixed costs, so by cutting salaries, allowances, and performance related pay etc. countries should expect reductions in expenses.

However, these measures produce profound consequences. This has been covered extensively in the management, sociological and HRM literature and concerns the situation in the public and the private sector in the same way.

So far, there is too little empirical evidence suggesting that downsizing is effective or not in achieving the intended benefits. So far, the economic legitimacy of the strategy has been challenged in the literature, for example by Said et al. (2007)[208] who found that the expected positive effects of workforce reductions on labour productivity did not materialize. The authors noted, however, that the nil-impact of workforce reductions on organisational performance whilst raising questions about the economic legitimacy of downsizing, also indirectly raises important questions about many behavioural assumptions in the downsizing literature: "it is possible that the negative impact of major job cuts on survivors' work behaviours were balanced by an improvement in organisational efficiency after personnel reductions"[209].

At one level, our findings support what the extant literature has long suggested: justice perceptions have a significant role in predicting the effects of downsizing. As we will see later on, people become demotivated and lose trust in leaders and in the organisation. Therefore, how organisations handle the procedures related to downsizing and how managers/supervisors treat employees before, during and after the downsizing is very important in predicting survivors' attitudinal and behavioural responses. "Survivors" expect a fair procedure and fair treatment from the organisation. When this expectation of fairness is not met, they perceive the organisation as not fulfilling their obligation[210].

---

208 T. Said/J. Le Louarn/M.Trembly.: The performance effects of major workforce reductions *International Journal of Human Resource Management*, Vol. 18 no 12. 2007, pp. 2075–2094.

209 Rasidah Arshada & Paul Sparrowb.: Downsizing and survivor reactions in Malaysia: modelling antecedents and outcomes of psychological contract violation. *The International Journal of Human Resource Management*, Vol. 21, No. 11, September 2010, p. 1793.

210 Arshada/Sparrowb, Downsizing and survivor reactions in Malaysia, op cit, p. 1807 and 1808.

Thus, the effects of downsizing extend far beyond those who lose their jobs[211]. Downsizing has implication on management, HR departments, staff representatives, survivors, organisational culture and trust levels. Studies have shown that downsizing affects job commitment levels, job satisfaction, stress and health levels and morale. Two concepts are central to understanding this: the psychological contract and organisational justice perceptions[212].

Generally, the literature distinguishes between the financial, organisational, and human consequences[213].

Economic and financial consequences

The overall evaluation of the reported economic effects of downsizing is rather negative. A multitude of studies have shown that most organisations in the public and in the private sector have not been able to improve levels of efficiency, effectiveness, productivity and profitability. The downsizing literature even portrays an overwhelmingly negative picture of the financial benefits of downsizing. There is strong evidence suggesting that a pure downsizing strategy is unlikely to be effective[214].

Organisational consequences

Besides the financial benefits, downsizing is expected to create organisational benefits. In the public sector, "anticipated organisational benefits include lower overheads, less bureaucracy, faster decision making, smoother communications, greater entrepreneurship, and increased productivity" (Burke & Cooper, 2000). However, as already discussed, most empirical findings suggest that the majority of restructurings and downsizings fall short of objectives and that implementation places heavy administrative burdens on organisations and managers. Overall, work demands increase significantly for middle managers during and after downsizing[215].

211 Cascio, Downsizing and Redundancy, op cit, p. 342.

212 Ibid.

213 Franco Gandolfi.: Unravelling Downsizing – What do we know about the Phenomenon? Volume 10, Issue 3, July 2009. *Review of International Comparative Management.*2009, p. 414.

214 Ibid.

215 Adrian Thornhill & Mark Saunders.: op cit, p. 289.

Human consequences

Many studies[216] have shown that downsizing has serious and negative effects on the public service workforce in terms of trust in the organisation, leadership, morale, job satisfaction, job engagement etc. We will discuss this issue separately later on in this topic. According to Gandolfi, "Downsizing-related human costs are extensive (Gandolfi, 2009) and far-reaching (Burke & Greenglass, 2000). Literature distinguishes between three categories of people directly impacted by downsizing; executioners, victims, and survivors. By definition, a downsizing executioner (Downs, 1995) or downsizer (Burke, 1998) is an individual entrusted with the conduct of downsizing. In contrast, a victim (Kettley, 1995) is a person who is downsized out of a job involuntarily (Allen, 1997), while a survivor (Littler, 1998) is a person that remains with the firm after involuntary employee reductions have taken place.

Downsizing scholars have identified and empirically studied the symptoms associated with the emotions, behaviours and attitudes of survivors. These symptoms have come to be known as "sicknesses". The most prominent sickness, the survivor syndrome, is a set of emotions, behaviours, and attitudes exhibited by surviving employees (Littler, 1998). Brockner (1988) asserts that downsizing engenders a variety of psychological states in survivors, namely, guilt, positive inequity, anger, relief and job insecurity. These mental states have the potential to influence the survivors' work behaviours and attitudes, such as motivation, commitment, satisfaction and job performance. The survivor syndrome is characterized by decreased levels of morale, employee involvement, work productivity and trust towards management (Cascio, 1993)[217].

4.4.3 Is downsizing inevitable?

Our survey did not collect data on alternatives to downsizing. Research into the effects of downsizing and restructuring over the past 20 years has consistently reported the need to consider alternatives to downsizing[218] However, during the last years, a considerable body of research focuses on downsizing and its

216 See for example OECD, Public Servants as Partners for Growth, op cit, p. 81.
217 Gandolfi.: Unravelling Downsizing – What do we know about the Phenomenon?, op cit.
218 Cascio, Employment Downsizing and Its Alternatives, op cit, p. 13.

effects, but much less on the impacts of alternatives to downsizing, for example, as regards the effects of redeployment, relocation and retraining. There is also little evidence as regards the relationship between downsizing and innovation[219].

Table 22: Employment Downsizing and Its Alternatives[220]: Strategies for Long-Term Success

Alternatives to Employment Downsizing for Temporary Downturns
• Cut Temporary Staff
• Eliminate Overtime
• Offer voluntary retirement
• Freeze salaries
• Cut Salaries
• Delay raises
• Freeze hiring
• Reduce work hours
• Use temporary layoffs (furloughs)
• Use furloughs with Incentives
• Cancel business trips and costly perquisites
• Reduce or suspend matching contributions to company-sponsored saving plans
• Raise employee contributions to benefit plans
• Postpone or eliminate bonuses

Source: Wayne F. Cascio, 2009.

The importance of doing research in the field of alternatives can be seen when taking the case of "furloughs". Although only few countries have reported to implement furloughs, scientific research shows that employees perceive this instrument as positive, as long as it is perceived as a fair instrument and saves employment levels[221].

Many experts have also pointed to the need to consider other issues than only efficiency considerations and not only to focus on the effects of downsizing and restructuring measures exclusively on employees. In fact, restructuring and downsizing is an organisational challenge, too.

---

219 Cascio, Downsizing and Redundancy, op cit, pp. 345–346.

220 See also, Cascio, Downsizing and Redundancy, op cit, p. 341.

221 Soohoo Lee & Robert Mark Sanders.: Fridays Are Furlough Days: The Impact of Furlough Policy and Strategies for Human Resource Management During a Severe Economic Recession September 2013; vol. 33, 3: pp. 299–311.

Overall, downsizing and restructuring policies are implemented with the objective to save resources. However, these policies, as such, are expensive and take time. Also restructuring as such can be an "administrative burden" and involves a series of interrelated processes which range from political decision-making, senior management planning, operational implementation, communication strategies, the organisation of numerous meetings, individually-focused or group-focused interventions, the management of conflicts, etc.

Similar to restructuring, managing downsizing also involves a strategy on alternative human resource planning, the determination of which downsizing strategies are to be used; the consultation with staff representatives and affected individuals and the training of those responsible for implementation, notification of redundant employees and the implementing of support programmes for leavers and survivors[222].

Consequently, in many cases, downsizing and restructuring programmes can turn out to be complex bureaucratic challenges. Similar paradoxical effects are known from deregulation and privatisation efforts (which create more red-tape) and debureaucratisation efforts (which create more bureaucracy)[223].

Therefore, an organisation's ability to minimise or alleviate negative consequences will depend on the approach adopted and a number of organisational factors[224]. Cascio[225] suggests that downsizing and restructuring measures should only be implemented of a number of questions have been answered.

---

222 Thornhill/Mark N.K. The meanings, consequences and implications of the management of downsizing, op cit, p. 285.

223 David Graeber. The Utopia of Rules. Melville House: London, 2016: p. 9.

224 Thornhill/Mark N.K. The meanings, consequences and implications of the management of downsizing, op cit, p. 278.

225 Cascio, Employment Downsizing and Its Alternatives, op cit, p. 12.

Figure 20: Employment Downsizing: The Hard Questions

Downsizing: The Hard Questions
Why does employment downsizing make sense for the organisation?
What is the business case for employment downsizing?
What is the problem that the organization is trying to solve?
If the problem is short-term cash flow, are there alternative way to cut costs?
Do prospective layoffs include hard-to-find skill sets?
How will the downsizing affect high performers who are difficult to replace?
What are the short-term-payoffs from a downsizing strategy?
What long-term treats to the organization's strategic success might be associated with employment downsizing?
What long-term costs might the organization incur by implementing employment downsizing?
Do the long-term benefits associated with employment downsizing outweigh its short-term costs?

Source: Cascio, 2009, Employment Downsizing and Its Alternatives: Strategies for Long-Term Success, op cit, p. 13

All of this shows that, failing to take into account interdependencies and fairness issues, the importance of core competencies, retention of skill, and maintenance of institutional memory, etc. are likely to result in negative organisational outcomes from downsizing[226]. The same is true as regards issues such as the loss of knowledge that occurs during downsizing and restructuring[227].

Therefore, organisations undertaking downsizing/restructuring should not only consider the impact on fairness perceptions but also on workload, necessary investments in order to avoid side effects, culture and climate of the organisation in regard to mechanisms for knowledge retention and how knowledge can be retained, within their implementation strategies[228]. Thus, while implementing

---

226 Sitlington, Do downsizing decisions affect organisational knowledge and performance? op cit, p. 118.

227 Sitlington, Do downsizing decisions affect organisational knowledge and performance? op cit, p. 117.

228 Sitlington, Do downsizing decisions affect organisational knowledge and performance?, op cit, p. 126.

downsizing and restructuring measures, one should consider the direct and indirect costs of the "whole package"[229].

Table 23: Employment Downsizing and Its Alternatives: Direct and Indirect Costs of Downsizing

Direct and Indirect Costs of Downsizing	
Direct costs	**Indirect costs**
• **Severance pay, in lieu of notice** • **Accrued vacation and sick pay** • **Supplemental unemployment benefits** • **Outplacement** • **Pension and benefits pay-outs** • **Administrative processing costs** • **Costs of rehiring former employees**	• Recruiting and employment costs of new hires • Low morale, risk-averse survivors • Decreased productivity among survivors • Increase in unemployment tax rate. • Lak of staff when economy rebounds • Start-up costs (recruiting, training, staffing) • Voluntary terminations of those who remain • Potential lawsuits from aggrieved employees • Potential strikes by unions in some countries • Loss of institutional memory and trust in management • Brand equity cost damage to the company's brand as an employer of choice

Source: Cascio, 2009, Employment Downsizing and Its Alternatives: Strategies for Long-Term Success, op cit, p. 12

4.5 Reform of other HR bundles and policies

4.5.1 The reform of job security

Writers on public administration have long suggested that without a specific status, legal protection, lifetime tenure and special ethical rules, our societies would be open to terrible corruption (*furchtbarer Korruption* – Weber) and this would

229 Cascio, Employment Downsizing and Its Alternatives, op cit, p. 12.

undermine the capacity of the state to rule society. From this point of view, job security is most important in times of economic crisis.

While – in times of new public management euphoria – life time tenure has often been associated with poor performance, another often neglected aspect of public service employment is the function of job security as a motivational instrument. In most countries, job security in the public sector is also an important (motivational) element for the recruitment and the retention of staff. At present, therefore, most countries still agree with this argument that job security is important, but also argue that more job security can only be justified for specific positions and functions. Moreover, in times of economic constraints and performance orientation, the importance of job security seems to be widely underestimated as an important motivational factor and the attractiveness of the public sector as an employer. This is also in line with many studies that show the detrimental effects of job insecurity.

Yet, as we have seen, lifetime employment seems to be less important than it was some decades ago. During the past years, many countries have been moving away from the classical lifetime-tenure principle. In more countries it is now possible to dismiss civil servants for various reasons (and more often also in cases of poor performance). Countries with a more traditional bureaucratic career system still have a higher degree of job security. Thus, if a country decides to reform its traditional career structure, it is also likely that it will reform traditional job security patterns. Here, one case is Portugal, which has completely reformed traditional bureaucratic employment features, including job security.

The current downsizing trends in many countries also show that it would be misleading to speak in a general way about the "stability of public service employment". In fact, people often have a false image of employment in the public sector, since they believe that public employment is more stable than employment in the private sector. Austria, Columbia, Latvia, United Kingdom, Portugal, Poland, Spain and Austria reported that personnel cuts were stronger in the central public administrations than in the private sector.

In the meantime, it seems, a bureaucratic country like Greece has provided for less job security than a post-bureaucratic like Sweden although, by tradition, many countries with a bureaucratic career structure allow dismissals only for disciplinary reasons. Thus, increasingly, restructuring, downsizing and reorganisation enable governments to terminate the employment relationship.

On the other hand, the case of Ireland shows that countries have choices independently of the economic situation. Ireland implemented a high number of reforms in all HR bundles. However, this was not the case in the field of job security and the dismissal of staff.

Still, the trend towards the relaxation of job security is not towards a continuous weakening of job protection for civil servants. Overall, (only) five countries have reported that it has become easier to dismiss public employees and (only) four countries have also eased job protection for civil servants. Thus, despite the trend towards less job security, many countries seem to maintain a high degree of job security for central administration employees.

Figure 21: Dismissals of public employees and civil servants

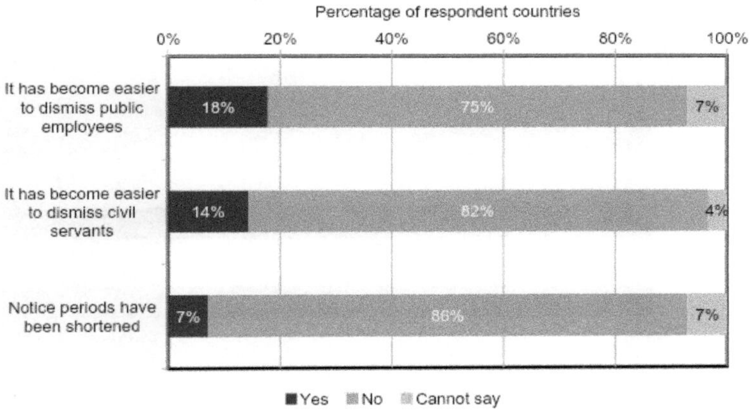

From this, one may derive the conclusion that the degree of job security is still high but "relative" and closely connected to the national context, status, the national social dialogue etc. However, as long as budgetary pressures persist or are even increasing, this may also a reason for reforming job security levels and abandon old, established practices.

4.5.2 Reform paths in the field of compensation and salary systems

Remuneration is arguably one of the most critical influences on the quality and effectiveness of human resources. Compensation influences job satisfaction, job motivation, job performance, turnover, fairness perceptions and the quality of the work. In virtually every aspect of organisational functioning, compensation can shape employee behaviour and organisational effectiveness[230].

230 Nina Gupta & Jason D. Shaw.: Employee compensation: The neglected area of HRM research: *Human Resource Management Review* 24. 2014, p. 1.

As already mentioned earlier in this survey, our data suggest that remuneration systems were subject to very strong reform activities in the field of HRM. Whereas other issues such as working time and leave were only changed moderately, the remuneration systems were subject to massive reforms. Between 2008 and 2013, almost 75% of all countries have introduced reforms of their remuneration systems.

Here, it is important to note that the reform of remuneration systems is an "EU dominated" reform topic. 71, 4% of all countries that have implemented reforms in the field of remuneration are EU-Member States.

Figure 22: Reform of remuneration system

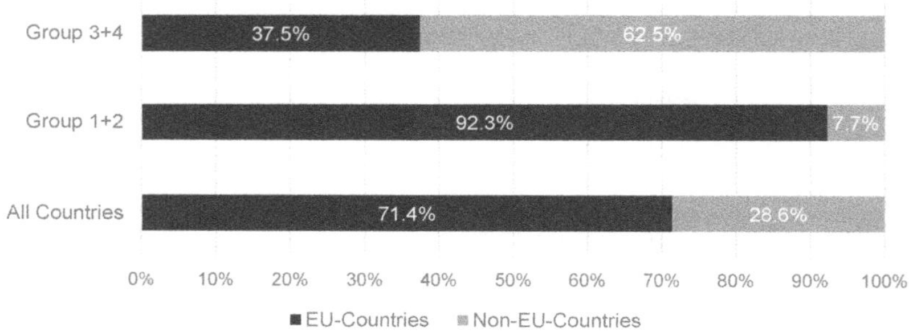

Some examples may illustrate the changes:

Portugal implemented wage cuts, suspensions of performance bonuses and decreases of overtime pay. Since 2010, Spain implemented a salary cut. Moreover, in 2012 there has been an elimination of one of the two annual extra pay scales. In Poland, since 2009 pay in the civil service has been frozen. In addition, it has been decided to extend this freeze until 2016. Secondly, in 2009 the scale which serves to determine the basic pay of civil service corps members and so-called civil service bonus (paid to the civil servants only) has been changed. This change has been preceded by a substantial research conducted by the Civil Service Department in the scope of individual pay of civil service corps members. Thirdly, a special bonus—one of optional components of pay—was eliminated. The background document which prolongs the freeze on civil service pay till 2016 is the Multiannual Financial Plan of the State (it comprises also the Convergence Programme). Hungary eliminated the 13th salary. Estonia abolished career-based salary components, such as additional remuneration for tenure, foreign languages and academic degree. In Belgium the reforms slowed down the temporal advancement by spreading the increases over more periods and in slowing down advancement if unsatisfactory performance. In Germany, seniority is not anymore taken into account. For the remuneration of agents in professional and secretarial positions and technical support, pay regularly increases in eight levels in line with experience. Remuneration is also based on performance: Agents effecting extraordinary performance can enter new levels faster; agents with low performance may not reach a new level in the regular periodic interval. Finally, in the Czech Republic the average salaries for top level actually increased due to non-systematic changes introduced in 2011. The overall budget for state employee's remuneration was decreased by 10%. This resulted in decrease of salaries for a vast number of regular staff and increase in salaries for some managers.

Figure 23: Instruments used in Remuneration Reforms

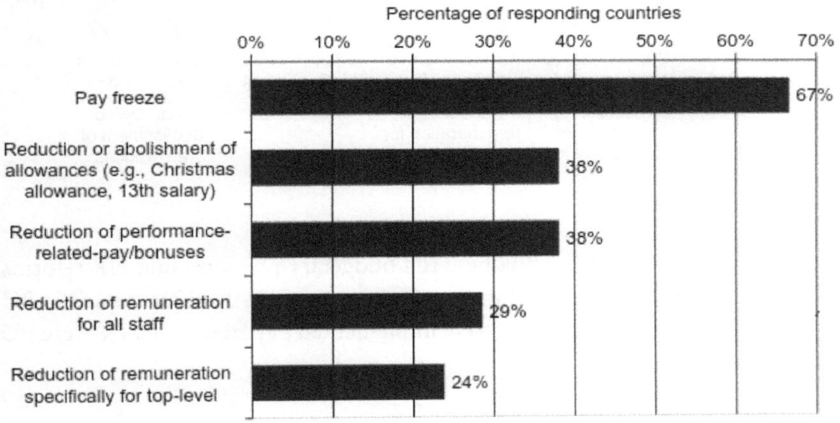

Altogether 14 OECD countries have implemented measures in order to freeze remuneration (sometimes for certain categories of staff), seven countries even cut remuneration levels for all categories of staff, in nine countries allowances and bonuses were reduced as well as performance related pay. The latter was the case in those countries with high and highest budgetary pressures. However, some countries with modest budgetary pressures did not implement drastic reforms or did not even implement any reforms at all. Chile, Norway, Sweden, Australia, Switzerland, Austria, Belgium, New Zealand, Germany and the United States did not cut remuneration levels. 67% of countries in the sample (43% of countries with low budgetary constraints and 100% of those with high budgetary constraints) implemented remuneration reforms since 2008.

Figure 24: Remuneration reforms in central public administration since 2008 per category of countries

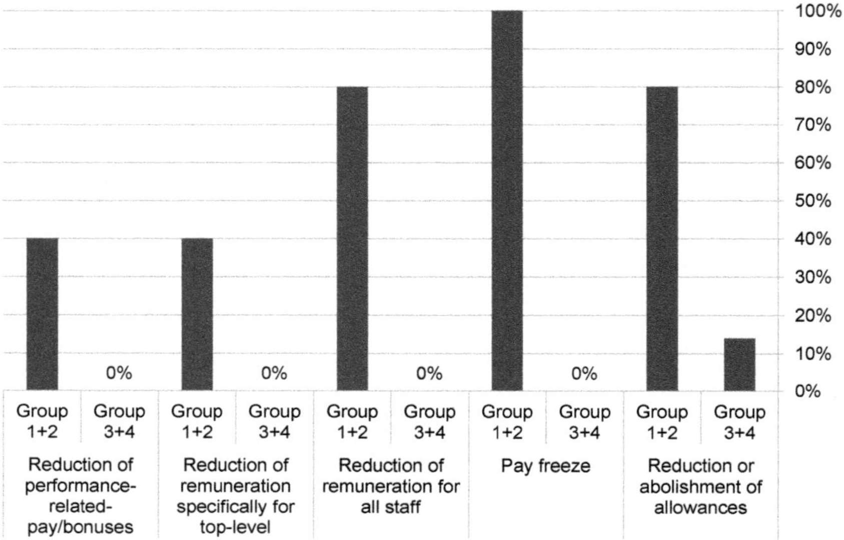

Thus, one could say that the link between budgetary pressures and HR reforms is strongest in the field of pay. Moreover, freezing pay mostly implemented in EU countries. From all countries that have implemented pay freezes, 85, 7% were EU Member States.

Figure 25: Payment freeze

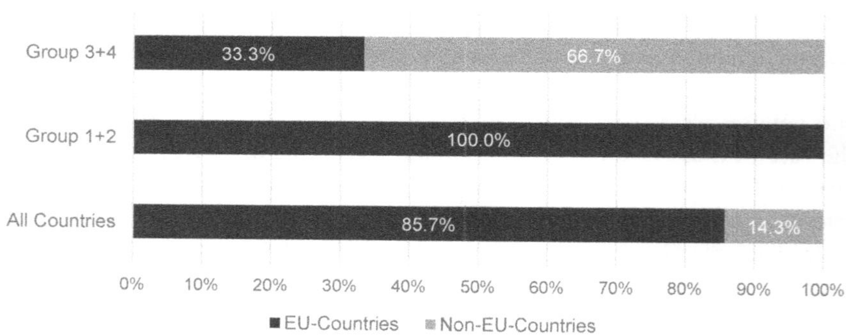

Pay reforms are often subject to very emotional (and not often rational) debates, especially if discussions focus on senior pay, comparisons between public and private pay and performance-related pay.

In his philosophical study, Dekkers[231] compared the pay debate in 17 European, Asian and American democracies, including the Netherlands. Dekkers extracted seven arguments (for example *higher pay will improve performance of top officials*) that figure prominently in all of the discussions. He then analysed these issues using philosophical techniques and empirical research. Dekker concludes that often popular arguments are based on perceptions and clichés and not the exchange of a rational discussion.

4.5.3 What happens to performance related pay in times of budgetary constraints?

As countries struggle to balance their budgets, increased attention is focusing on how public employees are compensated. OECD countries are also facing considerable pension and retiree health care obligations that have significantly contributed to their financial problems.

Traditional remuneration systems were established decades ago and for a long time they changed very little. The traditional focus on careers, stability, seniority and positions made sense when the vast majority in the public service had similar qualifications and jobs. The classical pay system was adapted to the dominant values at the time: bureaucratization, standardization and equality. Consequently, civil service systems were still predominantly based on the principle of automatic pay progression, immaterial incentives and (more or less) automatic promotion as a motivator. Thus, whereas public pay systems were based on the principle of equality, private sector pay systems were based on the principle of autonomy: "In terms of Hofstede's cultural framework, the civil service culture differs from the prevalent business culture in the United States on the dimension of individualism versus collectivism. The civil service subculture tends to be more security-oriented than competitive and can be described as more collectivist than individualist favoring equality over equity"[232].

---

231 Teun J. Dekker.: Paying Our High Public Officials – Evaluating the Moral Justifications of Top Wages in the Public Sector, Routledge.2013.

232 Brigitte W. Schay & Sidney F. Fisher.: The Challenge of Making Performance-Based Pay Systems Work in the Public Sector. *Public Personnel Management*, No. 42(3). 2013, p. 379.

As the scrutiny of public sector pay has increased, renewed attention has focused on the longstanding debate on whether private sector workers earn more than their public sector counterparts. Conclusions from past comparison studies of pay and total compensation vary due to different approaches, methods, and data leading to disagreements over their applicability[233]. In order to offer comparable data and with the objective to contribute to a rational debate on the issue, the OECD has also started to work on the issue as such[234].

During the last years, the workforce, the work and values have also changed greatly. In particular, qualifications have become much more diverse and work has become highly skilled and increasingly specialized knowledge work. In addition, important changes in values have taken place. Today, civil servants want to be seen as "individuals" and to be treated individually. In Dubet's research 72.9% of all people interviewed find performance-related pay fairer than seniority pay[235].

Consequently, traditional pay systems with their career ladders, time-based pay increases and specific allowances are increasingly reflecting a slowly disappearing concept of employment: "That model is designed to reward loyalty by providing stable and secure employment, reflecting and meeting those needs"[236]. Today, employees themselves expect immediate rewards and recognition for their individual accomplishments.

Thus, although traditional pay systems may better correspond to the principle of equality, they do not match with new expectations and value changes. Today, more public employees want to combine the principle of equality with the principle of autonomy and individual performance. In short: they want to be treated more as individuals. Consequently, during the last years the reform of *incentive systems has* played a major role in motivating employees towards performance orientation. Many countries have introduced a pluralist incentive sys-tem ("cafeteria system") which offers a broad choice of extrinsic and intrinsic incentives and rewards. For example, most OECD countries have

233 Thom Reilly.: Comparing Public-Versus-Private Sector Pay and Benefits: Examining Lifetime Compensation. *Public Personnel Management* 42(4). 2013, pp. 521–544.

234 OECD.: Public Sector Compensation in Times of Austerity, OECD Publishing, Paris. 2012.

235 Francois Dubet et al. : Injustices: L'expérience des inégalités au travail, 2013.

236 US Office of Personnel Management.:, Performance Related Pay, Washington D.C., April 2002, p. 4.

implemented performance-related pay systems in recent years[237]. The main reason for introducing PRP cited in most cases is to enhance the motivation of employees and thus to improve performance and efficiency[238].

Figure 26: Geographical distribution of performance related-pay in central public administrations

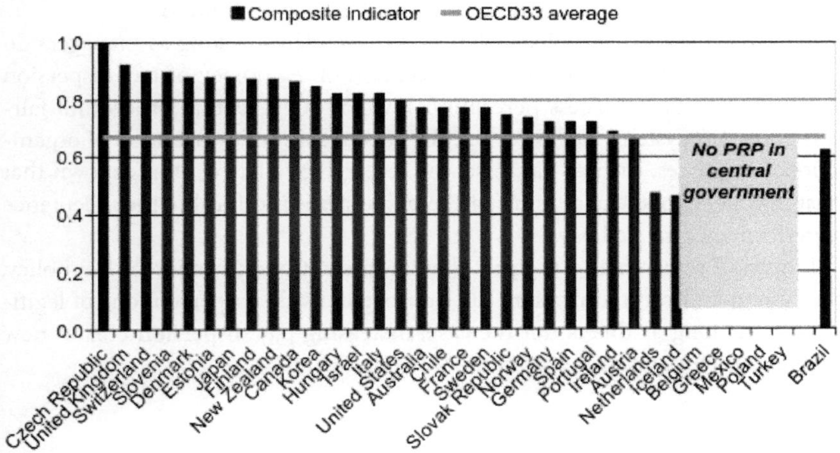

Source: Information provided by governments in response to a request for information issued by the OECD Public Governance and Territorial Development Directorate to national delegates to the Public Employment and Management Network in June 2012; 2010 OECD Survey on Strategic Human Resources Management in Central/Federal Governments

The reform of pay systems is followed by a strong tendency to decentralise the remuneration system to regional and local authorities, or to agencies and even to line management. Thus, in most OECD countries processes of responsbilisation, individualization, flexibilisation and decentralization can also be seen in the field of pay.

---

237 Brigitte W. Schay & Sidney F. Fisher.: The Challenge of Making Performance-Based Pay Systems Work in the Public Sector. *Public Personnel Management*, No. 42(3). 2013, pp. 359–384.

238 David Marsden & Ray Richardson, Motivation and Performance Related Pay in the public Sector, Centre for Economic Performance, London School of Economics, Discussion Paper No.75, May 1992.

In the meantime, not only the national pay systems differ but also the various systems of performance related pay. Overall, pay diversity as such has increased within the national systems and amongst the different occupations and ranks[239]. Also the structure of the systems has become more diverse[240]. Whereas Sweden has a relatively individualized pay system (every agency negotiates individually with its employees), pay is decentralized between the federal and the regional level in Germany. In other countries pay is still rather centralized.

This trend towards pay dispersion creates problems as long as managers do not succeed to increase employees' perception of legitimacy of pay dispersion (and organisational fairness perceptions), which suggests that procedural fairness of the HR systems can maximize the effectiveness of distribution of organisational resources, such as pay. Also, the research by Shay et al has shown that trust in supervisors who administer the pay systems is critical to the acceptance of performance-related pay.

Empirical research also suggests that an integrative and coherent HR policy, pay system and communication, can improve individuals' perceptions of legitimacy[241]. As long as this is not the case, increasing pay dispersion creates new conflicts and unfairness perceptions.

---

239 Patrick E. Downes & Daejeong Choi.: Employee reactions to pay dispersion: A typology of existing research, in: Human Resource Management Review, Vol. 24. 2014, pp. 53–66; Matt Bloom, The Performance effects of Pay Dispersion on Individuals and Organisations. *The Academy of Management Journal*, Vol. 42, No. 1. 1999, pp. 25–40.

240 Knut Rexed/Chris Moll/Nick Manning/Jennifer Allain.: Governance of Decentralised Pay Setting in Selected OECD Countries, *OECD Working Paper*, No.3. 2007.

241 Ibid, p. 65.

Figure 27: The use of PRP in Central Government

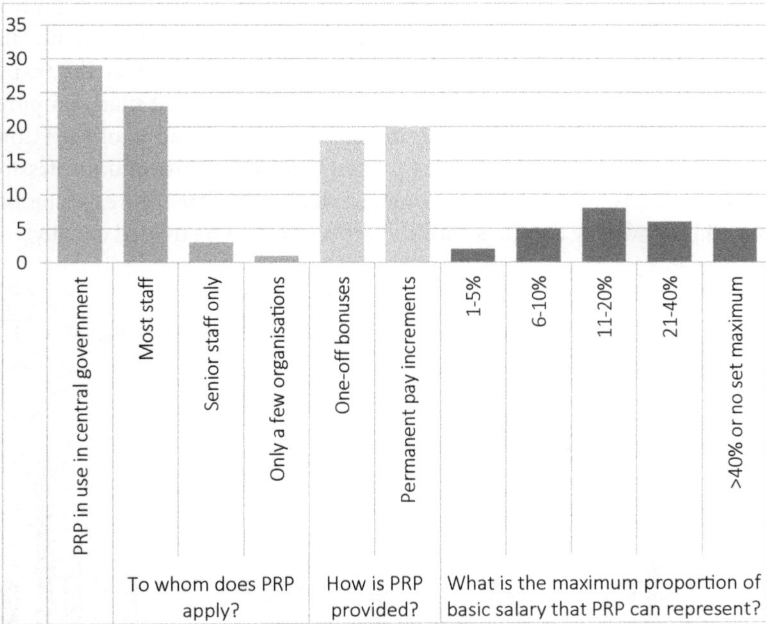

Source: Information provided by governments in response to a request for information issued by the OECD Public Governance and Territorial Development Directorate to national delegates to the Public Employment and Management Network in June 2012; 2010 OECD Survey on Strategic Human Resources Management in Central/Federal Governments.

Still, public employees constantly compare their performance with the performance of their colleagues (Note: most believe that they are better than others). In the case of standardized pay, many employees believe that their pay is not fair since they perform better than their colleagues. Many also believe that their performance is not managed and measured in a professional way. Consequently, fairness problems differ from the past. However, they are not solved once PRP is introduced and civil servants are paid according to performance[242].

From now on, new feelings of being treated unfairly (for example, by those who measure performance levels) emerge and, in many instances, people are

242 Kirsten Bregn.: Detrimental Effects of Performance-Related Pay in the Public Sector? On the Need for a Broader Theoretical Perspective. *Public Organization Review*. 2013, No. 13, pp. 21–35.

even more demotivated and frustrated after the introduction of PRP. Since people constantly compare themselves with other colleagues, they also tend to believe that colleagues who receive bonuses and PRP do not deserve them. Often, employees who do not receive PRP are becoming demotivated since they expected to get bonuses etc. Another dilemma concerns the fact that many employees do not trust their superiors to take fair decisions on the allocation of PRP. Consequently, many people feel that they are treated unfairly because of unprofessional or unfair pay decisions of their superiors. In all of these cases, the expectation to be treated individually conflicts with the expectation to be treated equally.

Figure 28: Compensation of central government middle managers (2011)

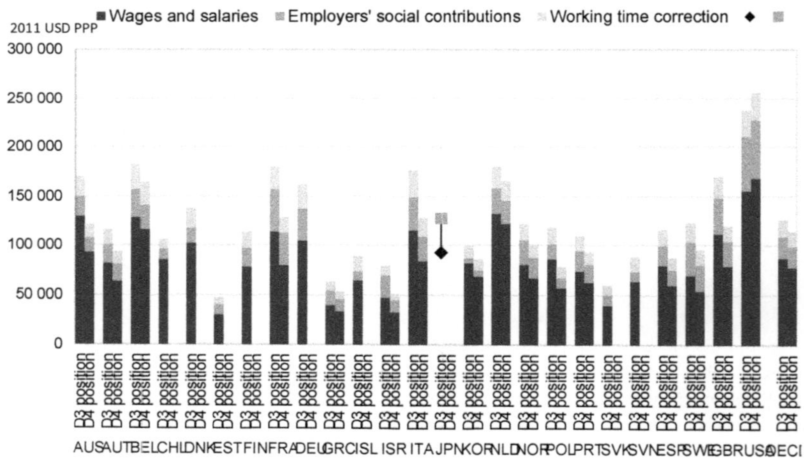

Source: OECD, 2011

Thus, as long as traditional pay systems exist they will always be seen as unfair and not corresponding to new value developments. However, any alternative may not be better. In the future one main challenge will be to better balance the three principles of equality, autonomy and performance in the field of performance-related pay.

The complexity surrounding reward management is just one of the difficulties faced by human resource management. The main argument put forward in favour of PRP is that it acts as a motivator, by providing extrinsic rewards in the form of pay and intrinsic rewards through the recognition of effort and achievement. PRP is also seen as helping employees to identify closely with the goals of the organisation, leading to increased productivity, quality, flexibility and teamwork. In addition, PRP is seen to be useful in the recruitment and retention of staff.

For the past 50 years, many researchers, however, have questioned whether PRP actually acts as a motivator, or, indeed, if money can motivate. Empirical evidence in the USA, Australia and Malaysia even questions whether PRP has enhanced individual performance[243].

Demmke[244] suggests that modern Performance-Related Pay Schemes are not necessarily fairer than traditional seniority pay. Rather questions of unfair and fair pay are simply different in centralised, standardised and decentralised systems. Whereas in the former system, the principle of seniority (everybody receives salary increases independently of his or her performance) may be at the centre of the "unfairness" debate in systems with PRP and individual pay setting, the problem is the pay discretion of managers (and the subjective allocation of PRP to those people who are supposed to perform better) and the perception of employees" (different) pay to that of their colleagues.

However, returning to the traditional centralized and seniority pay schemes is not an option. Rather, it is important to design fairer pay systems under decentralized conditions. For this, one major challenge will also be to avoid discrimination in allocating bonuses and PRP. In 2008, a study by the European Foundation for the Improvement of Living and Working Conditions revealed that "men are not only paid bonuses more often but the sums they are paid are also larger. Some 13% of male wage and salary earners had received at least €1,000 as a bonus for the previous year, whereas only 5% of women received such a bonus. A significant gender pay gap is also evident with respect to medium-sized bonuses of between €500 and €1,000"305. So far, only few empirical studies have analysed the pay gap between full-time employees and part-time employees, older versus younger employees, top-civil servants versus line managers and other employees etc. In the future, the legitimacy of performance-related pay systems will very

243 Jeanette Taylor & LooSee Beh.: The Impact of Pay-for-Performance Schemes on the Performance of Australian and Malaysian Government Employees. *Public Management Review*, Vol. 15, No. 8.2013, pp. 1090–1115; Edward Kellough & Lloyd Nigro.: Pay for Performance in Georgia State Government. *Review of Public Personnel Administration*, Vol. 22, No. 2. 2002, pp. 146–166; James Perry &T.A. Engbers/S.Y. Jun.: Back to the Future? Performance Related Pay, Empirical research, and the Perils of Persistance. *Public Administration Review*, Vol. 69, No. 1. 2009, pp. 39–51.

244 Christoph Demmke.: Leistungsbezahlung in den öffentlichen Diensten der EU-Mitgliedstaaten – eine Reformbaustelle. *der moderne Staat*, No. 1/2009.

much depend on the question whether bonuses are paid as a result of a non-discriminatory process. One may doubt whether this is the case today.

The data to our survey even suggests that performance related pay has already seen its "best times" and the difference between theory and practice is increasing. 9 countries have reduced bonuses, allowances and performance related pay.

However, interestingly, Greece has introduced a performance related pay system in 2014.

Overall, current trends in the field of pay are complex and contradictory. Whereas pay disparity and pay flexibility are increasing, feelings of being treated unfairly may be rising if performance related pay is not implemented properly. At the same time, there is still wide support for decentralised and flexible pay systems and the need to align public and private pay settings (especially for top-managers).

4.5.4 Skill development and training – investments instead of saving resources?

Today, politicians and managers repeat the mantra that economic competitiveness depends crucially on the skills and investments in training of the workforce. Whereas in the past "skill development and training" were underfunded "underdogs" in the field of HRM, today they have become top priorities policies, and not only in the field of HRM, but as a policy in general.

Everywhere, governments, politicians and management experts agree upon the key role that skills, training and long-life-learning play in securing competitiveness and social cohesion. Within this discourse, it seems that skills are the answer to a whole set of economic and social problems.

In fact, education is a key element as regards the economic growth capabilities of an economy[245]. However, education does not automatically lead to an educated workforce. At the beginning of their study, Hanushek & Woessman wondered, why South America was never able to profit from, compared with parts of Asia, their good institutions, good infrastructure and the superflux of resources. The answer seems to be the rather poor quality of the education[246] Similar studies have been carried out – from an neo-institutional logic—explaining why potentially "rich" countries are performing poorly. Explanatory variables ranged from poor education systems, lack of resources and capacities, corrupt political elites

245 E.A. Hanushek & L. Woessmann, L.: The Knowledge Capital of Nations: Education and the Economics of Growth. London: MIT Press. Massachusetts. 2015.

246 Hanushek & Woessmann, 2015, op cit, p. 2f.

to the lack of good governance. Thus, education and skills are indeed an important factor, but not the only one.

With the increasing importance of skill policies, also the notion of skills has also become considerably broader than it was in the past[247]. Today, the popular skill discourse uses very different notions like enlarging basic skills, employability skills, adapting skills, key skills, management skills, future skills, IT skills and leadership skills. Today, the term skill includes a variety of meanings such as soft-skills, transferable skills, interactional skills, problem solving skills social skills, IT skills and networking skills. The term "skill" as such has become indistinguishable from personal characteristics, traits, competences, behaviours and attitudes[248]. Consequently, policy makers increasing insistence upon the diffuse using of skills has not been matched by strategic approaches in the field of training policies.

Why have skill development policies become so important, other than because of economic factors?

One of the main reasons is the shift from traditional and hierarchical industry towards "flat" services, with the need for employees to have more relational, communicative and problem solving soft skills. However, technological developments and organisational renewal are not the only factors that require skill renewal. Overall, the decentralization, fragmentation and individualization of structures and processes also require the decentralization and individualization of skill development and training policies. In "Training and Human Resource Development in the European Union Member States", Bossaert et al (2008) observe that trends towards more individualistic HRM approaches can best be seen in the field of training, "where the 'catalogue' philosophy in the sense of standardized training activities is increasingly replaced by tailor-made 'action' programmes, which are more frequently based on concrete individual needs and whose main concern is the transfer of competence"[249].

New Public Management doctrines focused on efficiency, outputs and results-based performance management. This approach required managers to adapt quickly to the development of a new performance management bureaucracy and

---

247 John Payne.: The unbearable lightness of skill: the changing meaning of skill in UK policy discourses and some implications for education and training. *Journal of Education Policy*, Vol. 1, No. 3. 2000, pp. 353–369.

248 Ibid.

249 Daniel Bossaert (Editor).: Training and Human Resource Development in the European Union Member States, European Institute of Public Administration, Maastricht. 2008, p. 6.

the need to learn how to manage and to measure individual and organisational performance. Boxall adds that public employees face a fast-changing, ambiguous environment characterized by constrained funding. In this surrounding, managers need capabilities in organisational renewal and political and interpersonal skills to handle a complex network of stakeholders. Thus, the networking society and collaborative governance have become ever-important skill requirements as such, as "networking", "coordinating", "and communicating" and "co-working" become ever more important skill requirements. To this should be added the business environment, which is becoming ever more international and culturally diverse.

Finally, demographic challenges and budgetary constraints also mean that public sector organisations face particular challenges in attracting and retaining staff and the need to adapt the skills and develop older employees. In a context of financial constraints, public organisations simply cannot compete for talent by paying higher wages. In fact, they need to invest in the existing workforce.

According to Boxall, this "environment poses some major challenges for management development, which we have grouped into three broad categories: managing uncertainty and renewal, managing stakeholders and partners, and managing people and resources. The issues chief executives face, such as how to renew and restructure and organisation effectively, do not fall neatly into one disciplinary silo and are handled better by managers who have been equipped to deal with systemic problems. Now more than ever, HR specialists need to be focused on the development of line managers…"[250].

However, skill development requirement should not only focus on the top and on line managers. What is needed is investment in the whole workforce. But what do we know about concrete investments in training and skill development in OECD countries?

In fact, there are many reasons to expect that OECD countries reform training systems as such, but do not decrease the amount of training even in times of budgetary constraints, their investments in the field of training. In order to get an overview about the importance of training as such, we have therefore started to collect data on the length of training as such.

Our data reveals that training offered to public employees ranges from one day in Latvia, Spain and Costa Rica to twelve days in Norway and in Hungary

---

250 Peter Boxall.: The critical challenges facing New Zealand's chief executives: implications for management skills. *Asia Pacific Journal of Human Resources*, Vol. 52. 2014, p. 38.

and 14 days per year in Korea. Overall, only 18 countries replied to this question, as training is a decentralized service and reliable data is not always available. Moreover, in times of on-line training, it becomes more difficult to compare and to assess training (and costs) as such. Still, it seems that some countries offer many training opportunities. However, in other countries, training is still a neglected HR policy and even a rare HRM activity.

Figure 29: Length of training in days per year

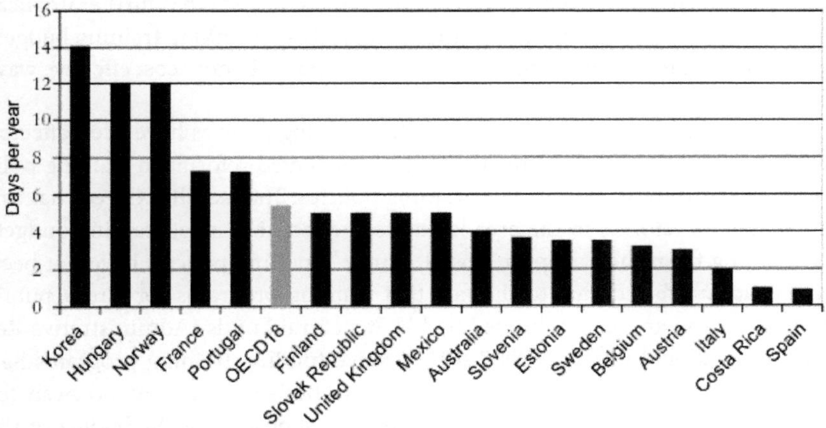

Training in the United States varies between one day and one week on average.

Often, literature on training is placing training into the context of lifelong learning, knowledge management and skill-development. Consequently, the importance of training as such is increasing. On the other hand, the literature on training is silent about cutbacks in civil service training budgets and what impact cutbacks have on training content and methods[251]. The latter can be explained by the fact that cuts in training contradict with official proclamations on the importance of competency development and skill training:

"In fact, training has many roles in central public administrations. Firstly, it is related to the implementation of tasks and focuses on developing skills and competencies in order to fulfil objectives of the organisation. Secondly, it is part of the motivation system and functions as an instrument to retain a high-quality

251 Merilin Metsma.: The Impact of Cutback Management on Civil-Service Training: The Case of Estonia. Administrative Culture 15 (1). 2014, 58–79, p. 74.

and high performing workforce. And thirdly, training is an instrument to raise civil servants' awareness of their role and responsibility and introduce shared values among civil service staff"[252]. Bossaert et al (2008) also claim that training is linked to organisational performance and as such an asset and an investment in human resources[253]. According to Stewart and Brown, training can also be aligned with strategy to help an organisation gain a competitive advantage over other organisations[254].

Contrary to these findings, our survey confirms that training budgets seem to be among the first items to be cut when fiscal stress hits. This has further implications for training programs and training methods as shrinking training budgets force organisations to prioritize training topics and seek more cost effective ways of delivering training[255].

Overall, 22 countries have reported that training policies have been affected by the financial crisis. 19 countries have implemented reforms in training policies in order to raise efficiency of training policies. The fact that Greece has not implemented reforms in the area is due to the fact that most training budgets are coming from the European Social Funds: "Training policies have not been significantly affected, due to the fact that training programs for Greek public administration are mainly funded by EU Structural Funds (Administrative Reform Operational Program 2007–2013). Since funding training programs had no, (or had just minor) impacts for the State Budget, there was no need for reduction/cuts. What is not certain is how the allocation of the budget of the next programming period (2014–2020) will affect the training programs" (Greek answer to the OECD survey).

In fact, our data illustrates that 16 OECD countries have reduced training budgets and ten countries have reduced the number of training days.

---

252 Merilin Metsma, op cit, p. 59.

253 Bossaert, Training, op cit, p. 164.

254 Greg L. Stewart &Kenneth G. Brown.: Human Resource Management, 2nd edition, John Wiley, New Baskerville. 2011, p. 335.

255 Merilin Metsma, op cit, p. 59.

Figure 30: Implementation of austerity reforms in training policies

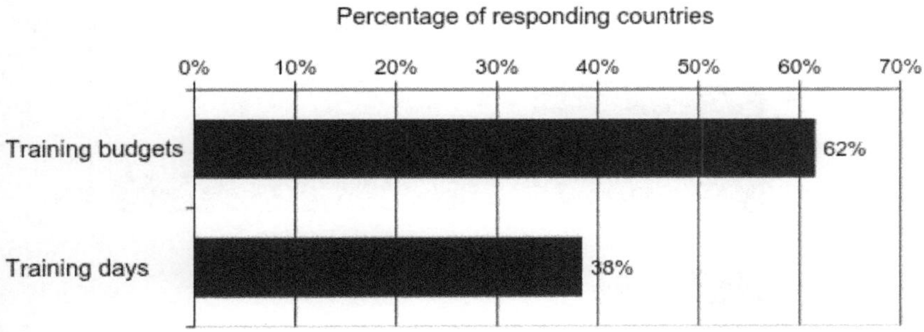

Again, important differences can be made between countries with high budgetary pressures and countries with lower budgetary pressures. Overall, countries belonging to category 3 and 4 also reduce budget and reduce training days. However, in almost two-thirds of all responding countries, training is considered as a cost factor, and many OECD countries seek to cut training budgets. For example, in Poland, the training budget for the whole civil service decreased by approximately 20% from 61,1 million PLN in 2009 to 48,8 million PLN in 2014 although the number of trainees stayed more or less the same. Thus, the effect of the financial crisis on the training budget is considerable. As already mentioned, our data also suggest that cuts in training budgets are influenced by the source of training funds 8as in the case of Greece).

Only in Sweden, France, Germany, Norway, Chile, Canada, Korea and Columbia training policies have not been affected by the financial crisis. All of these countries do not belong to our category 1 and 2 countries. On the other hand, 80% of those countries with high budgetary constraints (category 1 and 2) have implemented reforms in the field of training policies.

Figure 31: Austerity reforms in the field of training per category of countries

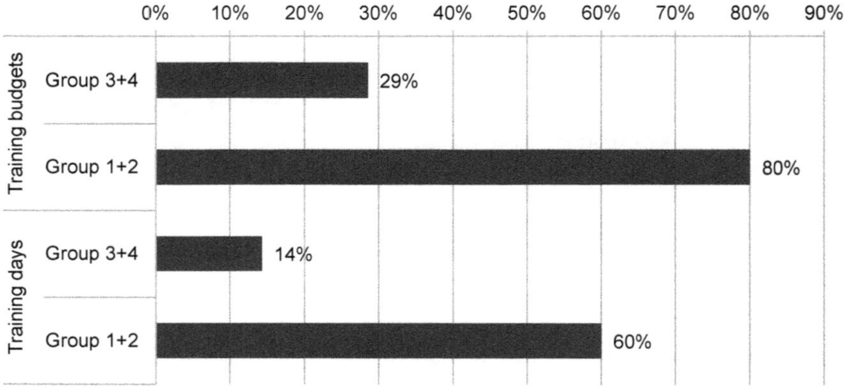

The case of France shows, again, that countries have choices. Although France belongs to those countries with high budgetary constraints (category 2), this country has chosen not to cut training budgets and not to reduce training days. On the other hand, Switzerland and Finland have introduced budget reforms and reduced training days.

Obviously, there are significant differences amongst countries as regards the choice of reform instruments in the field of training.

According to Stewart/Brown (2011), there are many possible reform options in order to reduce costs and raise efficiency of training. These measures can be divided into:

- Development Costs
- Delivery Costs
- Trainer Salary and Benefits
- Hidden costs (Trainee compensation, trainee productivity)
- Wasted Investments (offering training without needs assessments etc.)[256].

256 Stewart/Brown (2011), Human Resource Management, op cit, p. 338.

Figure 32: Implementation of measures to raise training policies' efficiency since 2008

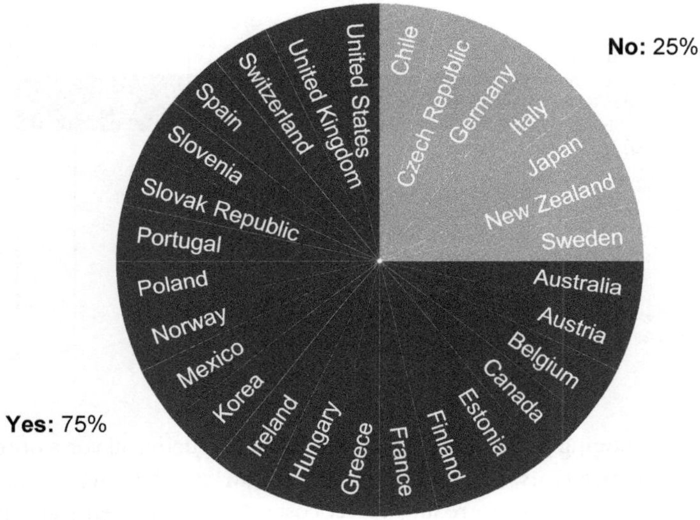

In our survey, there was no space to analyse all of these "efficiency instruments".

Still, OECD countries reported that they are introducing measures to make training more cost-effective, by reducing travel costs to training events (in eleven countries) or by centralising and streamlining training curricula (United Kingdom), by using training needs assessments to ensure that training is only provided when necessary (in 14 countries) and by shifting employees training to be readily available at employees' desks (computer-assisted e-training) (in 21 countries).

Figure 33: Measures introduced in order to raise efficiency

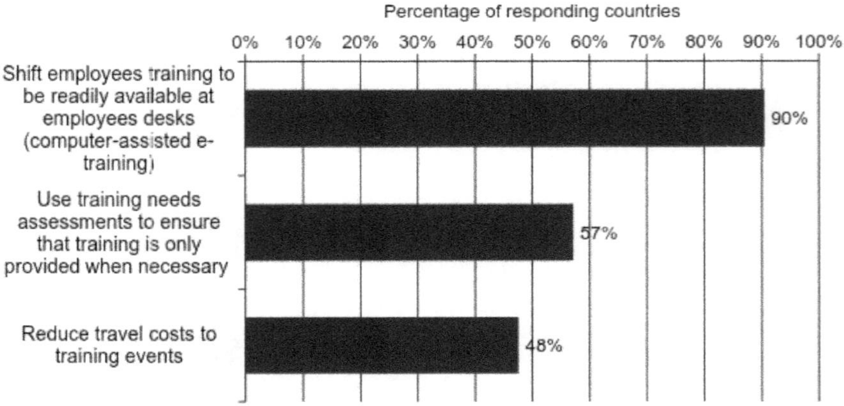

Countries belonging to the category 1 and 2 are introducing all sorts of reforms in order to reduce costs. On the other hand, countries belonging to category 3 and 4 are more reluctant to reduce travel costs to training events and to offer training only when it is necessary.

Figure 34: Reforms in the field of Training – use of instruments per category of countries

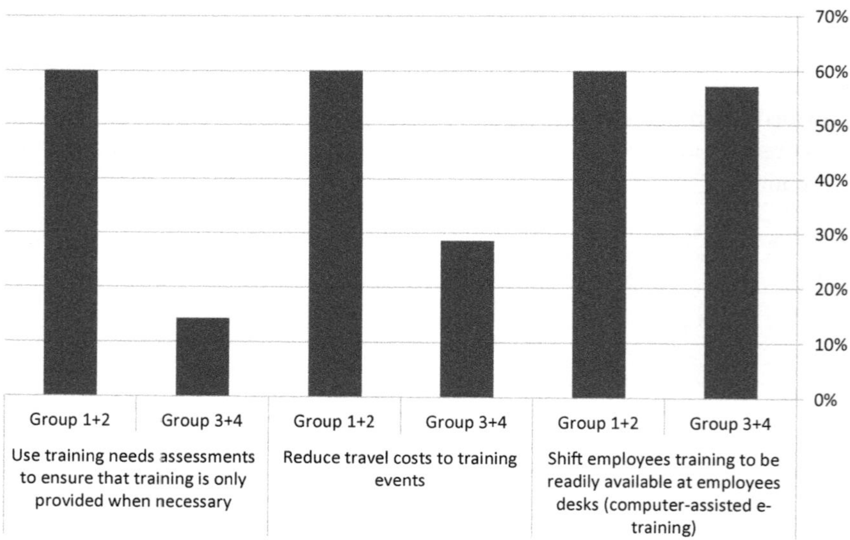

Often, it is difficult to separate cutting measures from efficiency measures. For example, in almost all OECD countries, in-house trainings became more widespread and outside-training activities were reduced. Other reforms concern the creation of synergies in order to save resources. For example, the United Kingdom has created a single training curriculum to change what people learn and what is on offer. Since 2010, the Australian Public Service (APS) has adopted a strategy-driven approach to prioritise its investment in learning and development for skills and capabilities that are shared across the Service (leadership development, talent development, core skills and management skills). The APS has also adopted a collective approach to designing and developing learning programs for shared learning needs. This approach was not the result of pressures from the 2008 financial crisis, but was driven by an internal APS agenda to ensure the APS has the capability required to continue meeting the needs of citizens, and by the recognition that there was an opportunity to improve the efficiency and effectiveness of the APS's collective investment in employee learning and development.

Thus, many reform trends in the field of training are contradictory in times when employers and employees are calling for the need to invest in skill development and competency development as parts of national competition strategies. Reducing training budgets may have negative effects on the individual, organisational and the level of central public administration as such. The latter also concerns leadership programs and the call for more investments in senior leadership training:

"On the individual level, training is part of the motivation system, as it provides civil servants with opportunities to move to new positions and develop their careers through developing their skills and competencies. On the positional/organisational level, training is related to the implementation of tasks and focuses on developing skills and competencies in order to fulfil the objectives of the organisation. The performance of organisations and their ability to implement policies depends by and large on the qualities of their members and on the organisations' ability to learn and adapt. On the state level, training is an instrument for retaining a high-quality and high-performing workforce, raising civil servants' awareness of their role and responsibility and introducing shared values that contribute to cross-departmental cooperation and public-service ethics"[257].

Overall, the trends towards more and standardised "cheap" training and continuous competency development programs seem to be over. Future developments

257 Merilin Metsma, op cit, p. 61.

are difficult to predict. However, given the increased need for saving public resources, could it be that in the future, calls for investments in skills and competences correlate with less financial resources available for training?

Unfortunately, our data sample is too small in order to give a full picture of the situation. However, as regards the available data, we have reasons to believe that many countries focus on cutting costs rather than on implementing a wider and more sophisticated menu of measures and instruments that may both reduce costs and raise the effectiveness of training as such[258].

4.5.5 Managing sickness levels

Workplace absenteeism is costly to the public sector. In many countries, sickness related costs are very high and public administrations experience longer sickness rates than the private sector.

The relationship between work, health and sickness rates is very complex and there is no space here to discuss these issues in more detail. For example, the link between demographic developments and health management, or the relationship between increased job intensity, stress levels and sickness rates.

The workplace has a significant impact on people's health and well-being. Poor management of workplace health can lead to work-related ill health and to high levels of sickness absence. This gives real cause for concern, not least because of the costs involved, the impact on service delivery and the consequences for individual staff.

Therefore, the management of health and sickness policies should a key HR issue. It is a key indicator of how well an organisation is managed. Committing resources to prevent people being made ill by work, or being absent from the workplace for health reasons, and placing an emphasis on prevention can benefit both employers and employees. Surprisingly, few countries focus on preventive measures. It is far better if the problem is prevented from occurring in the first place.

Overall, almost 60% of all participating countries in this survey have implemented measures in order to reduce absenteeism.

Most countries seem to focus on cost-reduction measures in order to curb costs related to the too high costs. Few countries like Germany (with very high sickness levels) have invested in preventive medical care programmes. For example, almost 30% of all countries have introduced measures in order to limit the number of paid sick days.

258 Stewart/Brown (2011), Human Resource Management, op cit, p. 335–369.

Figure 35: Have you introduced any policies directed to reduce absenteeism since 2008?

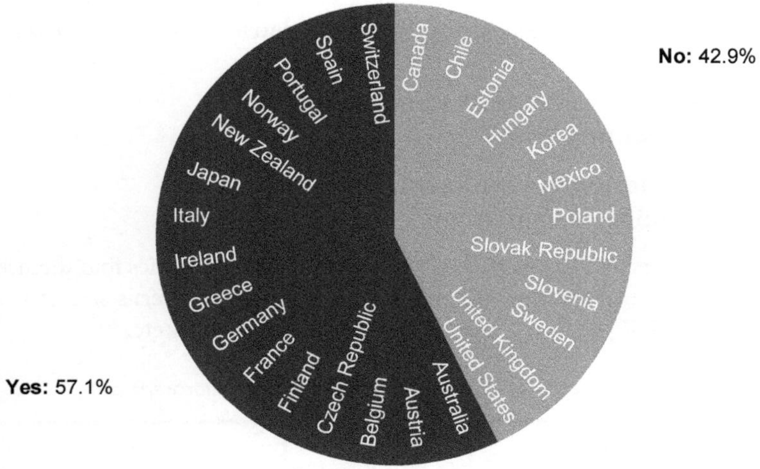

Figure 36: Implementation of policies in order to limit paid sick days

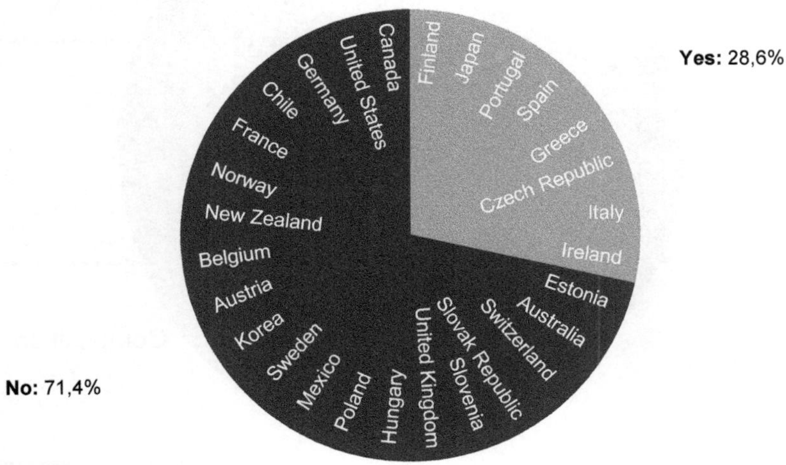

Obviously, the data does not allow for an evaluation of the effectiveness of sickness related HR policies. However, it indicates that countries are active in this policy field try to reduce too-high sickness rates and focus on cost-related issues.

4.6 Empirical evidence as to reform effects and outcomes of reforms

4.6.1 HR Reforms and the workforce – intentional and unintentional results

As a consequence of all of these reforms, most OECD countries find themselves in a process of massive changes of the workforce. This concerns size, structure, composition, HR policies, working conditions, age, diversity etc.

Figure 37: Changes as regards workforce composition and workforce structure

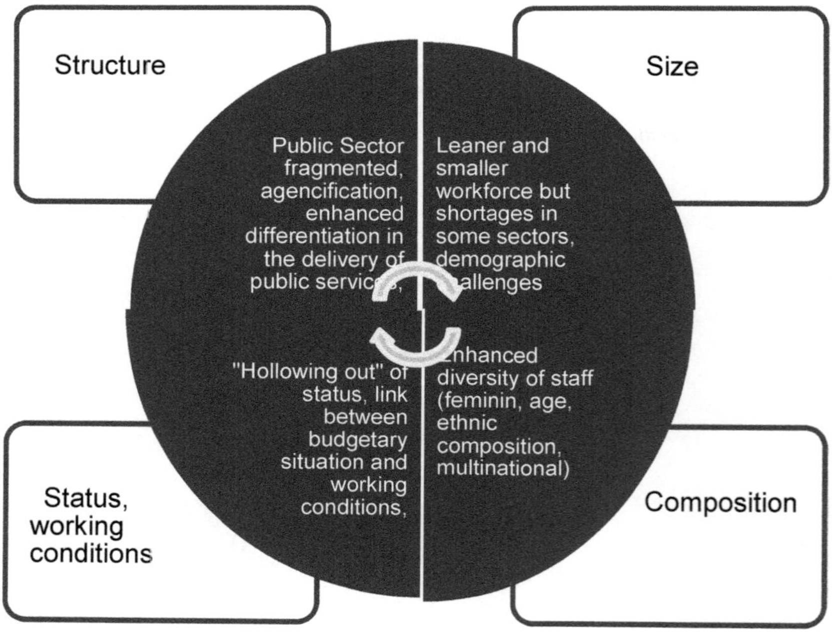

Source: Demmke/Moilanen, 2013, op cit, p. 75.

These trends go hand in hand with the hollowing out of the traditional civil service employment conditions (as discussed in the introduction of this study).

Reforms take place within the context of the restructuring of public employment. Still, the effects of this process are far from clear. As early as in 1996, in the first edition of *Civil Services in the Europe of 15*, the authors came to the conclusion that the differences between the working condition between civil servants, public employees and private sector employees were becoming less pronounced[259]. This trend continued until today. In fact, the differences between the working conditions in the public and the private sector have become less meaningful: in this sense, a partial harmonisation between labour regimes in the public and the private has already taken place in almost all Member States. Therefore, the current discussion focuses on the question whether or not the civil service status under public law should be aligned/abolished towards the status of employees in the private sector or not.

Today, most important differences relate mostly to job security, recruitment procedures, pay systems and career development policies. However, even these features are undergoing tremendous changes: Job security is being reduced, recruitment procedures are being flexibilised, pay systems are individualised and linked to individual performance and career structures are modified and, in some cases, even abolished. As a consequence, civil service employment differs less from private sector employment than ever before. Moreover, the differences between civil service employment and public service employment are becoming less clear.

In many OECD countries, job security levels differ amongst public law civil servants and labour law public employees. Consequently, countries with high budgetary pressures have focused on the relaxation of job security for public employees. In 60% of these countries (category 1), dismissals have become easier for public employees, but not for civil servants.

These figures suggest that—despite many alignment trends between the public and private sector and amongst civil servants and other public employees—differences in job security are increasing amongst the various employment categories. This is mostly the case in countries with high budgetary pressures because of the focus on dismissing public employees rather than civil servants.

---

259 Astrid Auer/Christoph Demmke/Robert Polet.: Civil Services in the Europe of Fifteen: Current Situation and Prospects, European Institute of Public Administration, Maastricht. 1996.

Figure 38: Dismissals of public employees and civil servants per category of countries

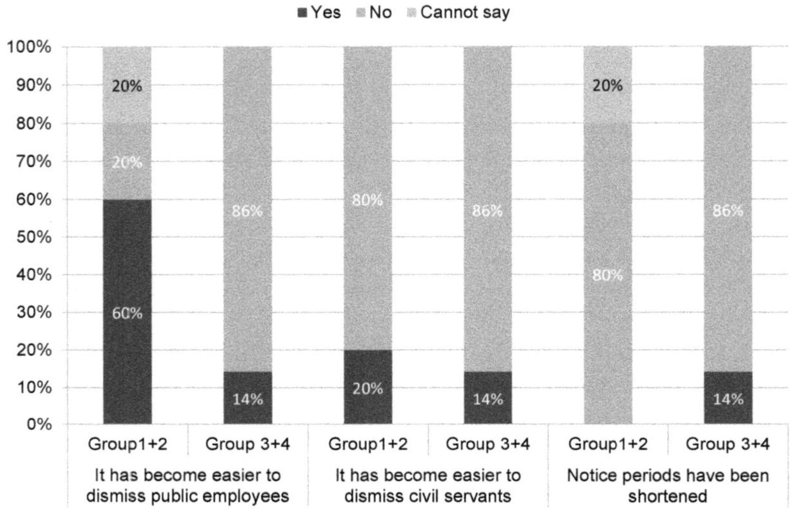

Thus, in most countries, HR reforms focus on the reform of organisational and career structures, public employment numbers, the composition of the workforce and the reform of working conditions. All of these issues are contested fields. On the other hand, whereas OECD countries reform working conditions, they do not touch upon one of the oldest civil service principle: the civil service status. In our survey, only few countries reported that they want to abolish the civil service status.

Whereas in some countries reforms are "creeping in" slowly but without major overhaul of long established structures, they lead in other countries to a completely new administrative landscape. Also, working conditions are changing differently and are deteriorating in many countries. However, in other countries they remain on a high level, at least in some countries with less budgetary constraints. Finally, job security is being reduced in some countries but remains on a high level in other countries. One should be more precise in this field: as regards the civil servants!

Moreover, governments and employers use a much wider menu of employment contracts and reform instruments in the field of public employment than before. In the future, it is also likely that the trend towards governance will continue to have an impact and produce new forms of employment relations and more diverse contractual relations.

Table 24: Dimensions of public employment restructuring[260]

Structure	Size	Composition	Status
From unified Civil service to differentiation, decentralisation and decomposition Different categories of staff (public and private law) Civil servants, public employees, short-term employees Shared services, outsourcing, agencification, PPP, privatisation Centralised coordination	Smaller Leaner Employment shifts to sectors with new/more recruitment needs (education, health) Recruitment shortages in some areas (ICT) Attractiveness according to countries and sectors is different	More women in top positions More diversity More public employees in civil service positions Age management (people stay longer) Lifelong learning (LLL) – focus on constant development of competences and skills Meritocracy and conflicts with equality, diversity, representativeness and democracy	Public law status remains Dual systems prevail, diversity and fragmentation of personnel are characteristic in most of the Member States Decline of numbers of CS, trend towards core CS "Hollowing out" of status substance, alignment of employment conditions More public employees in CS functions, new "unfairness perceptions" amongst categories of staff Some issues remain specific (job security, recruitment etc.) Overall: Identity crisis of specific civil service, public employees and private employees exercise public powers New discussions on need of specific working conditions

Source: Adapted from Demmke/Moilanen, 2013, op cit.

Enduring budgetary pressures will not stop another priority: the introduction of hasty austerity measures whose effects are not properly evaluated and whose outcomes may be worrying in many cases. "From one perspective, a recession might

260 Demmke/Moilanen, 2013, op cit., p. 92.

suggest that there is no longer a need for workforce planning. Suddenly, there is no 'war for talent'. Good people with scarce skills are in plentiful supply, the public sector is no longer seeing its trainees depart to better-paid jobs once qualified, and any organisation that has retained its graduate programme has seen applications skyrocket; they can take their pick from the most able. However, the recession also brings problems that require thoughtful workforce-planning attention. Labour turnover, already low in much of the public sector before the current round of budget pressures, is likely to come to a near standstill; few people will risk a job move unless absolutely necessary or extremely safe. In addition, older workers may choose to stay put rather than retire at 60 or 65. People staying put always presents difficulties: no injection of fresh blood, promotion blockages leading to frustration and disenchantment, and less scope for restructuring. Another issue is that financial and headcount constraints will impact on the ability to recruit; essentially this means that more will have to be done with fewer people"[261].

As an OECD study puts it, "There is little empirical analysis about which public administration reforms bring about efficiency and productivity gains... Although reductions in operational expenditure are "expected" to have a positive impact on the short-term budgetary aims of government, they may also act to the detriment of government's long term capacity for service delivery"[262]. Next, "fiscal consolidation plans normally involve reductions in staffing levels and in compensation of public employees, a situation that can have a significant impact on the motivation, engagement and commitment of public servants and leadership – which of course affects the quality of service delivery"[263].

It is also likely that the trend towards different work contracts, freezing of promotion opportunities, new working time arrangements pay and working conditions increases inequalities: "Lower pay levels for new recruits in Ireland, for instance, have increased inequalities and brought a sort of dual market in the public sector. Similarly, in France the less favourable pay levels and working conditions offered to new recruits de facto leads to a dual labour force in the public sector, despite the same skills and educational background. Germany also has a strong internal labour market with lifelong employment, but at the same time an increasing number of peripheral employees with temporary contracts... Another way of looking at inequality is also to identify whether the adjustments are having disproportionate effects on certain categories of workers, especially those

261 Dilys Robinson.: Workforce planning during bleak times, A public sector view Institute for Employment Studies, Brighton. 2010.

262 OECD (2009), Public Servants as Partners for Growth, Paris, 2009, p. 51.

263 OECD (2009), Public Servants as Partners for Growth, op cit, p. 10.

considered the most vulnerable. No doubt, certain categories of workers have been more affected by public sector adjustments. Lower employment prospects will directly hit those categories who tend to work in the public sector, especially women, young people and migrant workers”[264].

4.6.2 The changing composition of the workforce – the relationship between fixed-term employment and civil service employment

It is also possible that the central administrations are increasingly confronted with growing inconsistencies as regards the employment status and the employment of public employees in civil service employment positions.

On the one hand, in many countries with high budgetary constraints (category 1 and category 2 countries), fixed-term employees are the first victims of downsizing measures. Countries like Ireland, Greece, France, Portugal, Italy and Slovenia have focused on the reduction of fixed-term employees. Interestingly, these countries are all EU-Member States. Thus, overall, there is a clear relationship between budgetary constraints and the reduction of fixed-term employees.

Figure 39: Reduction of fixed-term employment in OECD countries

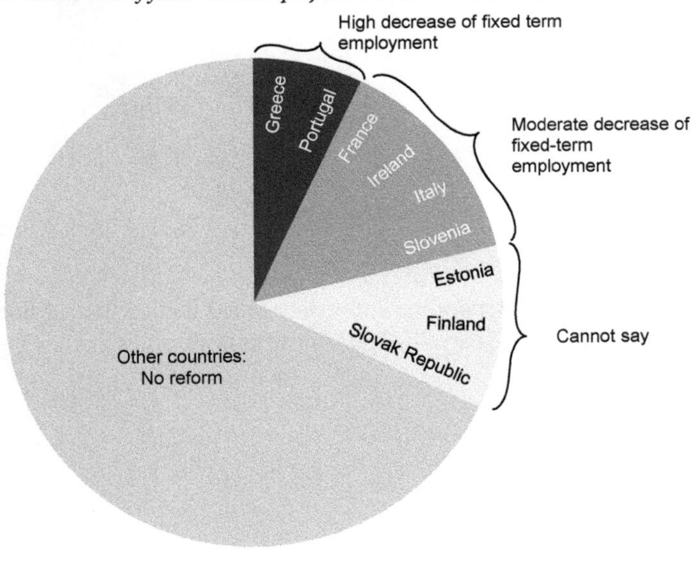

264 Daniel Vaughan-Whitehead (Editor):, Public Sector Shock: The Impact of Policy Retrenchment in Europe, Edward Elgar Publishing.2013, p. 22.

On the other hand, there is a strong trend to flexibilise civil service employment and to replace civil servants by fixed-term employees.

On the other hand, more than 50% of all responding countries have responded to the question, "What are the main reasons for the use of fixed-term employment contracts in the central public administration?" that they are in need for more flexible employment in order to save resources.

Figure 40: Need for more flexible employment in order to save resources

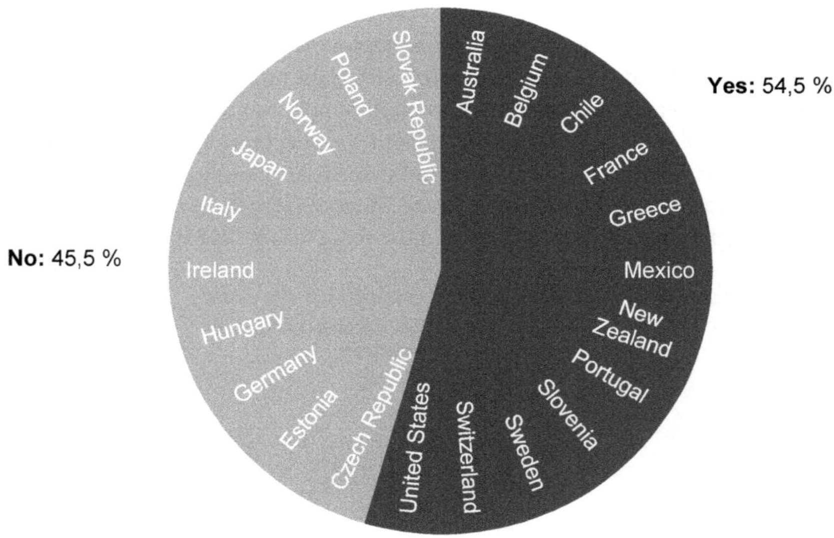

Moreover, 42, 9% of all responding countries replied that the use of fixed-term employment is a consequence of budgetary constraints.

Figure 41: Use of fixed-term employees as a consequence of budgetary constraints/ austerity measures

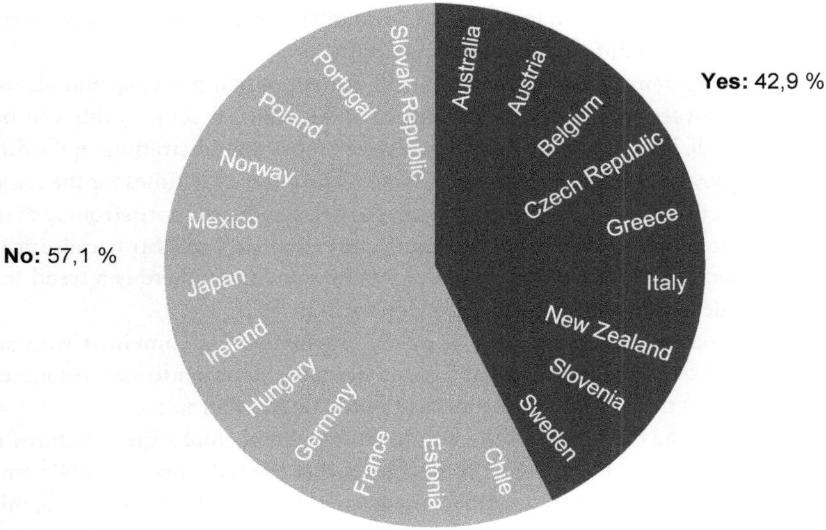

Thus, whereas fixed-term employees are the first victims in the downsizing process, countries also seek to flexibilise employment contracts and recruit more fixed-term employees at the same time.

This trend could lead to a hollowing-out of the civil service state and the reduction of the number of civil servants with high levels of job security. In some countries, however, fixed-term employees can also be recruited as civil servants. For example, in Ireland, "fixed-term employees are still civil servants. The difference between civil and public servants is a sectoral one" (Irish answer to the OECD survey).

As regards the question "Will budgetary constraints and the subsequent need for stabilizing national economies be an extra impetus to abolishing employment as civil servants?" approximately half of the responding countries answered with "very much" or "somewhat". Ireland responded, "Reduction of Public Service numbers (together with pay reductions) has played a significant part in the contribution made by the reduction in the public service pay bill to overall fiscal consolidation efforts and will continue to be a consideration in overall budgetary considerations for some time to come. However, given the significant reductions achieved to date potential for further reductions is limited".

From these data, one can derive the conclusion that the time of the "civil service state" seems to be over. Instead, OECD countries increasingly employ different categories with different employment contracts.

Thus, more central administrations will also employ a growing number of public employees with a different contractual situation, as long as this can be financed at all. This will lead to a situation where more administrations apply different employment relationships in the same sectors and sometimes for the same professions. Overall, fixed term employment is being reduced more strongly than civil service employment, mostly for budgetary reasons and also because it is easier to terminate fixed-term contracts. At the same time, there is a trend towards the flexibilisation of the civil service status.

Or, alternatively, the reduction of public employment is combined with an increase of fixed-term employment (like in Germany) in order to save resources if employment under unlimited contracts would be the alternative.

Because of the existence of different institutional and employment features, a comparison of our survey countries illustrates that the reduction of public employment concerns different employment groups in different countries. Still, this general trend towards the erosion of social cohesion and the standard employment model is taking many different ways on the central administrative level. For example, in the Irish central administration, despite all budgetary restraints and pay cuts, there is no trend towards a considerable increase of flexible contracts and the emergence of a so-called precarious employment model. On the other hand, in Germany, it is possible to observe a decline of the standardized employment model, both in the private sector and in the public sector (mostly in the field of education and research). In fact, as we will see later on, public employment trends on the central administration level have a "quantitative" and a "qualitative" dimension. Many jobs are still "good jobs" but they are getting less.

4.6.2 Impact on Workplace behaviour

The term "workplace behaviour" is very broad. In our study, we are interested whether and to what extent HR reform affect the ethical behaviour of public officials. The latter includes micro politics[265], and different forms of positive and critical forms of deviant behaviour. However, in this study, we restrict ourselves

---

265 Oswald Neuberger.:, Mikropolitik und Moral in Organisationen, 2. Editions, Lucius & Lucius, Opladen.2006.

to analysis of the implementation of HR reforms in the context of budgetary constraints and the impact on job satisfaction levels, job commitment, trust in leadership and justice and fairness perceptions.

In the 18th century Immanuel Kant concluded that nothing causes more indignation than injustice. Today, the OECD reports increasing levels of inequality in the OECD world[266]. However, this does not necessarily suggest that injustice also means that unfair treatment is also on the rise. All depends on how the principle of fairness is used[267]. People are naturally attentive to the justice of events and situations in their everyday lives across a variety of contexts. Individuals react to actions and decisions made by organisations every day[268]. Unjust and unfair treatment can strongly influence the individual behaviour and may exert a good or bad impact on individual and organisational performance[269].

Next, new "austerity" reforms may also support perceptions of organisational injustice. Experts in the field of organisational justice[270] often make a distinction between distributive justice, procedural justice and interactional justice. Distributive justice refers to the fairness of the allocation of outcomes. For example, "my unit's head endures the same harsh performance assessment conditions as the employees do, and the outcomes we get are fair, given our performance". Procedural justice refers to the fairness of the decision-making procedure behind the allocation of these outcomes. For instance, "my unit's head is consistent in the procedures s/he uses, and I have the opportunity to express my view during these procedures". Interactional justice pertains to the fairness of treatment throughout the process of decision-making and allocating outcomes. For example, "I am treated with respect, and the procedures applicable in the performance

266 http://www.oecd.org/social/inequality.htm (last time checked on 6 June 2016).

267 Marion Fortin/Martin R. Fellenz.: Hypocrisis of Fairness: Towards a more reflexive ethical Base in Organizational Justice Research and Practice. *Journal of Business Ethics*, Vol. 78. 2007, pp. 415–433.

268 Mark J. Martinko/Michael Gundlach/Scott Douglas.: Towards an integrative theory of counterproductive workplace behavior: A casual reasoning perspective. *International Journal of Selection and Assessment*, No. 1–2/2002, pp. 36–50.

269 A. de Schrijver/K. Delbeke/J. Maesschalck/S. Pleysier.: Fairness perceptions and organisational misbehaviour: An empirical study, *The American Review of Public Administration*, Vol. 40, No. 6/2010. 2010, pp. 691–703.

270 See for a good overview: Russel Cropanzano/David E. Bowen/Stephen W. Gillard.: The Management of Organizational Justice. *Academy of Management Practice*.2007, pp. 34–48; Maureen L. Ambrose/Russell Cropanzano.: A Longitudinal analysis of Organizational Fairness: An examination of reactions to Tenure and Promotion Decisions. *Journal of Applied Psychology*, Vol. 88, No. 2. 2003, pp. 266–275.

assessment have been explained in a timely manner and the explanations given in the feedback are reasonable".

In our study, we could notice that public employees in the central administrations are very attentive to the justice of events and reforms. As we will see, workplace behaviour is directly linked to budgetary constraints and HR reforms. Differences are huge as regards the effects of HR reforms in countries with high budgetary constraints and countries with modest constraints.

In the academic literature, experts have pointed to many negative effects of unprofessional performance assessments, job terminations, unfair promotion decisions, decisions not based on merit but personal considerations, salary cuts, unfair recruitment decisions, etc. on fairness perceptions.

What then happens to employees if national governments continue to introduce harsh pay cuts and pension reforms, decide on voluntary or obligatory job transfers, limit promotions, relax job security, reduce the scope of health schemes, reform the standard employment model, etc.? So far, little is known about the impact of reforms on individual workplace behaviour. Overall, the role and importance of changing emotions and fairness perceptions at the workplace as a consequence of the introduction of ever new reforms and austerity measures is still widely under-researched an, sometime, not even recognised in the whole public administration, including central public administration (Cropanzano/Stein/Nadisic 2011: xiii[271]).

From what is known in the academic field, compensation and benefit reductions and adjusted work schedules, which have a direct impact on an employee's personal finances, life and livelihood are most likely linked to increases in misconduct, disengagement and less work commitment. Cost-cutting reforms are also linked to reduced rates of employee commitment and disengagement, which has been linked to employee performance and engagement. Overall, economic pressures, budgetary cuts, the reduction in salaries and promotion opportunities may result in more stress, competition and a general decline in organisational culture (ethical climate). In these situations, issues such as fairness, courtesy, abuse of power and impartiality may be at risk. This again can result in more ethical violations, such as stealing organisational resources, misconduct at work, unwelcome behaviour, etc. Moreover, job satisfaction and organisational commitment is found to be negatively associated with overall perceptions of organisational

271 Russel Cropanzano/Jorgan H. Stein/Thierry Nadisc.: Social Justice and the Experience of Emotion, Routledge, New York.2011.

and procedural injustice (for example in the case of injustice unprofessional performance assessments and unfair recruitment decisions).

In a study by Demmke/Moilanen (2012)[272], officials from central administrations of all EU Member States were asked whether reform policies which are introduced as a reaction to the financial crisis have effects on workplace behaviour. As regards this question one should obviously distinguish between those Member States which have not introduced austerity measures (yet), and those who have done so. For example, countries like Sweden, Luxemburg or Germany have not implemented austerity measures[273]. For instance, Sweden informs that it "has chosen not to worsen working conditions due to the crisis. Nor has structural change increased this time, since government finances are in order and there is little need to cut cost for monetary reasons". Bulgaria, the Czech Republic, Estonia, Greece, Hungary[274], Ireland, Latvia, Lithuania, Portugal, Romania, Slovenia, Spain and the United Kingdom have implemented very tough austerity measures. Other countries like Austria, the Netherlands, the Slovak Republic and Poland are more difficult to classify, and for practical reasons they were classified these Member States as non-austerity countries.

Still, some countries replied "hard to say"; because they had not introduced austerity measures or they did not have any empirical evidence as regards the relationship between austerity measures and workplace behaviour. The Netherlands replied: "Overall we have no cause for concern, although there is some debate on possible temporary effects on job satisfaction. We would like to point out that the effects might vary from organisation to organisation as a result of variations in the quality of management and the strength of the ethical culture". On the other hand, change is always going on and every year some thousands of staff are made redundant for structural reasons. A job security system, agreed between the social partners, supports noticed staff to find new jobs on the labour market.

The results of the Demmke/Moilanen study show a strong relationship between the introduction of austerity measures and workplace behaviour. For example, the impact of austerity measures is believed to be strongest in the field of lowering of job satisfaction. Eighty-three percent of countries that have

---

272 Demmke/Moilanen, Effectiveness of Good Governance, op cit.

273 In this study we are focusing on austerity measures that directly affect individual workplace behaviour, such as the reduction of salaries and relaxation of job security. To our knowledge, these three countries have also implemented austerity measures but not as regards the reduction of salaries and easing of job security.

274 Consequently, the answer to this study from Hungary states clearly that there seems to be an increased fear for losing one's job.

implemented austerity measures report lowering of job satisfaction. Austerity measures will also decrease of trust in leadership. 84% of austerity countries reported that the introduction of austerity measures leads to distrust in leadership.

Moreover, many Member States report a decrease in workplace commitment. As regards the austerity countries, 58% reported a decrease in workplace commitment compared to 36% of the non-austerity countries. Seventy-three percent of the austerity countries observe a decrease of trust in the organisation compared to 21% of the non-austerity countries. Also the degree of loyalty is influenced by the introduction of austerity measures. Whereas 58% of all austerity measures mention that loyalty levels are somewhat decreasing, only 14% of the non-austerity countries say that this is the case.

Basically, our survey confirms the Demmke/Moilanen findings. Overall, many countries report a decrease of trust in the own organisation, in leadership and decreasing job commitment and job satisfaction as a result of the implementation of new reforms.

Figure 42: Effects of reforms on workplace behaviour

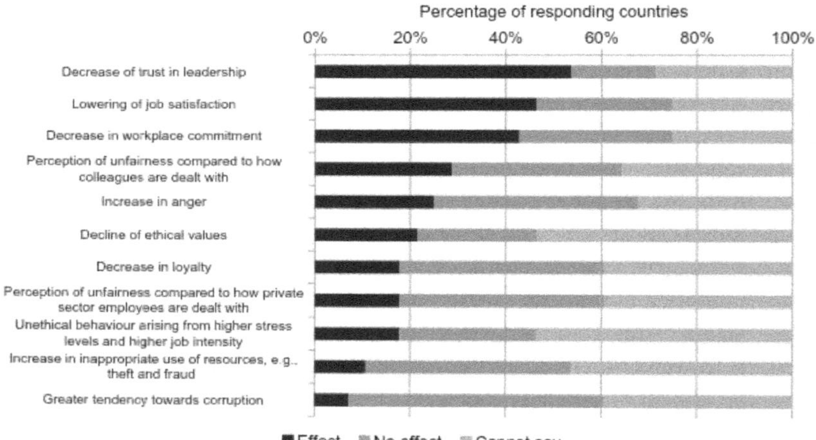

Interestingly, we can observe (again) a clear correlation between the degree of budgetary pressures and reform effects. The higher budgetary pressures, the more negative are effects on workplace behaviour. Ultimately, these trends may have critical effects on the integrity of governance[275] as such.

275 Leo Huberts.: The Integrity of Governance, Palgrave MacMillan. 2014.

Table 25: Effects of Reforms on Workplace Behaviour

	Group 1					Group 2									Group 3						Group 4							
	Czech Republic	Greece	Ireland	Portugal	Spain	Australia	Estonia	France	Hungary	Italy	Slovak Republic	Slovenia	United Kingdom	United States	Austria	Chile	Korea	Mexico	New Zealand	Poland	Belgium	Canada	Finland	Germany	Japan	Norway	Sweden	Switzerland
Decrease of trust in the organisation	●	●		●	●		○	○	○	○		○			●	○	●	●	○	○	○		●			○	●	●
Decrease of trust in leadership	●	●		●	○		●	○	●	○		○	●		●	○	●	●	○	○	○		●			○	●	●
Perception of unfairness compared to how private sector employees are dealt with		●		●	●		●			●					●	●	○		●	●	○					○	●	
Perception of unfairness compared to how colleagues are dealt with	○	●		●	●		○		●	●			●	●	●	●	●		○	●	○		●			●	●	●
Decline of ethical values	○			●	●		●	○	●	●		●			●	●	●	●	●	○	●					●	●	
Decrease in workplace commitment	○			●	○		○		●	○			●	○	●	●	●	●	○	●			●			●	●	●
Lowering of job satisfaction	○	●		●	●		○	○	●	○			●	○	●	●	●	●	○	○	○		●			●	●	●
Increase in inappropriate use of resources, e.g., theft and fraud	○			○	●		●	●	●			●		●	●	●	●	●	●	●			●			●	●	
Unethical behaviour arising from higher stress levels and higher job intensity	○	●		●	●			○	●			●			●	●	●		●	●			●			●	●	
Increase in anger		○		●	○				●			○			●	●	●			○			●			●	●	●
Decrease in loyalty	○			●	●		●		●			●	●	○	●	●	●	●		○			●			●	●	○
Greater tendency towards corruption				○	●				●			●			●	●	●	●		●						●	●	

● No effects ○ Some effects ● Strong effects

This again means a negative relationship between tough downsizing/cost containment approaches and workplace behaviour. This confirms our hypothesis 5 and also 6. Overall, the differences are huge between countries with high budgetary pressures (belonging to category 3 and 4) and countries with lower budgetary pressures (belonging to category 1 and 2). One can also conclude from these findings that current "austerity" HR reforms that are being implemented have an immediate and negative effect on workplace behaviour.

Figure 43: Effects of reforms on workplace behaviour and relationship low/high budgetary constraints

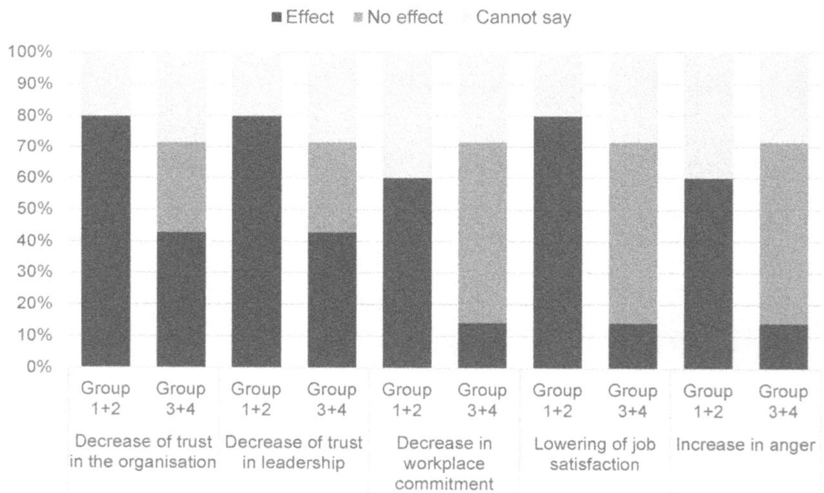

This is mostly the case as regards trust levels in the organisation, trust levels in leadership, workplace commitment, job satisfaction and the increase in anger. Still, our data do not allow for a more detailed analysis as regards the impact of HRM reforms on different categories of employees: for example, differences as regards technical staff and top-managers. As regards this question, empirical evidence is scarce. In their study on the impact of cutbacks and job satisfaction of top managers, Van der Voet and van de Walle (2014) come to the conclusion that job satisfaction of top managers is also declining, but for different reasons as for other public employees[276]. According to the authors, "cutback measures are negatively related to the perceived managerial autonomy of public managers and positively to the degree in which politicians interfere in the affairs of managers, autonomy may function as a mechanism to explain decreased job satisfaction as a result of cutback implementation"[277].

Next, a relatively high number of answers report that public employees perceive increased unfairness compared to how colleagues in the public or in the private sector are dealt with.

Interestingly, there seems to be no correlation between the introduction of austerity measures and the decline of ethical values as well as between austerity measures and unethical behaviour arising from higher stress levels and higher job intensity. As regards the latter, one explanation may be that causes for higher stress levels and job intensity can be found in many more factors than only in the introduction of austerity measures.

Whatever the right interpretation of reform effects, one thing is sure: the impact of HR reforms is also contextual and—sometimes—contradictory. Whereas some countries experience strong decreases in loyalty, unethical behaviour and job satisfaction, in other countries this is not the case. For example, comparing Norway, Portugal, Spain and Austria show similar but also hugely differently results.

276 Joris van der Voet/Steven van de Walle.: How cutbacks and job satisfaction are related: The role of top-level public managers' autonomy, FP7 COCOPS Final Academic Conference: Leuven, Belgium (2014, June, 10–2014, June 11).

277 Ibid.

Figure 44: National context and different effects on workplace behaviour

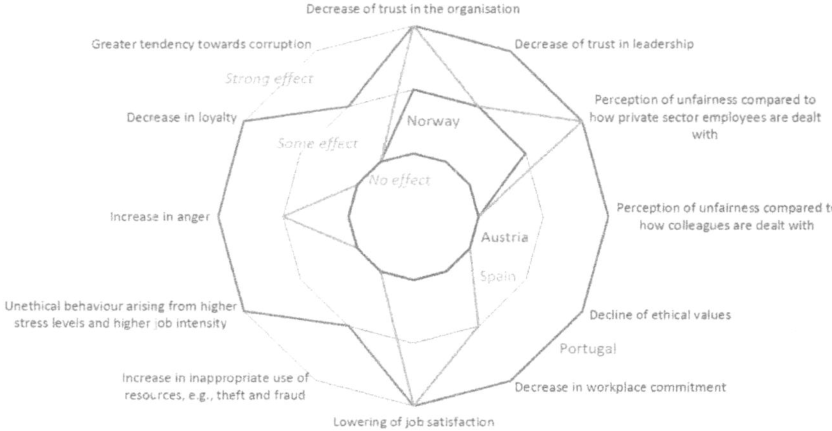

Thus, although it is possible to derive general conclusions as regards the effects of HR reforms on workplace behaviour, the impact of reforms is also influenced by other contextual factors such as culture and parallel developments in the private sector. Consequently, the term "public HR reform" is ambivalent in itself as it is perceived differently in the OECD countries.

4.6.3 Development of stress, job intensity and job quality

There is no need to discuss the relationship between downsizing and stress, as this relationship has been discussed many times. So far less discussed is the relationship between HR reforms, reform of work systems, job quality, job intensity and stress.

A number of countries did not produce empirical evidence as to the development of job quality. The reason is—as already discussed in this survey—it is very complicated to define and to analyse work quality and work systems. As long as countries have not agreed on common indicators how to measure work systems it is also difficult to evaluate the outcomes of work systems, such as job quality.

This explains why the survey results do not indicate clear trends but rather complex relationships. For example, job quality may improve while job intensity, stress and sickness levels increase.

According to the data, overall, almost half of all countries who answered to this question reported improvements in workplace quality. Only 18% reported deteriorations in this field.

However, it should also be noted that the situation becomes ever more diverse in OECD countries. Again, budgetary constraints are linked to the deterioration of workplace quality in the Czech Republic, Greece and in Portugal.

Table 26: Development of organisation of work and workplace quality in countries since 2008?

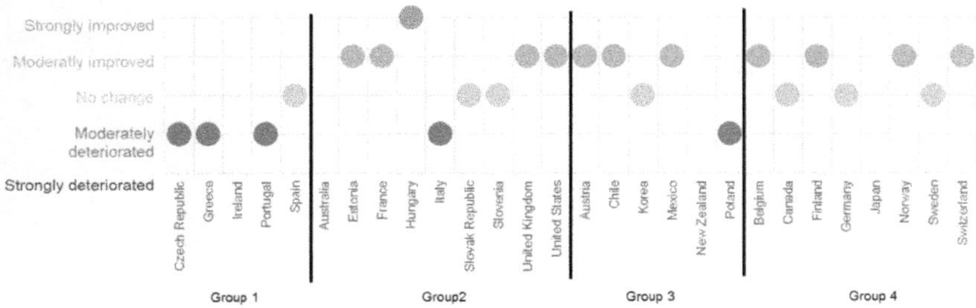

On the other hand, many countries report trends towards more job intensity and higher stress levels. Most surprising is that almost no country reports decreasing levels of stress and job intensity. Thus, rising stress levels and job intensity are global trends.

Figure 45: Development of Job intensity and stress

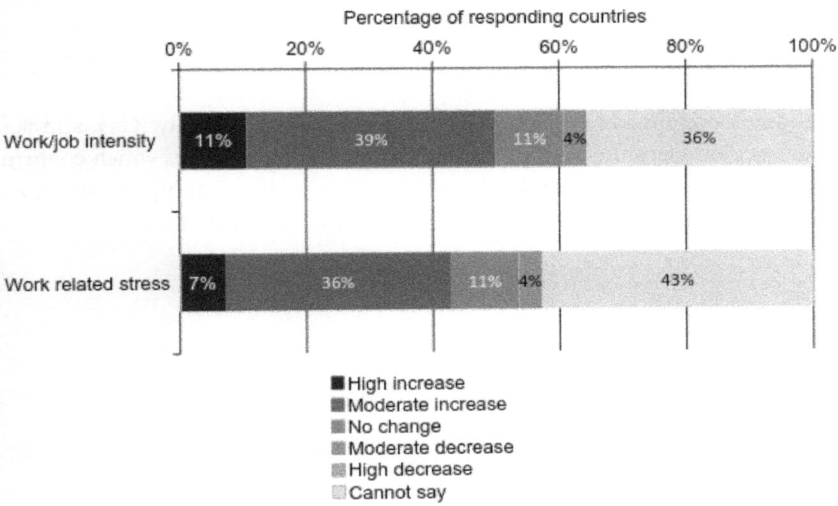

There is no space here to discuss the full range of issues. We are more concerned with the analysis of the presented data in the context of budgetary constraints. Here, we cannot observe a direct link between stress levels and budgetary constraints. However, as already mentioned, the data suggests that stress levels are increasing in almost all countries. Thus, these trends are not necessarily linked to budgetary constraints but also to other developments.

Figure 46: Relationship Budgetary constraints and Stress

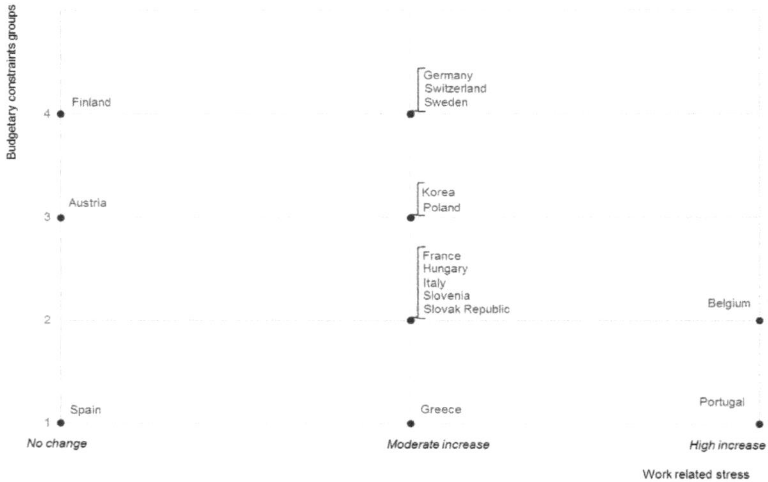

The same development can be seen in the field of job intensity. This is in accordance with literature on high performance working practices which confirm that "doing more with less" and the emergence of new forms of high-performing workplaces produce more stress and have higher levels of job intensity.

Figure 47: Relationship Budgetary Constraints and Job Intensity

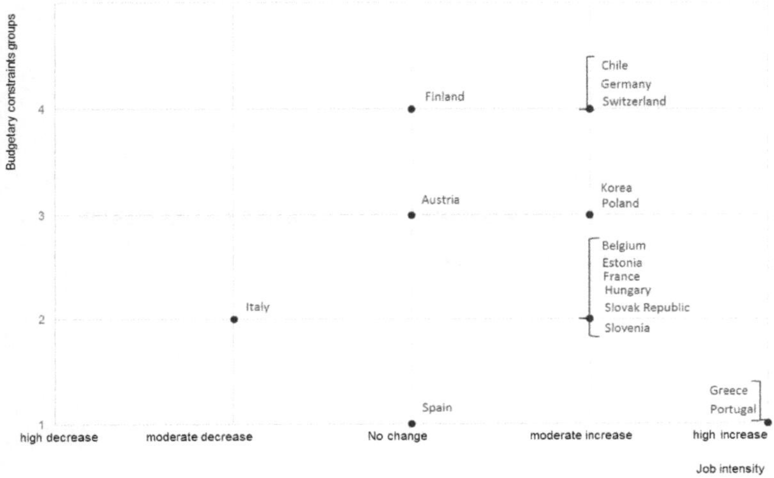

The latter findings are important as the development of stress levels, job intensity, job quality and sickness levels is highly contextual and not linked to budgetary challenges. Overall, there is a trend in almost all OECD countries towards more stress and more job intensity. There is no place here to discuss the reasons for this trend. However, OECD countries are advised to closely monitor this trend as it seems only a matter of time until these trends show more side-effects such as higher turnover rates, higher sickness rates, lower productivity levels, less job satisfaction and less job engagement.

Figure 48: Comparisons of Country categories 1 and 2 versus 3 and 4 and stress/job intensity

Work related stress

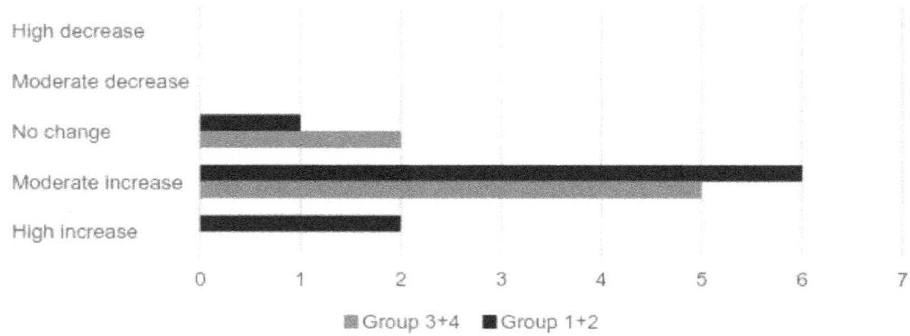

Job intensity

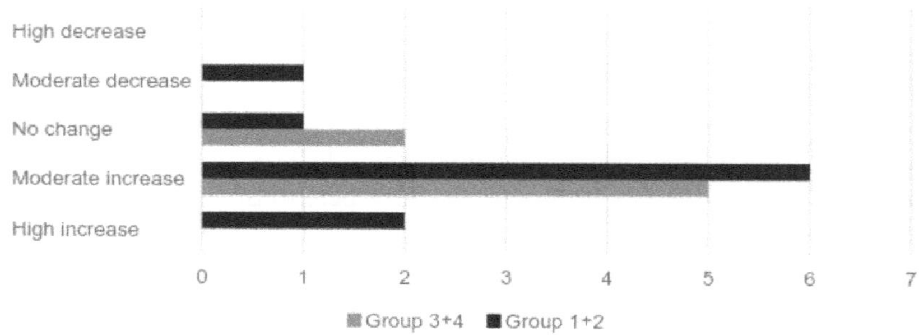

Still, one should also mention that more job intensity and more stress are not necessarily bad things as long as job control, job autonomy and job engagement are also increasing. However, problems start when rising job intensity and stress levels are linked to more workload, less job control and more job constraints.

These trends are not necessarily linked to working time issues. Overall, average working time is around 40 hrs in most countries (and ranging from 35 hrs in France to 48 hrs in Costa Rica). Only five countries have increased working time during the last years. These were Japan, the United Kingdom, Greece, Portugal and Ireland. Portugal increased working hours from 35h to 40h per week, in order to be the same as in private sector. In Greece, working hours were increased from 37, 5 hours per week to 40 hours per week (2011). In Ireland, in July 2013 net hours for civil servants were increased from 34.75 hours per week to 37 hours. The United Kingdom has a maximum working hour of 48 hours. In

2012 all departments were requested to undertake a review of working hours. As a result of this a number of departments have increased working hours for new starters and employees on promotion from 36 hours to 37 hours. The standard number of working hours is 36/37 hours per week. Japan has adjusted working hours in the context of its demographic ageing strategies.

Thus, central public employees do not necessarily work longer. However, work pressure seems to increase within the same amount of working time.

4.6.4 Two steps back, one step forward – positive and critical developments

The situation in many OECD reflects what Levine illustrated already thirty years ago: "We are entering a new era of public budgeting, personnel, and program management. It is an era dominated by resource scarcity. It will be a period of hard times for government managers that will require them to manage cut-backs, trade-offs, reallocations, organisational contractions, program terminations, sacrifice, and the unfreezing and freeing up of grants and privileges that have come to be regarded as unnegotiable rights, entitlements, and contracts. It will be a period desperately in need of the development of a methodology for what I call 'cutback management'"[278].

Overall, the answers of many countries reveal some worrying trends that should give reason to investigate the effects of current reforms: Deteriorations could be noted in the following HR policies:

- Negative effects of downsizing policies
- Increase in stress
- Negative impact of remuneration reforms (less pay, less motivational pay)
- Reduced career opportunities and reduced promotion opportunities and policies
- Negative effects of cutting of training policies on skill levels
- Increased job intensity
- Decreasing attractiveness of public sector employment

In more countries officials are dissatisfied with restricted career opportunities and slow advancement in the hierarchies. The case of restricted promotion opportunities show that organisational change is most easily accomplished when the people affected have something to gain, but under conditions of budgetary pressures the acceptance of change will be unlikely because there is only little to

278 Charles H. Levine, More on Cutback Management, op cit, p. 179.

win: "Under these conditions, creativity diminishes, innovation and risk taking decline, and the sense of excitement that comes from doing new things disappears. Simply put, it just is not as much fun working and managing in a contracting organisation as it is in an expanding one"[279].

4.6.5 The positive side of it

Studying cases of good HRM and *successes* take us to the heart of current debates about the modern public service capacities to govern and to manage public services in an increasingly difficult context. To affix the label "successes" to HRM is risky business. The risk is doubled when "successes" is attributed to new ideas, innovation and improvements in the field of HRM whereas—at the same time—ideas are widespread that HRM is not innovative and the poor performance of public services is a major reason for public distrust. Not surprisingly, many researchers are more interested in cases that are likely attract a lot of attention, such as cases of corruption, public scandals, waste of public money, poor performance and quality management etc.

Although not intended, also this survey focuses on a problematic link—the relationship between budgetary constraints and HR policies. Of course, our hypothesis is that this link is not necessarily a positive one.

Even though this focus on "challenges" is understandable, it clearly hinders the development of evidence, knowledge and awareness of positive developments and cases of "good administration". What is clearly missing is realistic literature and studies about improvements in the field of HRM in the context of budgetary constraints and the attitude of public employees about the nature and effects of recent developments in this area.

This is not only the fault of perceptions and clichés. In fact, lack of evidence about positive developments is also "the fault" of public administrations and HR managers.

For example, one important instrument to generate more evidence on the effects of reforms on personnel is the implementation of employee surveys. There is no space here to discuss the different methodologies used in carrying out employee surveys (and discussing the existing flaws in this respect). However, suffice to know that a number of countries reported that they do not carry out employee surveys at all. Moreover, employee surveys are only carried out in a restricted number of policy fields. For example, whereas all of those countries who

279 Levine, 1979, op cit, p. 180.

carry out surveys job satisfaction is being analysed, only a minority of countries analyse employee perceptions as regards the effectiveness of HRM systems.

Figure 49: Employee surveys – in which areas?

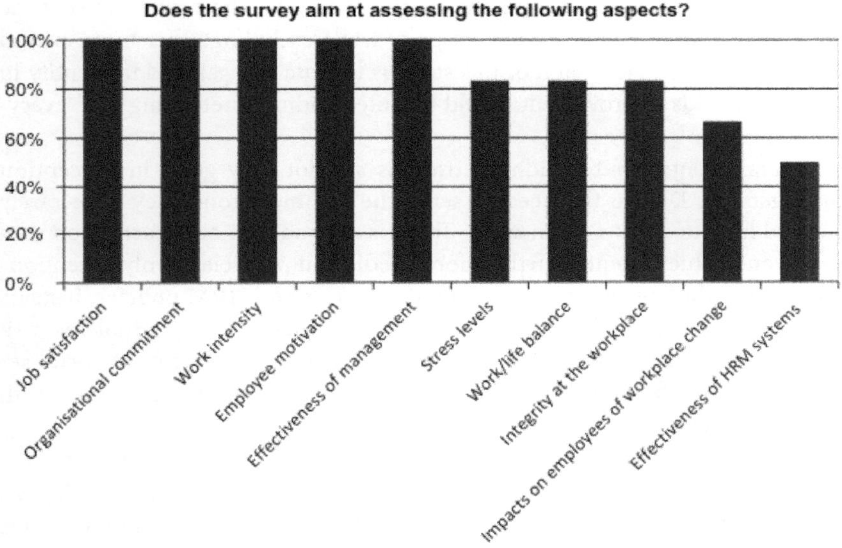

One should conclude, therefore, that evidence on reform effects is thin in some HR policies and that our data only allows for a discussion on what can be observed and measured: The tip of the iceberg.

Overall, OECD countries invest in employee surveys in a number of fields. However, there is often a complete lack of surveys (and consequently—data!) in fields like the effectiveness of HR reforms on the effectiveness of HR systems, ethical behaviour, fairness perception and fluctuations of trust levels, developments in working conditions and as well as recruitment and HR policies in comparison to the private sector. Moreover, little is known on horizontal public employee comparisons (for example whether certain categories of staff (managers, older employees, women, minorities etc.) have witnessed improvements over the last years whereas other categories of staff have not. As already discussed, central administrations have also done too little in order to evaluate and to compare the effects of different work systems on organisational effectiveness, as discussed earlier in the theoretical part of this survey.

Finally, too little is known on the decision-making and the use of employee surveys as such!

Given the limited attention and knowledge to the dimension of positive developments, it is not surprising that there is no specific theory on "good administration" and "successes". Discussing successes may also be seen as naïve if the emphasis is put purely on positive aspects while excluding other more critical issues. Thus, one modest aim of this study is to close this gap and to identify in which HR fields improvements could be noted without pretending that "everything is golden".

Overall, central public administrations are not very good in perception management. Due to the need to serve the common good they have rarely learned how to market themselves. There is no tradition of reporting on successes and achievements. Furthermore, media and politicians only exceptionally discuss the positive aspects of public services and HRM policies. Instead, the media focus on deficiencies and public service failures (e.g. problems with waiting lists in hospitals, poor education systems, inefficiencies in social security systems, failures in security, cases of corruption, waste of money in construction etc.).

After years of public service bashing and discussions around the existence (or not) of a specific public service motivation, what seems to be missing today is a public affirmation about the importance of the public services and the people who work for the common good.

Obviously, discussing public service successes is also difficult since citizens have a right to expect that public servants perform well anyway. Public Officials are paid with tax payers' money and they spend (amongst others) tax payers' money. Consequently, people have a right to expect that public servants perform well. However, it is precisely because of this (high) expectation that it is difficult to talk (and research) about successes. Furthermore, discussing successes is risky business. Public services do not have a specific purpose like profit making (in the private sector). Rather "goal achievement" and "fulfilment of duties" and "working for the common good" are more important objectives. In all public administration systems, the most important public service values (such as fair and standardised treatment, neutrality, stability, hierarchy and impartiality) are "static" and "conservative" whereas the societal values are "fluent", "modern" and call for efficiency, reform, change, innovation, flexibility and performance. The tension between these two concepts and values explain another difficulty in identifying positive developments.

Today, it is easier to define and to introduce principles of good administration than to identify successes in the field Human Resource Management and the implementation and enforcement of these principles. Identifying successes also involves a number of qualitative and quantitative criteria and variables. Moreover, positive results of HR reforms are more difficult to define in the public services than in the private sector because performance standards are not limited to economic, quality and customer satisfaction criteria. Instead they also include constitutional, regulatory and political standards, as well as the common interest. Efficiency and effectiveness are necessary but not sufficient conditions for gaining public trust. In many cases, the public is confronted with ethics and integrity issues in the public services. Trust, as we have seen in this survey, is a precious resource which can easily be destroyed but is difficult to be restored.

Consequently, there is no "absolute" set of theoretical approaches to this topic. This needs to be changed.

In our survey, OECD countries were very reluctant to report positive developments. If so, they believe that the crisis produces opportunities, rather than successes. One opportunity is the possibility to improve workforce planning and to improve data management practices. Another opportunity is to better anticipate demographic changes and become more professional and more strategic in anticipating future HR and employment trends.

Figure 50: Positive side effects of reforms

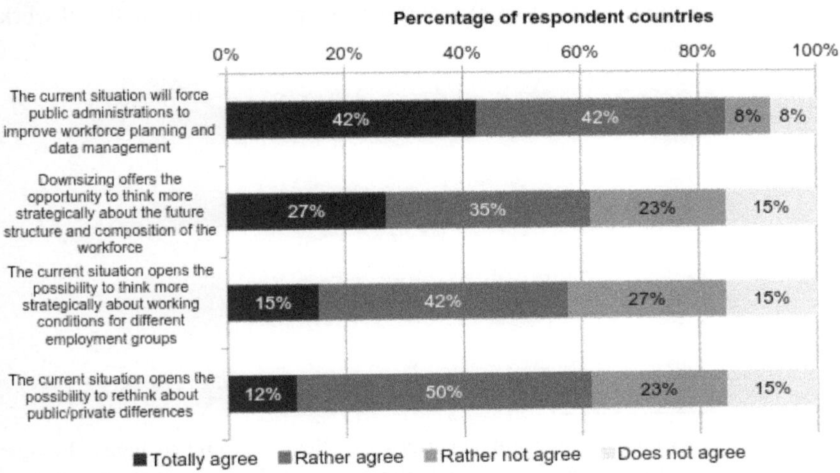

The difficulties involved in reporting about successes and positive developments may also be related with many ambivalent developments and paradoxes. Here, we come back to the Hesse/Hood matrix (in chapter 3.1) which discusses the many unintentional and intentional effects of reforms.

For example, more stress may be related to better job quality. Or, higher levels of job intensity and stress levels may be also a result of more and tougher performance management and performance measurement practices.

On the other hand, tougher performance management practices do not mean that public employees are performing better, as a consequence of the introduction of these instruments. In the field of HRM, too often, reform initiatives make proposals on how to improve the individual performance of the employees without considering that most of them are actually performing very well. A number of HRM studies in the public sector also ignore why public employees are mostly satisfied with their work and perform well, even when——they are poorly paid. In the United States, Al Gore (1993) argued that the fundamental problem of managing the public sector would be the "system" but not the people ("civil servants")[280].

As already mentioned, work quality improves in a number of countries. This should be marketed as a "success" and a positive development. In fact, little seems to be known about this important trend. Also, many countries have answered to this survey that the question as such is too broad and they could not reply to the question given the fact that the development of work and work quality is a result of many factors which are difficult to measure. Still, many countries have acknowledged the importance to measure the development of the quality of work and the organisation of work.

280 see also the whole report: National Performance Review, From Red Tape to Results: Creating a Government that Works Better and Costs Less, Government Printing Office, Washington D.C., 1993.

Figure 51: Change in overall organisation of work and workplace quality since 2008

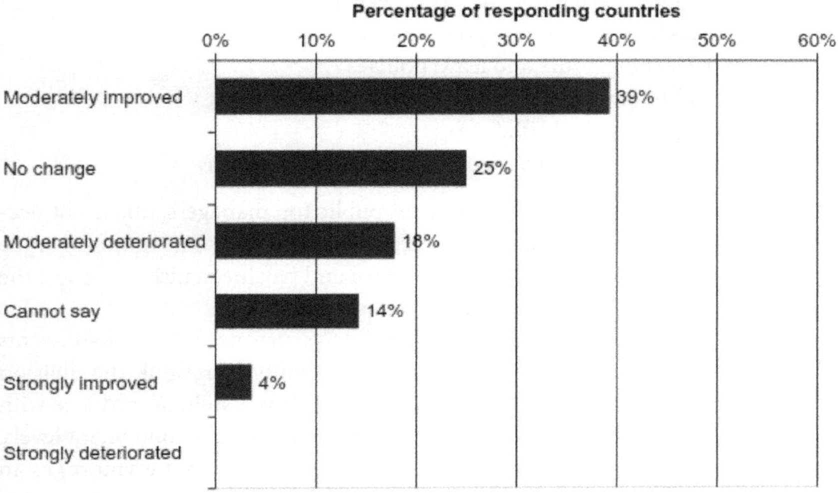

Still, as already discussed in the theoretical part of this survey, we acknowledge the lack of comparative approaches and the lack of comparative studies in the field of work systems in central public administrations. Further research is badly needed as regards the development of the organisation of work and the quality of work in the national central public administrations. The available findings in our survey also point to some positive developments in the field.

Next, it is also important to mention that in most OECD countries working in central public administration is still more secure and attractive than working in the private sector (although job security as such is decreasing and cob contracts are being flexibilised). Moreover, in many countries, employees in central public administration enjoy[281]:

- high levels of job and employment security
- good opportunities to combine private and professional lives[282]

281 Eurofound (2013), Working Conditions in Central Public Administration, op cit.

282 Jaekwon Ko/SeungUk Hur/Aaron Smith-Walter, Family-Friendly Work.: Practices and Job Satisfaction and Organizational Performance: Moderating Effects of Managerial Support and Performance-Oriented Management. *Public Personnel Management*, No. 42(4). 2013, pp. 545–565; Laura den Dulk/Sandra Groeneveld., Work–Life

- an interesting job, including a challenging job content (not all levels)
- high levels of job satisfaction and job engagement[283]
- very high levels of employee representation
- reasonable working hours and leave policies
- competitive holiday arrangements
- low exposure to physical risks
- often, relative high percentages of women in top-positions

Although pay levels are generally lower for public top managers, this is not necessarily the case for middle managers and professional staff. One may also argue that pay is not as diverse as in the private sector and pay inequalities amongst the lowest and the highest paid categories are reasonable[284].

Still, the grand (and often ideological) public vs. private sector debate seems to be over. Most countries do not value the possibility to rethink the division of labour between the public and private sector. This is also in accordance with the data on using "privatisation" as an instrument to control employment levels. Here, our data suggest that countries do not use "privatisation" (anymore) as an important instrument to manage employment levels. Our survey confirms this trend, although most countries are very reluctant to further privatise public services on the central level. In our survey, only slightly more than 20% of all countries reported that they use privatisation as a mean to reduce public employment.

Again, this is also in line with increased criticism towards the so-called "New Public Management" doctrine, which we discussed in the beginning of this survey. After all, this also suggests a positive trend: HR reform has become less ideological and more pragmatic.

Of course, Governance is a fuzzy word and difficult to define. As such it includes changes as regards public service delivery through non-public actors, changes in decision and rule making, the choice of new instruments, broader participation channels, more transparency, decentralisation, delegation, agencification etc. Only a detailed analysis of all these different components of Governance and their impact on HR reforms will reveal the strengths and weaknesses of this concept.

Balance Support in the Public Sector in Europe. *Review of Public Personnel Administration*, No. 33(4). 2012, pp. 384–405.

283 J. Scott Frampton.Public Sector Job Satisfaction: A Conversation with Impact. *Public Administration Review*, Vol. 74, Issue. 3. 2014, pp. 396–397.

284 OECD.: Public Sector Compensation in Times of Austerity, OECD Publishing, Paris. 2012.

According to Enroth, "Governance in this brave new world, involves a plurality of actors interacting in networks that cut across the organisational and conceptual divides by means of which the modern state has conventionally and all too conveniently been understood"[285].

The preference for outsourcing and the establishment of shared services may be because of mixed experiences with the "privatisation" of public services and services of general (economic) interest during the last years and the end of the market euphoria in the 1990's. Still, there can be no doubt that—compared to decades ago—the marketization process has continued.

In fact, it is difficult to draw clear lines and establish clear criteria for those issues which could be outsourced, decentralized, delegated and marketised, or better not? Why should the provision of energy be privatized, but not water? Why should flying be privatized, but not the railways? Why privatize nuclear power stations but not governmental agencies or even ministries? Should we allow, as it is already the case, to pay money for shorter waiting times in hospitals and preferential treatment of doctors, fast tracks on motor ways, support in getting better school notes, better access to lobbyism channels—but not to central public service delivery? In fact, answering these questions is difficult. Unfortunately, there is no time here to discuss what experts in the field (Rawls, Sandel, Walzer, and Sen) would advise us to. Should—at the end—government be separated from economy as it was separated from religion 200 years ago? As a consequence, should government employment be reduced to a minimum as this would be the radical consequence of present developments?

Still, governments apply a mixture of measures and instruments (see the overview below) but all of them involve huge challenges and side effects.

For example, Public Private Partnerships (PPP) were introduced many years ago: "PPPs are extremely popular, they enjoy a positive image and they fit neatly into discussions about administrative reform. Administrators all over the world like PPPs. Using them is a sign of a modernizing bureaucracy, and that they are taking advantage of an organisational arrangement which represents a win-win situation: the private sector is making profits; the public partner improves the provision of public services by bringing together the specific capacities and capabilities of state and non-state sectors"[286]. Unfortunately, PPP reviews are mostly

285 Henrik Enroth, Policy Network Theory. In: Marc Bevir (Ed.):, The SAGE Handbook of Governance. Sage 2011, p. 19.

286 Gunnar Folke Schuppert, Partnerships. In: Bevir (Ed.), The SAGE Handbook of Governance, op. cit., p. 286.

reflecting the particular view of the author. The whole debate is still characterised by rather ideological discussions.

The same can be said about the successes and failures of outsourcing, contracting out, nudging and shared-services. As Cohen and Eimicke state, "contracting to downsize is really an illusion as the displaced public workforce has been replaced with a contractor workforce, often located across the street or down the block; sometimes it is the same worker paid more or less to do the same work he or she did for the government"[287]. However, it may also be true that downsizing and cost reductions have indeed been achieved but without significant improvements in quality delivery.

It is beyond the scope of this survey to discuss the pros and cons of all of the existing restructuring elements in all countries.

287 Steven Cohen and William Eimicke, Contracting Out. In: Mark Bevir (Ed.), The SAGE Handbook of Governance, op. cit., pp. 238–239.

Table 27: Effectiveness of restructuring measures

Categories/Instruments	Measures	Challenges
Structural/Organisational Reforms	Privatisation, outsourcing, delegating tasks to agencies, decentralisation, PPP, reduction of hierarchies, shared services, fusion of organisations, task evaluation, team working, enhancing efficiency through ICT, organisational streamlining	Privatisation, agencification and decentralisation may only lead to shifts in employment, effectiveness of outsourcing and privatisation differs and should be decided on a case by case basis, still too little evidence on the link between organisational reforms and workplace behaviour, more ex-ante evaluations are needed: what happens to staff in terms of status, working conditions, social security, what are the transfer costs?
Budgetary instruments	Ad hoc job cuts, long term reductions, re-allocation of staff, arbitrary job cuts, job cuts based on performance appraisals, job cuts based on age and gender, last recruited leaves first	Political driven cuts are often across-the board, often, governments reacting to fiscal situations through cut backs etc. did not reduce public expenditure, although reductions in expenditures may have a positive short-term impact, they may also have negative side effects on the long run (for example as to a high-quality service delivery)
HR Instruments	Workforce planning, workforce reviews, early retirement measures, recruitment freezes, promotion freezes, non-replacement of retired officials' redeployment measures	Impact on morale, commitment, job satisfaction, voluntary or involuntary, early retirement and impact on employment rate and public budgets

Source: OECD, Public Servants as Partners for Growth, op. cit.

5. Conclusions: Reform Trends in the Field of HRM

Budgetary constraints have caused a more radical, but arguably less strategic, way of managing expenses in HRM policies. Today, cutback management is once again a central issue in both public management practice and research. We conclude that, in many cases, cutback management is generally not part of a well-thought government or organisation's long-term strategy, but takes the form of a short-term, reactive reform agenda. Whereas, theoretically, it is possible to do "more with less" and even "better with less", it is very difficult to achieve these objectives as long as saving resources are the prime objective of all reforms. In fact, in most cases Human Resource Management is subordinated to other policy objectives. Given the lack of empirical evidence in this study, it is difficult to say whether the accumulated knowledge in the field of HRM is taken into account in the policies of strategic public management.

Overall, countries are implementing many reforms in the field of HRM. As a consequence, HRM as such is changing dramatically.

From a more neutral point of view, HR policies in most OECD countries are moving through a fascinating but also a disorienting period. Whereas the past organisational reform trends were characterized by a move away from the classical bureaucratic model, current reforms do not indicate convergence towards a new administrative best-practice model and even the varieties of New Public Management thesis may be unconvincing. In fact, several reform trajectories exist in the field of HRM which lead to a modernisation of structures, processes and employment conditions, but these highlight the existence of alternative models rather than a shift towards one common HR reform model. Neither is there a common trend towards one employment model.

In fact, there can have been few times when it has been a greater challenge to understand the changing nature of the employment relationship. The old conception of the typical full-time employed male employee with life-time tenure, and between those with and without stable jobs has long been outdated. Instead, it is often unclear who is even to count as an employee, in the face of the disappearance of distinctions between civil servants, employees, independent contractors, self-employed, and fixed-term and the spread of "triangular" relationships mediated by employment agencies.

Overall, public employment is changing as regards size, structure, composition and status. The national central public administrations are also becoming more open, flexible, diverse, feminine, fragmented and smaller. All countries are eager to enhance efficiency, productivity and innovation by cutting budgets although there is no best-practice blueprint how to do this. The current trend seems to be rather towards bestfit than to best-practice developments. This again leads to more diversity than to more convergence.

Still, developments are different in different parts of the world and are strongly related to budgetary pressures. Overall, many countries in the European Union have become the "sick man" of the OECD world. Overall, those countries which are pursuing a tough cost control paths are all belonging to the European Union.

In most cases, European countries have implemented tough HR reforms that have resulted in many hard choices, paradoxes and negative side-effects. The negative effects of these reforms on public employees' morale, job satisfaction, stress levels, trust in leaders etc. have been well documented in the literature, for example by Levine and Cascio (amongst many others). Overall, the situation of many central public employees in the European Union is worrying. This may be even more the case when considering the situation of all public sector workers, as working and employment conditions of central public employees are often better than the situation of other public sector workers.

Overall, OECD countries are following different reform paths. According to our model (in the theoretical part of our survey) and the analysis of the data, we are in the position to classify OECD countries in the framework for budgetary constraints, HR bundles and reform trajectories. However, we wish to highlight that it is much easier to place countries in the "tough cost control" category than into the two other categories. The reason for this is the focus on technical bundles in this survey and, consequently, the lack of data on behavioural bundles.

Because of the focus on the implementation of technical cost-control bundles, we have decided to refrain from a classification of countries into the second category, "Responsible restructuring". As regards the first category, "Soft employee focused reform path", we have classified those countries which have not implemented tough cost control measures, did not increase working time and maintained public employment levels. This category of countries also did not show negative effects on HR reforms on workplace behaviour and employee reactions as a result of reforms.

Table 28: Reform path in OECD countries

Soft employee focused reform path	Responsible restructuring	Tough cost control / downsizing path
Norway, Germany, Sweden, Chile, Japan, Canada	No data available	Greece, Portugal, Ireland, Spain, United Kingdom, Czech Republic, Slovenia

Thus, we can confirm Hypothesis 7 to which only a minority of countries have implemented a soft employee focused reform path (which basically means no implementation of severe cuts in employment levels, pay, no cuts in training and no changes as regards job security etc.) (Hypothesis 7). However, in this survey, we could not verify hypothesis 8 ("More common are responsible restructuring paths that combine technical and behavioural HR bundles and a pure downsizing path") because of the lack of data.

However, this all does not mean that OECD countries are copying private sector models. In fact, many working and employment conditions in central administrations could also be seen as an example of best practice as they are fairer, less prone to discrimination, or even better and more efficient. However, as a consequence of newly implemented reforms, the attractiveness of employment on central public administration is shrinking and cases of best practices are becoming less.

Table 29: Reforms in HR and general development

Reforms in HRM	General developments
• Central public employees with public law status	• Further restriction to few categories (e.g., judges, police, military) in most countries, further alignment of employment conditions and status with public and private sector
• Central public employees with private law status	• Large majority of employees in public service delivery jobs, further alignment of employment conditions and status with private sector
• Administrative principles and ethical standards	• Classical values such as legality and impartiality remain in place, on-going trend towards conflicting values, as a consequence, more detailed ethics rules, controls and accountability mechanisms, politicization remains challenge (due to decentralization and individualization trends partly increasing)

Reforms in HRM	General developments
• Merit principle	• Ongoing focus on Merit principle, increasing (pay) injustices linked to merit, social mobility remains great challenge
• Trends in public employment	• Generally further reduction of central public employment, need for additional recruitment in certain sectors and in some countries, need for demographic-sensitive age management, more evidence on negative side-effects on popular downsizing measures
• Job security	• Depending on national context, relaxation of lifetime tenure, importance of job security returns on agenda
• Bureaucratic career and post-bureaucratic systems	• No trend towards a best practice model, move away from pure forms and more diversity of different systems; often emergence of "bureaucracy-lite" systems, more innovations as regards work systems
• Principle of hierarchy	• Remains important, although trend towards more communication, participation and teamwork
• Decentralisation of responsibilities	• Depending on context, growing awareness of the need for more consistency and coherence in standards, working conditions and HR policies, need for more for discussions on accountability in HR settings
• Mobility between the public and private sector	• Further enhanced, difficult in some countries because of difficult competitive situation of the public sector, conflicts of interests increasing
• Leadership	• Ever growing expectations as to transformational, ethical and transactional leadership, gap between leadership expectations and the leadership reality growing, ongoing distrust in leadership, more differentiation in approaches, increased focus on new skill requirements
• Career development	• More focus on individual development plans, competency management, lifelong learning, management of older employees more important, parallel less career development opportunities and promotions due to austerity measures, remain a challenge in times of budgetary constraints

Reforms in HRM	General developments
• Work systems	• Investments in innovative and learning workplaces, more evidence on relationship work systems and organisational performance; no new universal model
• Anti-discrimination and diversity	• Context depending, On-going importance, greater focus on new areas such as age discrimination
• Recruitment procedures, selection of top officials	• Context depending, further opening up of public sector, move away from recruitment to entry level in traditional countries, more flexible recruitment (also at mid-career), context depending creation of senior civil services
• Pay and Pay according to performance	• Ongoing criticism of performance-related pay but also as regards standardized pay systems, trend towards more pay differentiation and related unfairness perceptions, reduction of allowances
• Performance management and personnel appraisal	• Ongoing management and measurement challenges, context depending increase of performance management bureaucracy, greater focus on communication and trust, call for more fairness and more professional leadership of line managers
• Working conditions	• Enhanced pressure on in some countries due to austerity measures; reconciliation of work and family life; in some countries deterioration of working conditions; context depending attractiveness of central public administration in many countries
• Working time	• Flexible working times, in some countries increase of weekly working hours
• Social dialogue and distribution of competence in HRM	• Further decentralization and fragmentation, context depending forms of SD, Weakening of SD
• HRM and role of Personnel Department; psychologisation of HRM	• In theory increased role of HRM in Strategic Management, trend towards individual responsibility of employees as regards engagement, skill development, satisfaction, performance, competence development, increased focus on emotions and fairness perceptions, in reality HR still seen as cost factors

Reforms in HRM	General developments
• Training	• Increasing differences between call for more investments in skill development and training and training seen as cost factor, great reforms as regards ICT used in training and skill development, on-going trend towards lifelong learning, more focus on training for older officials
• Specific pension system	• Further alignment with private sector, increase of retirement age, early retirement more difficult, calculation not on basis of last salary, more old age poverty
• Health related policies	• Increase in stress and job intensity in many countries, more investments in preventive measures

Source: adapted from Demmke/Moilanen, 2013 op cit., pp. 132–135

5.1 Is public HR still different to private sector HR – should it be?

There has been an ongoing discussion in the scientific community for many decades about the differences between public and private organisations and the impact of HR reforms on individual workplace behaviour, status, work motivation and character traits. The discussion is not only of theoretical importance. In fact, it is of great practical importance for the future design of HRM policies because it clarifies a number of highly relevant issues: For example, should performance related pay be introduced in the public sector if motivational incentives are different for public employees than for private sector employees? Or, does a specific Public sector motivation exist as such? And if so, how is public sector motivation changing in times of crisis? Is intrinsic public sector motivation becoming less important and being replaced by more extrinsic public sector motivation?[288]

All of these questions are related to one overriding topic: Is government specific in relation to the private sector? Should it be? How is government changing? Are we moving towards a "privatization" of government? And, if so, is this

288 Steven van de Walle/Bram Steijn/S.Jilke.: Extrinsic motivation, PSM and labour market characteristics: A multilevel model of public sector employment preference in 26 countries. *International Review of Administrative Sciences,* 81(4).2015.

a problem? Is "Collaborate Government" a forerunner in a long term process of a complete "blurring of boundaries" between the public and the private sector?

Will "merit", "skills", "competence" and "ethics" become the ultimate HR policy issues, both in the private and in the public sectors?

Interestingly, the position that public organisations are different was always in striking contrast to the opinion of major public administration experts such as Herbert Simon and Max Weber who underlined the commonalities among organisations and suggested that public and private organisations are more alike than different. For example, Weber applied his concept of bureaucracy to private organisations, too. Simon was of the opinion that it was false to assume that public and non-profit organisations cannot, and on average do not, operate as efficiently as private business.[289]. Simon was also convinced that public employees were not distinct from private employees. In "Administrative behaviour"[290], Simon wrote, "I used to think that organisation was important, but now I think that it is much more a matter of personality. The important thing is the man. If he has drive, ability, imagination, he can work in almost any organisation."[291] These findings are logical. Many people in both types of organisations virtually perform the same functions as "managers, secretaries, computer programmers, auditors, personnel officers, maintenance workers," etc.[292] or, more concretely, "A government-owned hospital, for example, obviously resembles a private hospital more than it resembles a government-owned utility."[293]

Moreover, Simon agreed with Merton who argued that purposive action does not imply "rationality" of human action[294]. In both, the public and in the private sector, the most important limitation to a correct anticipation of consequences of action is provided by the existing state of (limited) knowledge[295]. Because of

289 Herbert Simon.: Public Administration, Alfred Knopf, New York. 1973.

290 Ibid.

291 Ibid.

292 Ibid.

293 James L. Perry.: Measuring Public Service Motivation: An Assessment of Construct Reliability and Validity. *Journal of Public Administration Research and Theory*, Vol. 6, No. 6, 1996, pp. 5–22.

294 R.K. Merton.: The Unanticipated Consequences of Purposive Social Action. *American Sociological Review*, Vol. 1, Issue 6. 1936, p. 896.

295 Merton, op cit, p. 898.

this, behavioural economics have grown in importance and have increasingly informed politics, both in the private and in the public sector[296].

Today, Thaler and Sunstein are enthusiastic about libertarian, paternalist nudging in the private and in the public sector because they are impressed by the imperfection in individual decision-making and the low costs of nudging. They catalogue many factors that can lead to mistakes in human judgment and decision-making such as optimism, overconfidence, loss aversion, a status quo bias, framing, inertia, inattention, error etc.[297]

Thus, why should public and private HRM differ if people do not differ? Decades ago, Goodsell, in his polemic *The Case for Bureaucracy*[298], revealed that "the empirical evidence reviewed to verify the "bureaucratic mentality" does very little to assure us that it actually exists. Bureaucrats have not shown to be less flexible and open-minded than non-bureaucrats, and they do not appear more rule-oriented. Indeed, much evidence points to little difference between bureaucrats and ordinary people[299]". Goodsell presented interesting socio-demographic information and data about the average civil servant. He concluded that the average civil servant is in fact not much different to other citizens. Goodsell concluded that bureaucrats are ordinary people. They teach children, manage forests, program computers, chase speeders, arbitrate labour disputes, calculate benefit-cost ratios, inspect meat, enforce environmental permits, conduct research, negotiate contracts, prepare laws and fight wars: Within a point or two, bureaucrats as a whole are identical with the general public in their concern about crime, drugs, the environment, welfare, and the condition of the cities. Their views are similar close on capital punishment, premarital sex, school bussing, and fundamentalist religion. Overall, comparability out-weighs contrast"[300].

Despite these findings and the growing importance of behavioural economics, many scholars still argue that the public sector attracts a specific type of public employees with specific traits and a specific public sector motivation.

---

296 A. Oliver.:, Nudging, Shoving, and Budging: Behavioural Economic Informed Policy. *Public Administration*, Vol. 93, No. 3.2015, pp. 700–714; D. Kahneman.: Think Fast and Slow, Farrar, Straus and Giroux. 2013.

297 Richard H. Thaler & Cass Sunstein.: Nudge: Improving Decisions about Health, Wealth and Happiness, Penguin Books.2009.

298 Charles E. Goodsell.: The Case for Bureaucracy, A Public Administration Polemic, Third Edition, Chatham, New Jersey. 1994.

299 Charles E. Goodsell (1994), The Case for Bureaucracy, op cit, p. 123.

300 Charles E. Goodsell (1994), The Case for Bureaucracy, op cit, p. 114.

Other experts point to the need of having specific employment features and a specific employment status because of the fact that public sector tasks and values differ to private sector tasks. This discussion is important and "very real" as more countries are in a process of reforming the employment status of public employees and align this status towards more private sectors like features. Will this trend affect public service ethics, principles of hierarchy and rationality in decision-making, and the attractiveness of public sector jobs? If so, positively or negatively?

Our survey reveals that a number of countries link budgetary constraints and the need for abolishing the specific civil service status. Almost half of all OECD countries are considering the abolishment or reform of the classical civil service status.

Figure 52: Budgetary constraints as extra impetus to abolishing employment as civil servants?

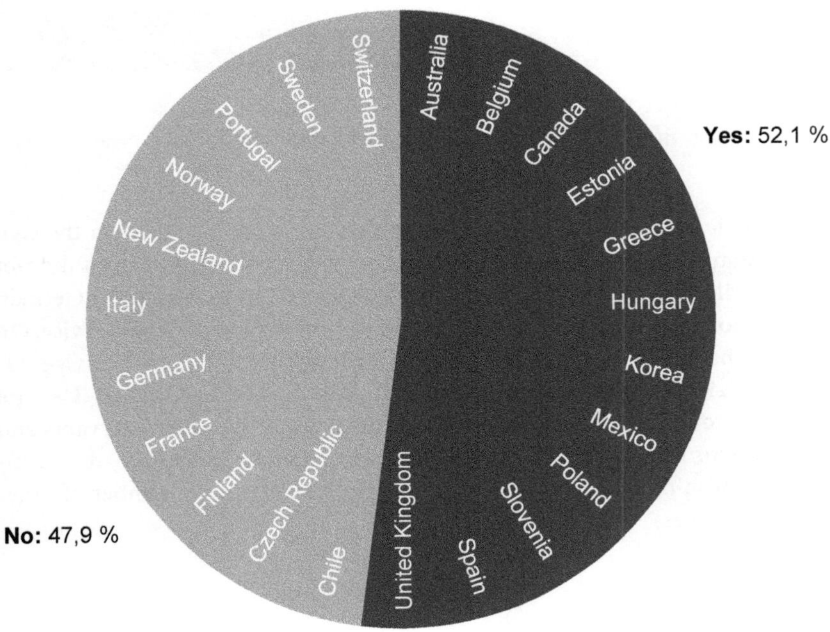

Interestingly, the answers to this question are also related to the budgetary situation of a country. However, the (constitutional, legal, cultural and political) context is more decisive for the question whether and how the civil service status differs to other complement relationships. And whether the status should be reformed or abolished, or not changed at all.

Figure 53: Abolishment of civil service and relation with categories of countries

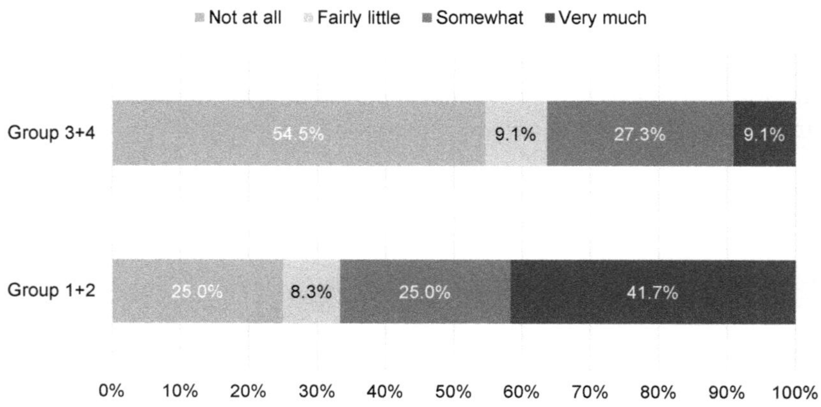

For example, in some countries, the budgetary crisis has no effect on the civil service status. For example, for a long time, the Czech Republic even did not have a Civil Service Law. Therefore, why abolishing it? In Germany, the German Constitution (Grundgesetz) requires the existence of a specific civil service. On the other hand, Portugal and Italy have already reformed the civil service status in the 1990's (Italy) and during the last years (Portugal). Sweden does not see a need to abolish the civil service as differences between civil servants and private sector employees (almost) do not exist anymore. Therefore, the intention to abolish the civil service status is strongly related to a number of other contextual issues.

Figure 54: Budgetary constraints as extra impetus to abolishing employment as civil servants – countries

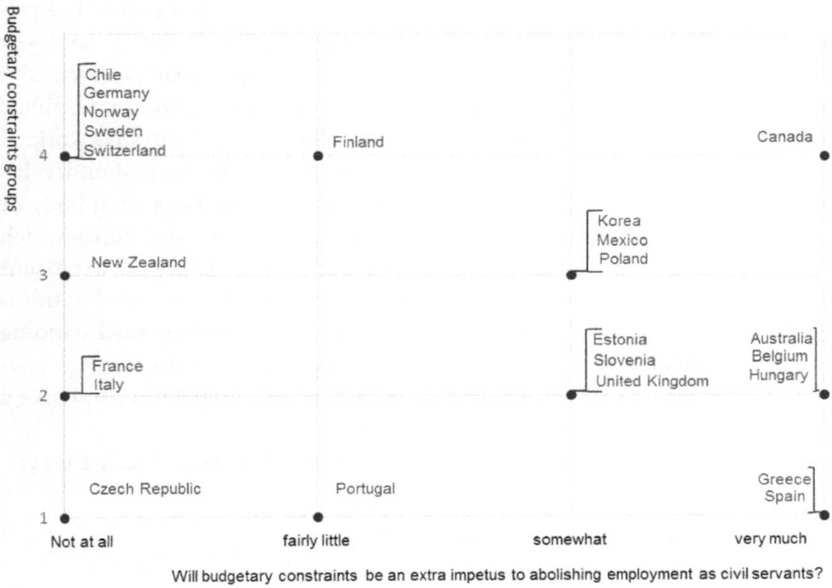

Still, in some countries, the civil service status is linked to a long tradition and a number of legal and philosophical arguments, such as the principles of hierarchy and rationality. Hierarchy and rationality are the cornerstone of the traditional bureaucracy, and these principles are still alive and doing well in many countries. From the ethical point of view, acting rational and following the law or the superior's orders is usually not problematic. It still is a very relevant guideline for public officials, as it highlights the importance of the rule of law and loyalty to democratically elected government. However, the problem with the Weberian concept is that as an ethical guideline it is simply too narrow for today's multi-level governance. Today, the level of awareness is growing that work in the public sphere is much more complex and no longer dominated by the principle of rationality, as Weber predicted. Instead, the individualization of HRM is an ongoing process. As we have seen behavioural economies have become an integral part of HRM theories and "Nudging" experts like Thaler, Sunstein[301] have become popular.

301 D. H. Hausman & B. Welch.: To Nudge or Not to Nudge, in: The Journal of Philosophy, Vol. 18, No. 1. 2010, pp. 123–136.

Still, classical bureaucratic countries such as France or Germany with a long established civil service tradition do not wish to abolish the classical civil service systems. These proponents of maintaining differences between public and private sector employees argue that work in the public service is specific and—by nature—different from work in the private sector. In *Government is Different*[302], Appleby noted the differences among organisational structures within the public sector: "government administration differs from all other administrative work…". For example, a ministry works in a totally different work climate and under different parameters than a police station, a judicial court, an inspection body or a local authority. Ministries, in particular, have special tasks and duties which differ from those in the private sector. For example, offering services to citizens (clients) may not be one of the most important priorities of a ministry, but this is the case for most of the private companies. Therefore, the professional standing of a governmental official is specific in many countries. In some countries, governmental officials still enjoy a different prestige, a special reputation and have a different motivation than private sector employees.

Consequently, civil servants should also be treated differently because they:

- Are given considerable power and responsibilities
- Set legal and normative standards for citizens
- Have a responsibility to provide leadership
- May intervene directly in the basic rights of citizens, e.g. police
- Are financed and paid from the public budget in order to carry out work for the public
- Have different values, ethos and (public sector) motivation

Therefore, civil servants bear special responsibilities for the public. They exercise public powers on behalf of the country. They spend public money for important government projects. They raise taxes. They hunt down criminals. They protect people. They take decisions which have an impact on the fundamental rights of citizens. They decide on health and on risk protection. The level of power or responsibility awarded to the public officials can be seen as requiring the imposition of some specific duties, rights and obligations for carrying out that role properly. For all these tasks, it is important that the public servants exercise their role properly, and act lawfully, honestly and loyally without acquiring any personal advantage. In

302 Paul Appleby.: Government is different, in: Shafritz J. M., Hyde A. C. (Eds.) (1987), Classics of Public Administration, 2nd Edition The Dorsey Press, Chicago, Illinois. 1945.

short, this means that they must have a specific ethos because the exercise of public tasks requires fairness and leadership as regards a number of principles (equity, equality, non-discrimination, impartiality, loyalty and neutrality).

Therefore, for proponents of "differences" amongst public and private sector organisation and between civil servants and private sector employees, the specific public tasks also require specific working conditions and in some case a specific legal status or legal status which links the person to the state. In particular, those employees who are directly participating in the exercise of powers, who are intervening in the fundamental rights of the citizens, who spend public money and who are safeguarding the general interest of the state (or of other public authorities) should have a specific status which binds them to the public interest.

In fact, our data allow for a geographical analysis which shows that—in relative percentages—the intention to abolish civil service employment is not linked to geography and only partly to the budgetary situation of a country. In fact, almost 50% of all countries belonging to category 3 and 4 seem to be more willing to abolish civil service employment in times of budgetary constraints.

Figure 55: Geography and the intention to stop employment as civil servants in case of budgetary constraints

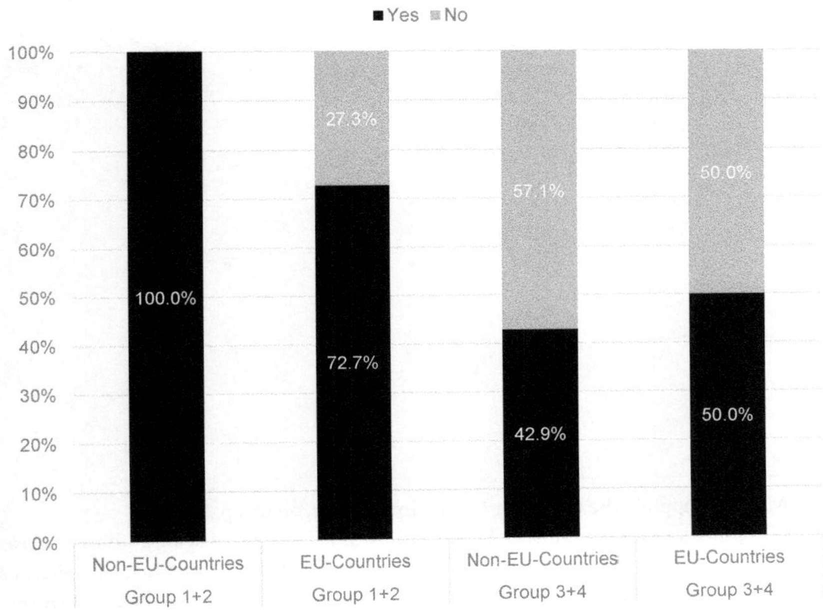

Countries with less-traditional systems and fewer differences between public and private employment features argue that there is no automatic link between the institutional structure and corruption levels. Thus, bureaucratic countries are not less corrupt than countries with other organisational features, because other explanatory factors play a more important role. For example, in her study on the *Quest for Good Governance*, Mungiu-Pippidi concludes that countries with a higher power-distance culture (Hofstede) have higher levels of corruption[303]. On the other hand, one explanatory variable for high levels of corruption is also the blurring of boundaries between the public and the private sector. The latter also applies to those countries with an open access order[304].

In order to shed some light on these questions, we have analysed the link between budgetary constraints and corruption as well as between institutional structure and corruption levels.

Figure 56: Budgetary constraints, categories of countries and corruption levels

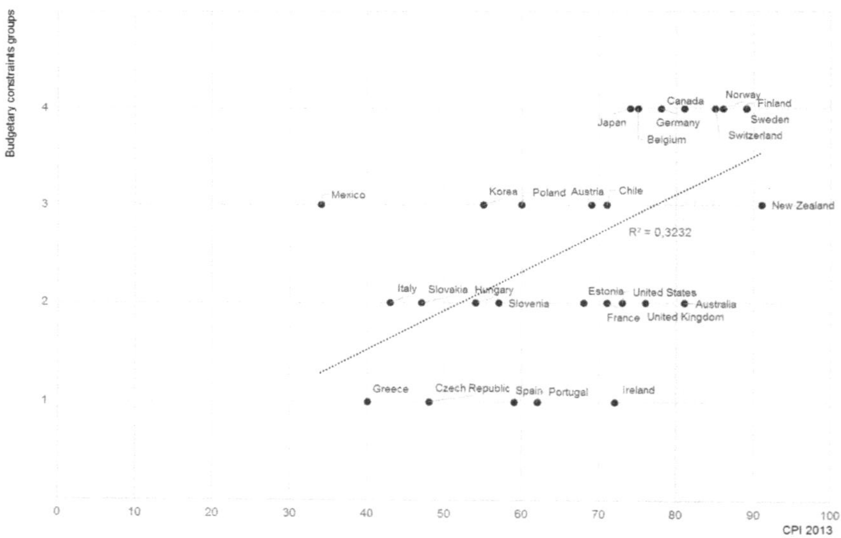

303 Mungiu-Pippidi, The Quest for Good Governance, op cit., p. 21.

304 Mungiu-Pippidi distinguishes between Governance regimes with a limited access order and an open access order and believes that the latter countries have a sharper separation between the public and the private sector, in: The Quest for Good Governance, op cit, p. 29.

The data reveals a relationship between budgetary constraints and corruption levels. For example, category 1 countries have higher levels of corruption than category 4 level countries. However, we cannot observe a link between institutional structure and corruption levels. For example, post-bureaucratic countries like Finland and Sweden have very low levels of corruption. However, this is also the case for a classical bureaucratic country like Germany with low levels of corruption. On the other hand, other classical bureaucratic countries like Greece and Mexico but also post-bureaucratic countries like the Czech Republic (and partly Italy) have very high levels of corruption. Thus, we conclude from here that the institutional structure as such is not decisive for the level of corruption. However, this does not exclude that some classical features such as merit-based recruitment procedures have a strong influence on the level of politicisation and also on corruption[305]. Moreover, according to Kwon, intrinsic motivation and public service motivation are negatively linked to corruptibility[306]. These findings suggest that any reform that aims at focusing on extrinsic motivators should consider potential negative side-effect.

In order to get more clarity about the link between budgetary constraints and the development of corruption, we have looked at the link between budgetary constraints and the development of corruption, as defined by the control of corruption data by the World Bank[307].

305 Meyer-Sahling, Jan-Hinrik & Tim Veen.: Governing the Post-Communist State: Government Alternation and Senior Civil Service Politicisation in Central and Eastern Europe. *East European Politics* 28(1). 2012, pp. 1–19; Carl Dahlström/Victor Lapuente/Jan Teorell (2012), The Merit of Meritocratization, op cit, pp. 656–668; Peter Evans & James E. Rauch, Bureaucracy and Growth: A Cross-National Analysis of the Effects of "Weberian" State Structures on Economic Growth. *American Sociological Review*, Vol. 64, No. 5 (Oct., 1999), pp. 748–765.

306 Illoong Kwon.: Motivation, Discretion and Corruption, in: Journal of Public Administration Research and Theory, No. 24. 2012, pp. 765–794.

307 According to this definition, "control of corruption captures perceptions of the extent to which public power is exercised for private gain, including both petty and grand forms of corruption, as well as 'capture' of the state by elites and private interests". We have taken this definition and not the one of transparency international, as definitions by TI have changed in 2012.

Figure 57: Development of Corruption and budgetary constraints – Changes in corruption between 2008 and 2013

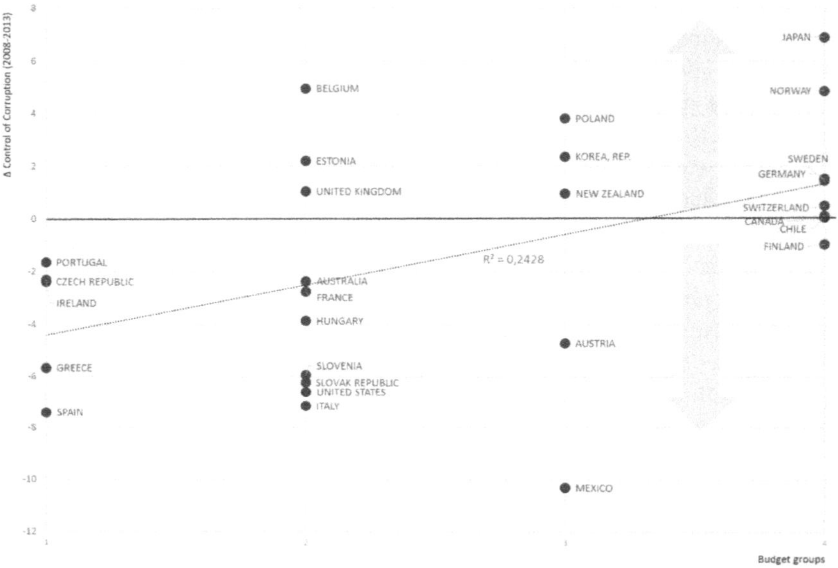

Again, the results are striking, as there is indeed a link between budgetary constraints and the development of corruption. According to the data, almost all countries belonging to category 1 have seen an increase in corruption levels during the last years, whereas this is not the case for category 4 countries. There is no link between budgetary constraints and the development of corruption as regards the other two groups, with Mexico showing the worst development of all countries.

These findings support opponents of a specific civil service status and specific public HR features who argue that the tasks of civil servants are not more specific or more valuable than those carried out in the private sector. Their arguments can be summarised as follows[308].

- First, even if public tasks are specific, this does not require a specific civil service status or specific legal contractual status. For example, any specific requirements can be easily arranged in an ordinary employment law contract (which is often based on collective agreements). The terms "essential functions of the state" and "safeguarding the general interest" are difficult to interpret.

308 Demmke/Moilanen (2010, 2012, 2013), op cit.

- Second, it is also not possible to argue that civil servants carry out more important tasks than private employees. Are doctors, workers in chemical companies, nuclear power station employees, farmers, bank and biotechnology staff not carrying out public interest tasks?
- Third, many current reform trends reveal an enormous paradox in many Member States with a specific career system. In these countries, working processes, working conditions and organisation structures are different in private and public organisations. However, there is very little evidence that the actual behaviour of public employees differs from those working in the private sector. In addition, traditional career models suffer from many well-known shortcomings. But what is then the point of having public employees who are treated differently than other employees?
- Fourth, in some countries civil servants carry out exactly the same tasks and functions as public employees (and sometimes work in the same organisation and the same office). For example, some countries employ teachers as civil servants and as public employees in the same school. However, performance level and ethical behaviour are actually the same whereas working conditions differ. This practice is as simple as it is unfair!

There is no clear answer to judge which arguments are "better". Answers should be linked to an understanding of the national context and administrative tradition. However, current trends are relatively clear in most countries: Many experts in the field point to the growing difficulties in identifying clear differences between the two sectors in times of governance, outsourcing, public-private partnerships and bounded rationality.

In fact, clear demarcations between public and private organisations have become more difficult and therefore oversimplified distinctions between public and private organisations are misleading[309]. Moreover, it is not easy at all to find benchmarks in public-private comparisons as the subject of comparison is becoming ever complex and diverse.

Would this suggest that, for example, the introduction of performance related pay has the same effects in the public than in the private sector? This important discussion immediately leads to Public Service Motivation theory (PSM). PSM theory refers to specific elements that motivate individuals to seek and continue employment in the public sector. Perry and Wise define it as "an individual predisposition to motives grounded primarily or uniquely in public

309 Hal Rainey.: Understanding and Managing Public Organizations, Third Edition, Jossey Bass, San Francisco. 2003.

institutions"[310]. Although some have suggested that prestige may be a factor for the desire of public service, this also applies to those working in the private sector.

The theory of public service motivation assumes that there are other motives unique to public employees, mainly that the public employee places the mission of the organisation and the betterment of society over financial rewards, when compared to private sector workers. In 1996, Perry developed a tool to define and measure PSM, a set of 35 statements relating to an employee's predisposition to seeking work in and remaining in the public sector. These items are associated with six dimensions related PSM: attraction to public policy-making, commitment to public interest, social justice, civic duty, compassion, and self-sacrifice. Respondents state their level of agreement or disagreement for each of the 35 items on a five-point scale. Employees that score high on the scale show a greater level of PSM

Despite the ongoing discussions on the (non-) existence of public service motivation, only few experts discuss how these differences develop in different regions, public sector organisations, as regards different administrative cultures, sex, age and positions, if existing, where and how these justify the existence of specific employment features for public officials[311].

On the other hand, people easily confuse the concept of public sector motivation with the concept of integrity and ethics, although it is not clear at all whether people with high levels of public sector motivation also act more ethically.

On the other hand, recent research in the USA shows that the level of public sector motivation is related to organisational effectiveness—however, not necessarily in a positive way. Hassan (2014) shows that "when employees perceive that their work has a positive impact on the welfare of others in their organisation and the community, they become highly motivated to perform well in their jobs"[312]. However, this form of emotional job involvement may also lead to higher sickness levels, burn out and self-exploitation[313].

310 Ibid.

311 W. Vandenabeele/Steven Van de Walle, International differences in public service motivation – the call of public service, Comparing regions across the world. In: James L. Perry/Annie Hondeghem (Editors).: Motivation in Public Management, Oxford University Press. 2008, pp. 223–247.

312 Shahidul Hassan.: Sources of Professional Employees' Job Involvement: An Empirical Assessment in a Government Agency. *Review of Public Personnel Administration*, Vol. 34, No. 4. 2014, p. 372.

313 Chih-wei Hsieh.:Burnout among Public service Workers: The role of Emotional Labor Requirements and Job Resources. *Review of Public Personnel Administration*, Vol. 34 (4). 2014, pp. 379–402.

In their research on *The Transformation of Governance – Who Are the New Public Servants and What Difference Does It Make for Democratic Governance?*, Park and Perry examine the relationship between the transformation of governance on the emergence of new public servants for service delivery and policy implementation[314]: "But who are now the agents of the state? How might the changed makeup of a new public service alter our expectations about democratic governance? "[315]

According to Park and Perry, "the most surprising result is how similar government public servants were to *both* for-profit public servants and for-profit, non-public services workers (…). We found that government and for-profit public servants were surprisingly alike, but, for the most part, very similar to for-profit, non-public servants. In contrast, non-profit public servants were more likely to conform to stereotypes often associated with government bureaucrats"[316].

As a consequence, overall, the conviction is growing that public employees can exercise important state tasks just as well or badly as civil servants under public law. Moreover, more countries are of the opinion that specific legal and ethical requirements in the national civil services can also be adopted under labour law, e.g., the rule of law, impartiality, equal treatment and fairness.

Still, all countries still follow a specific, not always rational, national logic. As regards public employment and the employment of civil servants and other public employees, different national models have developed and brought their own paradoxes and complexities. As a consequence, more countries are confronted with growing inconsistencies as regards the employment of public employees in civil service positions. For example, some countries employ a growing number of fixed-term employees in positions which should normally be offered only to civil servants with unlimited contracts. This has led to the fact that several countries apply different employment relationships in the same sectors, sometimes for the same professions and for employees who are working in the same office.

Here, little is known on the fairness perceptions and ethical behaviour of civil servants, public employees and employees under short-term contracts. Do the different categories of staff show different behaviour patterns because of different employment statuses?

When considering the situation, the following conclusion can be drawn: although most of the OECD-countries still apply a distinction between civil servants and other

314 Hun Myoung Park/James L. Perry.: The Transformation of Governance, Who Are the New Public Servants and What Difference Does It Make for Democratic Governance? *The American Review of Public Administration,* January 2013 vol. 43 no. 1 pp. 26–49.

315 Charles E. Goodsell (1994), The Case of Bureaucracy, op cit, p. 123.

316 Hun Myoung Park/James L. Perry, The Transformation of Governance, op cit. p. 44.

public employees, this distinction as such is no longer decisive for deciding which tasks are carried out by whom. In many cases, public employees subject to labour law can exercise important state tasks just as good or bad as civil servants. In addition, specific job requirements can be arranged in an ordinary labour contract: qualification requirements, powers, ethical requirements, fairness, professionalism and working conditions, etc. The logical consequence for some countries is to align the various employment conditions of all public employees under same law(s) or collective bargaining agreement(s) which is applicable to all public employees. Overall, this solution sounds practical and logical. However, in many countries the danger could be that this process could also be combined with a process that leads to a deterioration of working and employment conditions for civil servants.

5.2 How to evaluate future HR reform trends? Successes, failures, grey zones and context

The discussion of what has been achieved throughout the last decades is the most controversial issue of all. Many experts feel strongly on what to conclude about performance and successes but also about public services failures[317], even though it turns out to be very difficult to find clear answers. Yet, it is important to find responses to the effects of all HRM reforms within the last decades. As we will see later on it is easier to identify failures than to identify successes in the field Human Resource Management. For example, identifying successes[318] involves a number qualitative and quantitative criteria and variables (such as political and legal issues (constitutional issues, political strategies, attitudes of politicians, role of the legislator), financial indicators (resources available, management of resources, personnel costs), organisational criteria (organisational efficiency, organisational attractiveness, image etc.) and HR indicators (goal achievement, individual performance, motivation, satisfaction etc.[319]. Consequently, there is no "absolute" set of theoretical approaches to the subject of reform effects. Furthermore, the extent/nature/pace of HR reform is dependent on a range of factors which differ from country to country *vis-à-vis* the particular objectives chosen

317 Mark Bovens & Paul t'Hart, Revisiting the study of policy failures. Journal of European Public Policy, Vol. 3, No. 5, 2016, pp. 653–666.

318 Guy Peters.: Advanced Introduction to Public Policy, Edward Elgar. 2015; Allen Mc Connell.: Policy Success, Policy Failure and Grey Areas in Between. *Journal of Public Policy*, Vol. 30. 2010, pp. 345–362.

319 C. Talbot, Performance Management, in: Handbook of Public Management, op. cit., p. 494.

initially for the reform programme, the industrial relations environment, the power of public service unions, consensus on the need to maintain a partnership approach to modernisation, differing national priorities etc. Administrative reform must reflect the reality of these variables in particular countries, resulting inevitably in different mixes of private and public HR Management Systems".

This study also shows the importance of "context" driven reforms and the existence of a variety of national reform paths. Whereas in the past, many experts were searching for a new "best-practice" universal HR model, our survey shows that there is no one "single" best-practice Human Resource Management reform path. In fact, the trend is towards the diversification of HRM reforms and – in some cases – towards the individualization of HR-instruments (such as competency management, engagement policies, performance assessment, individualization of pay systems etc.).

HRM does not develop in a vacuum. In particular, HRM in central public administration is heavily influenced by political developments and changes as regards the nature of the state and government, socio-structural developments and reform pressures, public management fashions and organisational innovations.

HRM and context

Moreover, positive results of HR reforms are more difficult to define in the public services than in the private sector because performance standards are not limited to economic, quality and customer satisfaction criteria. Instead they also include constitutional, regulatory and political standards, as well as the common interest. Efficiency and effectiveness are necessary but not sufficient conditions for gaining public trust. In many cases, the public is confronted with ethics and integrity issues in the public services. Trust, as we know, is a precious resource which can easily be destroyed but is difficult to be restored.

To affix the label "failures" to HR policies is risky business. Even though this focus is understandable, it clearly hinders the development of evidence, knowledge and awareness of positive developments and cases of "good administration" in a complex context.

Before we enter into the discussion on concrete conclusions to our findings, it is interesting to examine the paradoxical context in which our study has been analysed:

- Today, work in the public sphere is no longer dominated by the principle of rationality as Weber predicted (and civil servants are also not seen any more as cogs in the machine). On the other hand, most public organisations keep a number of bureaucratic features. But work in the public sector is also more individual, value-laden, emotional, pluralistic and more unpredictable than ever. At the same time, HRM reform continues to affirm its significance for efficiency purposes and HRM is subordinated to economic and organisational imperatives. Thus, whereas the reform process as such is rather "simplistic", HRM as such is gaining in complexity.
- Boudreau and Lawler claim that "the more organisations pursue a bureaucratic and low-cost-operator approach to management, the less their HR organisation engages in advanced strategic activities"[320]. In fact, during the past years, many OECD-countries have focused on the introduction of many HR reforms. On the other hand, budgetary constraints, restructuring programmes and effects of austerity measures have not been a subject of rigorous scrutiny as regards the impact and the outcomes of individual HR policies and public employment trends. If this happened in the past, the focus of attention has been entirely on issues like the reduction of employment levels and the development of wages, but to a lesser extent as regards the link between consolidation measures and the impact of job intensity, sickness levels, quality of work,

320 J. Boudreau & E. Lawler III.: Stubborn traditionalism in HRM: Causes and Consequences. *Human Resource Management Review*, Vol. 24. 2014, pp. 232–244.

job motivation, job satisfaction, levels of trust in the own organisation and in leadership, job commitment, (un-) ethical behaviour and so forth. Another major obstacle to giving more prominence to the link between HRM and reform outcomes so far has been the difficulty to show that any HR reform will inevitably have an impact on governance as such.

What kind of further conclusions can be drawn from this survey? Is the impact of the financial crisis which started in 2008 and of budgetary constraints *new*? Is it special? Governments in the world have always had to cope with social and economic crises. War, depression, large-scale social conflicts, and a host of other significant challenges to the capacity of the public sector to govern have been all-too-frequent events facing governments[321].

Although we agree that some aspects of the current crisis are not new, some of them are *special*. The financial crisis beginning in 2008 has been posing a number of important new challenges to governments, even to those of the most affluent and seemingly most successful countries. For example, the need to reform pension systems and to tackle demographic challenges. Another challenge concerns the need to restructure and to downsize the public workforce. In many countries, this happened for the first time since the second World War.

Next, despite the fact that the economical context has improved during the last years, most countries continue apply "saving" measures in HR policies.

In all OECD countries, HR reforms in central public administration have become more pragmatic and less ideological. More public service employees do not perceive working in the public sector as distinct to working in the private sector. Instead, many public service professions are perceived as jobs and less as a vocation. At the same time, there is a clear danger that the public sector, public officials and public money are seen as causes, rather than as solutions for problems. Is this a sign for the return of "bureaucracy bashing"? Answering this question is more difficult as it seems, as many current developments in the private sector (for example in the field of applying the merit principle, fairness issues, the link between pay and performance) contradict the objectives of the state as an employer. Government needs employment systems that guarantee adherence to the core values, administrative law principles and ensure a focus on effectiveness, efficiency and accountability. They must ensure equal treatment and fairness while ensuring the merit principle and the equality of chances. They must be attractive

321 B. Guy Peters.: Governance responses to the fiscal crisis—comparative perspectives. *Public Money and Management*, January 2011, p. 76.

and competitive with respect to the private sector policies while managing tax payers' money as prudently as possible.

This can be best seen by the development of pay systems and the changing understanding of the merit principle: Overall, pay is being reduced. This is one of the most important results in our survey. However, another trend in the field is a "hidden trend".

In the past, pay systems were based on the principle of procedural fairness, the principle of transparency, standardisation and seniority. They were not designed as a direct payment for individual work done, but compensation for their service as a whole, in other words, for civil servants making their entire working capacity available to the general public and carrying out their duties to the best of their ability.

Today, most of the pay systems are based on the principle of individual performance and distributional fairness. The new pay systems are flexible and designed as a direct payment for individual work done. However, this does not suggest that flexible and performance related pay systems are fairer (and produce less conflicts) than the traditional systems. Instead, they are based on a different understanding of fairness and reflect the current value changes. The case of pay illustrates that many reforms also bring a greater number and variety of conflicting values.

Pay is closely related to the merit principle. The latter principle is "changing without being changed". Owing to the merit principle, most public administrations have become more meritocratic and, at the same time, more polarized. The more the concept of meritocracy is becoming a reality, the more it seems to legitimate a hierarchy of privilege. The paradox with the principle of meritocracy lies with the problem that our systems which reward talented people leave no hiding place for those who do not succeed in the competitive struggle. Today, rising levels of inequality and problems with social mobility can lead to a loss of social capital, frustration, discontentment and alienation. A further serious deficiency in the ethical grounds of meritocracy is its virtual absence of discourse on what areas of "merit do not do justice to vast differences in status, reward and power"[322]. Another problem is that the principle of meritocracy can, at times, be self-defeating, "The more opportunity there is for people to succeed in society, the less value such success is likely to have for them"[323]. If all people invest in more and better education and invest in their competences and skills,

322 Donald Menzel.: Ethics and Integrity in the public service. In: Donald Menzel/Harvey L White (eds.).: The State of Public Administration, Sharpe, London. 2011, p. 131.

323 Georg Dench (editor).:The rise and rise of Meritocracy, Blackwell, Oxford. 2006, p. 190.

the process ends as a race to the top. Everybody is likely to become disappointed quickly. Robert Merton showed that career satisfaction was higher in those units in which the promotion rates were low than in those with high ones. "If there is one thing worse than being blocked, it is seeing others succeed where you have failed"[324]. Merit, as the basis for employment decisions, is one of the core values. Yet employee faith in the application of merit principle is relatively low and appears to be in decline in many countries. "Even allowing for the fact that perceptions vary according to whether respondents were successful in obtaining a job, the results are still unsatisfactory"[325].

Thus, the consequent application of the merit principle seems to undermine one of the most important foundations of the national public administrations: the principles of equality and equity. In their publication *Diploma Democracy – On the Tensions between Meritocracy and Democracy*[326], Bovens and Wille show that Plato's ideal of the state which is run by the best and the brightest has (almost) become a reality. However, this new state is neither fairer, nor representative nor politically stable. Instead, the social cohesion is at stake.

Moreover, the application of the merit principle is threatened by the flexibilisation of HR policies, increased individual treatment and cases of politicisation in pay, promotion, recruitment and career development policies.

This survey illustrates worrying trends in the field of training. It is often suggested that fast changes that are taking place can also be seen in the field of skill development, lifelong learning and competency development. Whereas in the past civil servants were experts who held diplomas and received little training, today civil servants are required to continuously develop their skills and competencies. Policy-makers and academics keenly debate the importance of skills as a lever for boosting individual employability, organisational productivity and national competitiveness. Training is an important instrument in this process. This is in striking contrast to the results in our survey which shows that training budgets and training days are being reduced.

This survey also shows that, yet, it is important to find responses to the complex effects of all reforms within the last decades and the recent impact of the financial crisis. New questions and challenges arise in times of growing inequalities and the emergence of new forms of employment models in our societies. The

324 Ibid.

325 Lyonelle Briggs.: Testing APS ethics: Where is the integrity? *The American Journal of Public Administration*, Vol. 68, No. 2/2009, p. 134.

326 Mark Bovens &A. Wille.: Diploma Democracy – On the Tensions between Meritocracy and Democracy, Utrecht/Leiden. 2009.

pace of change and growing uncertainties about the reform results also generate more discussions on the need to preserve traditional structures, to keep the identity of civil servants and to maintain some specific features that are different to the private sector and other public sectors.

As already discussed in the previous chapters, despite all current developments away from the bureaucratic model, it is difficult to say whether the trend is towards the end of the bureaucratic paradigm or the beginning of a new post-bureaucratic, high-performance work system paradigm. Despite the popularity to criticise the over-emphasis on laws and rules in contemporary civil services, the primacy of law is likely to remain in the future. However, the classical bureaucracies are about to change. However, some bureaucratic features are not vanishing. It is not yet clear what the post-bureaucratic paradigm is, apart from remedies to the weaknesses of the classical bureaucratic model. Still, developments like decentralisation, responsbilisation, flexibilisation, skill development, engagement, mobility etc. are too wide and too fluid concepts. These developments are also full of paradoxes and ambivalences. Consequently, they represent alternatives to the classical models. But do this also mean improvement?[327]

What is sure is that contemporary central public administrations are increasingly complex. In the future, they will most likely become more complicated and probably more contradictory all the time. Consequently, value conflicts are increasing, too[328].

While expectations of government are increasing, the resources available to meet these expectations are diminishing. Civil servants of the future will have to be at ease with more job intensity, stress, complexity and flexibility. They will have to be comfortable with change, often rapid change. At the same time, they will take more autonomous decisions, be more responsible, accountable, performance-oriented, and subject to new competency and skill requirements.

The central workforce will be smaller, mobile, better qualified and more diverse than ever before. In some HR bundles, working conditions will deteriorate and this will have negative consequences on the attractiveness of central public administration jobs. This again will pose new challenges in the "war for talents" with the private sector and in the context of demographic changes.

If budgetary constraints persist, it is likely that levels of job satisfaction, job commitment, trust in the organisation and trust in leadership will further

---

327 Demmke/Moilanen (2010), Civil Services in the EU of 27, op cit.

328 Gjalt de Graf.: The Bright Future of Value Pluralism in Public Administration. *Administration & Society*, Vol. 47 (9). 2015, pp. 1094–1102.

decline. Countries must take these developments serious and introduce measures to halt these preoccupying trends.

Otherwise, it is difficult to see how countries suffering from tough budgetary constraints can maintain and deliver effective public policies. Some of these countries will experience that downsizing is not only a cost-saving operation. Instead, what is needed is saving resources while introducing "smart" austerity measures, create innovative workplaces, reform and modernise work systems and professionalise HR policies. As regards the latter, this can only be done together with the employees and not—in a top-down manner—without employees. For example, if organisations want engaged, satisfied and committed employees they must accept that "employee engagement is best seen as an outcome of managerial activity to build perceptions of trust, fairness and organisational justice, especially procedural and interactional or interpersonal justice. These are the antecedents of engagement. The question remains on how trust, fairness and justice are built. Each are essentially processes of the quality of interactions between management and employees" (Purcell, 2012)[329]. Unfortunately, HR policies in times of budgetary constraints rather lead to less trust and, often, the quality of interactions is lacking. Consequently, the concept of engagement is becoming an ambivalent concept. Although the concept as such is a purely positive concept (and focuses on the importance of employees), why should employees be engaged if HR policies are poor and demotivating? At the end, engagement can also turn into a punitive instrument if line managers believe that employees are not sufficiently engaged, whatever the definition of engagement may be. We do not go as far as this. In fact, we believe that employee engagement is worth pursuing, not only as a normative concept (or even as a new fad), but as a means of improving working conditions and organisational performance.

Will "engagement" replace the classical public service ethos concept? Here, the circle comes to an end and we come back to the beginning of this survey.

Whereas most governments agree that politics should not try to form the character or cultivate the virtue of its citizens, the case of engagement policies shows that current trends in HR policies are leading towards a "psychologisation" of HRM.

Our survey shows that it is time to recognize HRM as an important strategical policy. It is also important to recognize that work on central public administration is important and linked to organisational learning, organisational innovation and organisational performance. Overall, despite all popular images, work

329 John Purcell.: The limits and possibilities of employee engagement, Warwick Papers in Industrial Relations, University of Warwick, No. 96. 2012, p. 13.

in the civil services will remain interesting, challenging, important and "a key to a better society and world"[330]. It is likely that budgetary pressures and politics will continue to have a strong impact on reform fashions and reform agendas. The overall definition of what public administration should be in the future is likely to continue to be politically determined.

Therefore, it is likely to expect that the alignment trend between public and private HR policies will continue. However, central public employees will never be able to compete with private sector companies in terms of flexibility and pay. In a way, this is good news: Still, presently government employment systems are corresponding better to a Rawlsian principle of justice than current trends in the private sector which produce many forms of injustice and sometimes perverse results as regards the rewarding of individual performance.

Also, public HR policies will continue to apply some specific bureaucratic features that will remain in place in order to sustain core democratic values like equality, fairness and legal security. According to Peters and Pierre, "the challenge in the longer term… is to design organisations that combine the efficiency and service capacity of decentralised organisations with the uniform and legalistic nature of hierarchical organisations"[331].

So far, many reform paths have shown different degrees of successes and failures. All depends on what aspects of the reform process and what kind of trends and instruments are being considered: If the interest is in cost-cutting, many reforms are moving into the right direction. If the interest is in organisational performance, more should be done. If the interest is in the development of innovative work systems, "things have started to move". If the interest is in employee morale, employee productivity, trust levels (in leadership), ethics and skill development, countries are required to take worrying trends more serious. In the context, it is likely that employees and HR policies will not produce better outcomes with less (input, personal and finances).

Studying HR reforms take us to the heart of current debates about the change of Governance and the modern public service capacities to govern and to manage public services. HRM reflects the changing nature of political Governance. As this study illustrates, HR reforms in the public sector are the outcomes of a political process, the result of political choices and ever-changing values.

---

330 David H. Rosenbloom/Robert S. Kravchuk/Richard M. Clerkin.: Public Administration, Understanding Management, Politics, and Law in the Public Sector, 7th edition, Mc Grawhill, Singapore. 2009, p. 548.

331 Guy Peters &Jon Pierre (Editors).: Handbook of Public Administration, Second edition, Sage Publications. 2003, p. 6.

Bibliography

Aberbach Joel D. & Rockman, Bert A., In the Web of Politics – Three Decades of the U.S. Federal, Executive, Brookings Institution, Washington D. C. 2000.

Alagaraja, Meera, HRD and HRM Perspectives on Organisational Performance: A Review of Literature, in: Human Resource Development Review, Vol. 12 (2), 2012, pp. 117–143.

Amabile, T.M. The social psychology of creativity. New York, NY: Springer. 1983.

Amabile, T.M. A model of creativity and innovation in organisations, in: B. M. Staw. & L. L. Cummings (Eds.), Research in organisational behaviour (Vol. 10, pp. 123–167), Greenwich, CT: JAI Press 1988.

Amabile, T.M. Creativity in context. Oxford, Westview Press. 1996.

Amabile, T.M., Motivating creativity in organisations: On doing what you love and loving what you do, in: California Management Review, 40(1), 1997, pp. 39–58.

Amabile, T.M./Schatze, E.A./Moneta, G.B./Kramer, S.J., Leader behaviours and the work environment for creativity, in: Leadership Quarterly, 15, 2004, pp. 5–32.

Andersen, K./Cooper, B./Zhu, C. The effect of SHRM practices on perceived firm financial performance: Some initial evidence from Australia, in: Asia Pacific Journal of Human Resources, 45, 2007, pp. 168–179.

Appelbaum, E./Bailey, T./Berg, P./Kalleberg, A., Manufacturing advantage: Why high performance work systems pay off. Ithaca, Cornell University Press, New York 2000.

Arthur, J. Effects of human resource systems on manufacturing performance and turnover, in: Academy of Management Journal, 37, 1994, pp. 670–687.

Bakhtari, H. Cultural effects on management style: A comparative study of American and Middle East management style, in: International Studies of Management & Organisation, 25, 1995, pp. 97–119.

Bandura, A., Self-efficacy: Towards a Unifying Theory of Behavioral Change, in: Psychological Review, No. 84, 1997, pp. 191–215.

Bandura, A., Self-efficacy: The exercise of control, New York: W.H. Freeman 1997.

Barney, J. Firm resources and sustained competitive advantage, in: Journal of Management, 17, 1991, pp. 99–120.

Barney, J. & Wright, P.M. On becoming a strategic partner: The role of human resources in gaining competitive advantage, in: Human Resource Management, 37, 1997, pp. 31–46.

Baron, James & Kreps, David M.(eds.), Strategic Human Resources: Frameworks for General Managers, John Wiley & Sons 1999.

Barron, F. & Harrington, D.M. Creativity, intelligence and personality, in: Annual Review of Psychology, 32, 1981, pp. 439–476.

Beatty, R.W. & Schneier, C.E., New HR roles to impact organisational performance: From "partners" to "players.", in: Human Resource Management, 36, 1997, pp. 29–37.

Becker, B. & Gerhart, B. The impact of human resource management on organisational performance: Progress and prospects, in: Academy of Management Journal, 39, 1996, pp. 779–801.

Beer, M. The transformation of the human resource function: Resolving the tension between a traditional administrative and a new strategic role, in: Human Resource Management, 1997, 36, pp. 49–56.

Benn, Stanley I. & Gaus, Gerald F, Public and Private in Social Life, Croom Helm 1983.

Bevir, Mark (Editor), The SAGE Handbook of Governance, London 2011.

Birdi, K. A clear idea of innovation: A practical approach to being creative and making sure your ideas stick. London, BPS 2012.

Bloom, Matt, The Performance effects of Pay Dispersion on Individuals and Organisations, in: The Academy of Management Journal, Vol. 42, No. 1, 1999, pp. 25–40.

Blyth, Mark, Austerity, Oxford University Press, Oxford 2013.

Bonazzi, Giuseppe, Geschichte des organisatorischen Denkens (Veronika Tacke (Editor), 2nd edition, Springer VS, Wiesbaden 2014.

Boivard, Tony & Löffler, Elke, Public Management and Governance, Routledge, Cheltenham 2015.

Boselie, P./Dietz, G./Boon, C. Commonalities and contradictions in HRM and performance research. In: Human Resource Management Journal, 15(3), 2005, pp. 67–94.

Bossaert, Danielle (Editor), Training and Human Resource Development in the European Union Member States, European Institute of Public Administration, Maastricht 2008.

Bouckaert, Geert & Pollitt, Christopher, Public Management Reform: A Comparative Analysis 2011.

Boudreau, J. & Lawler III, E., Stubborn traditionalism in HRM: Causes and Consequences, in: Human Resource Management Review, Vol. 24, 2014, pp. 232–244.

Bovens, Mark & Wille, A., Diploma Democracy – On the Tensions between Meritocracy an Democracy, Utrecht/Leiden 2009.

Mark Bovens & Paul t'Hart, Revisiting the study of policy failures. Journal of European Public Policy, Vol. 3, No. 5, 2016, pp. 653–666.

Boxall, Peter & Macky, K. High-performance work systems and organisational performance: Bridging theory and practice, in: Asia Pacific Journal of Human Resources, 45, 2007, pp. 261–270.

Boxall, Peter & Macky, K. Research and theory on high-performance work systems: progressing the high-involvement stream, in: Human Resource Management Journal, Volume 19, Issue 1, pages 3–23, January 2009.

Boxall, Peter/Purcell, John, Strategy and Human Resource Management, Hampshire, UK: Palgrave Macmillan., 3rd edition, London, 2011.

Bradley, L. Kirkman/Lowe, K.B./Young, D.P., High Performance Work Organisations, Center for Creative Leadership 1999.

Bregn, Kirstin, Detrimental Effects of Performance-Related Pay in the Public Sector? On the Need for a Broader Theoretical Perspective, in: Public Organisation Review, No. 13, 2013, pp. 21–35.

Brewster, C. & Larsen, H.H. Human resource management in Europe: Evidence from ten countries, in: International Journal of Human Resource Management, 3, 1992, pp. 409–434.

Brewster, C. & Larsen, H.H. Human resource management in Northern Europe: Trends, dilemmas, and strategy. Oxford, Blackwell 2000.

Briggs, Lyonelle, Testing APS ethics: Where is the integrity?, in: The American Journal Public Administration, Vol. 68, No. 2/2009.

Brunner, Dorothea, Die Wahrnehmung der Lohndisparität im Unternehmen und deren Wirkung auf die Kündigungsabsicht, Rainer Hamp, München 2009.

Cairney, Paul, Public Administration in an age of austerity: positive lessons from policy studies, in: Public Policy and Administration, No. 27, 2012, pp. 230–247.

Carter, Bob/Danford, Andy/Howcroft, Debra/Richardson, Helen/Smith, Andrew and Taylor, Phil, Lean and mean in the civil service: the case of processing in: HMRC Public Money & Management, Vol. 31, No. 2, 2011, pp. 115–122.

Chang, H.T./Chi, N.W. Human resource managers' role consistency and HR performance indicators: The moderating effect of interpersonal trust in Taiwan, in: International Journal of Human Resource Management, 18, 2007, pp. 665–683.

Chung-An Chen/Bozeman, Barry, Am I A Public Servant or am I a Pathogen?, Public Managers Sector Comparison of Workers Abilities, in: Public Administration, Vol. 92, No. 3, 2014, pp. 549–564.

Colakoglu, Saba/Hong, Ying and Lepak, David P., Models of Strategic Human Resource Management, in: Wilkinson, Adrian/Bacon, Nicolas/Redman, Tom and Snell, Scott (Eds.) (2010), The SAGE Handbook of Human Resource Management, London, 2010, pp. 32.

Collins, C.J./Clark, K.D. Strategic human resource practices, top management team social networks, and firm performance: The role of human resource practices in creating organisational competitive advantage, in: Academy of Management Journal, 46, 2003, pp. 740–751.

Conner, J./Ulrich, D. Human resource roles: Creating value, not rhetoric, in: Human Resource Planning, 19, 1996, 38–51.

Cropanzano, Russel/Stein, Jorgan H./Nadisc, Thierry, Social justice and the experience of emotion, Routledge, New York 2011.

Cropanzano, Russel/Bowen, David E./Gillard, Stephen W, The Management of Organisational Justice, in: Academy of Management Practice, 2007, pp. 34–48.

Crouch, Colin/Finegold, David and Sako, Mari, Are Skills the Answer? The Political Economy of Skill Creation in Advanced Industrial Countries, Oxford Press, Oxford 2001.

Crouch, Colin, The Knowledge Corruption, Hidden Consequences of the Financial Takeover of Public Life, John Wiley 2015.

Currie, G./Procter, S., Exploring the relationship between HR and middle managers, in: Human Resource Management Journal, 11(3), 2001, pp. 53–69.

Dahlström, Carl/Lapuente, Victor/Teorell, Jan, The Merit of Meritocratization: Politics, Bureaucracy, and the Institutional Deterrents of Corruption, in: Political Research Quarterly, Vol. 65(3), 2012, pp. 656–668.

Dahlström, Carl/Lapuente, Victor/Teorell, Jan, Dimensions of Bureaucracy, A Cross-National Dataset on the Structure and Behaviour of Public Administration, in: Quality of Government Working Paper Series 2010:13, University of Göteborg.

de Graf, Gjalt, The Bright Future of Value Pluralism in Public administration, in: Administration & Society, Vol. 47 (9), 2015, pp. 1094–1102.

Dekker, Teun J., Paying Our High Public Officials – Evaluating the Moral Justifications of Top Wages in the Public Sector, Routledge 2013.

Demmke, Christoph, Are civil servants different because they are civil servants?, EIPA, Maastricht 2006.

Demmke, Christoph/Moilanen, Timo, Civil Services in the EU of 27, Peter Lang, Frankfurt/M et al. 2010.

Demmke, Christoph/Moilanen, Timo, Effectiveness of Public Service Ethics and Good Governance, Peter Lang, Frankfurt/M. 2012.

Demmke, Christoph/Moilanen, Timo, Governmental Transformation and the Future of Public Employment, Peter Lang, Frankfurt/M. 2013.

den Dulk, Laura/Groeneveld, Sandra, Work–Life Balance Support in the Public Sector in Europe, in: Review of Public Personnel Administration, No. 33(4), 2012. pp. 384–405.

Desmarais, Celine/Abord de Chatillon, Emanuel, Are there Still Differences between the Roles of Private and Public Sector Managers, in: Public Management Review, Vol. 12:1, 2010, pp. 127–149.

DiMaggio, P.J./Powell, W., The iron cage revisited: Institutional isomorphism and collective rationality in organisational fields, in: American Sociological review, No. 48, 1983, pp. 147–160.

Downes, Patrick E. / Choi, Daejeong, Employee reactions to pay dispersion: A typology of existing research, in: Human Resource Management Review, Vol. 24, 2014, pp. 53–66.

Harris,L./ Doughty, D., & Kirk, S., The devolution of HR responsibilities—Perspectives from the UK's public sector, in: Journal of European Industrial Training, 26, 2002, pp. 218–229.

Dubet, Francois et al, Injustices: L'expérience des inégalités au travail, 2013.

Eichhorst, Werner/Marx, Paul & Tobsch, Verena, Institutional Arrangements, Employment Performance and the Quality of Work, Institute for the Future of Labour, Discussion Paper No. 4595, November 2009.

European Foundation for the Improvement of Living and Working Conditions, Dublin, Comparing sectors in Europe, 2014.

European Foundation for the Improvement of Living and Working Conditions, Working Conditions in Central Public Administration, Dublin, 2013.

European Foundation for the Improvement of Living and Working Conditions, Quality of employment conditions and employment relations in Europe, 2013.

European Foundation for the Improvement of Living and working Conditions, Work Organisation and Innovation, Dublin 2012.

European Foundation for the Improvement of Living and Working Conditions, Impact of the crisis on working conditions in Europe, Dublin 2012.

Evans, Mark, Beyond the Integrity Paradox – towards good enough Governance?, in: Policy Studies, No. 33:1, 2012, pp. 97–113.

Evans, Peter/Rauch, James. E., Bureaucracy and Growth: A Cross-National Analysis of the Effects of "Weberian" State Structures on Economic Growth, in: American Sociological Review, Vol. 64, No. 5 (Oct., 1999), pp. 748–765.

Fairlie, P. Meaningful work, employee engagement, and other key employee outcomes. Advances in: Developing Human Resources, 13, 2011, pp. 508–525.

Ferlie, Ewan/Lynn, Lawrence/Pollitt, Christopher, Introductory Remarks, in: Ewan Ferlie and Lawrence Lynn/Christopher Pollitt (Eds.), The Oxford Handbook of Public Management, Oxford University Press 2007.

Flood, P./Mkamwa, T./O'Regan, C./.Guthrie, G./Liu, W.Armstrong, C./MacCurtain, S. New models of high performance work system: The business case for strategic HRM, partnership and diversity and equality system. Dublin, Ireland: National 2008.

Folkestad, J./Gonzalez, R. Teamwork for innovation: A content analysis of the highly read and highly cited literature on innovation. Advances in Developing Human Resources, 12(1), 2010, pp. 115–136.

Fortin, Marion/Fellenz, Martin R., Hypocrisis of Fairness: Towards a more reflexive ethical Base in Organisational Justice research and Practice, in: Journal of Business Ethics, Vol. 78, 2007, pp. 415–433.

Frampton, J.S., Public Sector Job Satisfaction: A Conversation with Impact, in: Public Administration Review, Vol. 74, Issue. 3, 2014, pp. 396–397.

Frost, P.J./Egri, C. The political process of innovation. Research, in: Organisational Behaviour, 13, 1981, pp. 229–295.

Gerhart, B./Wright, P.M./Mahan, G.C.& Snell, S.A., Measurement error in research on human resources and firrm performance: How much error is there and how does it influence effect size estimates?, in: Personnel Psychology, 53, 2000, pp. 803–834.

Gibb, S., Imagination, creativity, and HRD: An aesthetic perspective, in: Human Resource Development Review, 3(1), 2004, pp. 53–74.

Gibb, S./Waight, C.L., Connecting HRD and creativity: From fragmentary insights to strategic significance. Advances in Developing Human Resources, 7, 2005, pp. 271–286.

Godard, John, A critical assessment of the high performance paradigm, in: British Journal of Industrial Relations, Vol. 42, No. 2, 2004. pp. 349–378.

Godard, John, The psychologisation of employment relations?, in: Human Resource Management Journal, Vol. 24, 2014, pp. 1–18.

Gollan, Paul J., HR on the line: human resource managers' contribution to organisational value and workplace performance, in: Asia Pacific Journal of Human Resources No. 50, 2012, pp. 288–307.

Gooderham, P.N./Nordhaug, O./Ringdal, K., Institutional and rational determinants of organisational practices: Human resource management in European firms, in: Administrative Science Quarterly, 44, 1999, pp. 507–531.

Goodsell, Charles E., The Case for Bureaucracy, A Public Administration Polemic, Third Edition, Chatham, New Jersey 1994.

Graeber, David., The Utopia of Rules. Paperback, Melville House, London, 2016.

Gros, Frederic, Die Politisierung der Sicherheit, Matthes & Seitz 2015.

Grugulis, Irena & Vincent, Steven, Whose skill is it anyway? Soft skills and polarisation, Work, in: Employment and Society 23 (4), 2009, pp. 597–615.

Gruman, Jamie A./Saks, Alan M., Performance management and employee engagement, in: Human Resource Management Review, Vol. 21, 2011, pp. 123–136.

Guest, David/Conway, N./Dewe, P., Using sequential tree analysis to search for bundles of HR practices, in: Human Resource Management Journal, 14(1), 2004, pp. 79–96.

Guest, David, Human resource management and performance: A review and research agenda, in: International Human Resource Management, 8, 1997, pp. 263–276.

Guest David, Human resource management: When research confronts theory, in: International Journal of Human Resource Management, 12, 2001, pp. 1092–1106.

Guest, David et al, Human resource management and performance', in: British Journal of Industrial Relations, Vol. 41, No. 2, 2003. pp. 291–314.

Guest, David, Employee engagement: a sceptical analysis, in: Journal of Organisational Effectiveness, People and Performance, Vol. 1, No. 2, 2014, pp. 141–156.

Gupta, Nina/Shaw, Jason D., Employee compensation: The neglected area of HRM research, in: Human Resource Management Review 24, 2014, pp. 1–4.

Guthrie, J.P., High-involvement work practices, turnover, and productivity: Evidence from New Zealand, in: Academy of Management Journal, 44, 2001, pp. 180–190.

Hackman, J.R./Oldham, G.R., Motivation through the design of work: Test of a theory. in: Organisational Behaviour and Human Performance, 16, 1976, pp. 250–279.

Hailey, V./Farndale, E./Truss, C., The HR department's role in organisational performance, in: Human Resource Management Journal, 15(3), 2005, pp. 49–66.

Hanushek, E.A. & Woessmann, L., The Knowledge Capital of Nations: Education and the Economics of Growth. London: MIT Press. Massachusetts 2015.

Hassan, Shahidul, Sources of Professional Employees' Job Involvement: An Empirical assessment in a Government Agency, in: Review of Public Personnel Administration, Vol. 34, No. 4, 2014, pp. 356–378.

Hassan, Shahidul/Wright, Bradley, E./Yukl, Gary, Does Ethical Leadership Matter in Government? Effects on Organisational Commitment, Absenteeism, and

Willingness to Report Ethical Problems, in: Public Administration Review, 2014, Vol. 74 Issue. 3, 2014, pp. 333–343.

Hausman, D.M. & Welch, Brynn, To Nudge or not to Nudge, in: The Journal of Political Philosophy, Vol. 18, No. 1, 2010, pp. 123–136.

Hayle, Colin, Bureaucracy-lite' and Continuities in Managerial Work, in: British Journal of Management, Vol. 13, 2002, pp. 51–66.

Hesse, Joachim/Hood, Christopher/Peters, Guy (Eds.), Paradoxes in public sector reform: An international comparison, Duncker & Humblot, Berlin 2003.

Hofstede, Geert, Culture's consequences – comparing values, behaviours, institutions and organisations across nations, Second edition, Thousand Oaks, London, New Delhi 2001.

Holman, D./Wall, T./Clegg, C./Sparrow, P./Howard, A. The New Workplace: A guide to the human impact of modern working practices. London, Wiley 2003.

Hood, Christopher, The Art of the State, Clarendon Press, Oxford University Press, Oxford 2000.

Hood, Christopher/Dixon, Ruth, A Model of Cost-Cutting in Government? The Great Management Revolution in UK Central Government Reconsidered, in: Public Administration, Vol. 91, No. 1, 2013, pp. 114–134.

Howell, J.M./Higgins, C.A., Champions of technological innovation, in: Administrative Science Quarterly, 35, 1990, pp. 317–341.

Hsieh, Chih-wei, Burnout among Public Service Workers: The Role of Emotional Labour Requirements and Job Resources, in: Review of Public Personnel Administration, Vol. 34 (4), 2014, pp. 379–402.

Huang, T.C., Are the human resource practices of effective firms distinctly different from those of poorly performing ones? Evidence from Taiwanese enterprises, in: International Journal of Human Resource Management, 11, 2000, pp. 436–451.

Huang, T.C., The effects of linkage between business and human resource management strategies, in: Personnel Review, 30, 2001, pp. 132–151.

Huberts, Leo, The Integrity of Governance, Palgrave MacMillan 2014.

Huselid, M.A., The impact of human resource management practices on turnover, productivity, and corporate financial performance, in: Academy of Management Journal, 38, 1995, pp. 635–672.

Huselid, M.A. & Becker, B.E., Comment on measurement error in research on human resources and firm performance: How much error is there and how does it influence effect size estimates. In: Personnel Psychology, 53, 2000, pp. 835–854.

Hutchison, Ann & Boxall, Peter, The critical challenges facing New Zealand's chief executives: implications for management skills, in: Asia Pacific Journal of Human Resources, Vol. 52, 2014, pp. 23–41.

Jackman, Jay M./Myra H. Strober, Fear of Feedback, in: Harvard Business Review, April 2003, p. 31.

Jennings, P.D., Viewing macro HRM from without: Political and institutional perspectives, in: Research in Personnel and Human Resources Management, 12, 1994, pp. 1–40.

Jordan, Sara R, The Innovation Imperative: an analysis of the ethics of the imperative to innovate in public sector delivery, in: Public Management Review, Vol. 16, No. 1, 2014, pp. 67–89.

Jordan, Todd & Battaglio, R.Paul, Are we there yet? The state of Public Human Resource Management Research, in: Public Personnel Management, Vol. 43 (1), 2014, pp. 25–57.

Jorgensen, F./Laugen, B.T./Boer, H., Human resource management for continuous improvement, in: Creativity & Innovation Management, 16, 2007, pp. 363–375.

Jørgensen, Torben Beck/Bozeman, Barry, Public Values, An Inventory, in: Administration and Society, Volume 39 Number 3, May 2007, pp. 354–381.

Kahneman, D., Think Fast and Slow, Farrar, Straus and Giroux 2013.

Kane, R.L., Perceptions of human resource management effectiveness. Presented at the Fourth Conference on International Human Resource Management. Gold Coast, Australia 1994.

Kanter, R.M., When a thousand flowers bloom: Structural, collective, and social conditions for innovation in organisation. Research in Organisational Behaviour, 10, 1988, pp. 169–211.

Katou, A.A. & Budhwar, P.S., Causal relationship between HRM policies and organisational performance: Evidence from the Greek manufacturing sector, in: European Management Journal, 28, 2010, pp. 25–39.

Kellough, Edward & Nigro, Lloyd, Pay for Performance in Georgia State Government, in: Review of Public Personnel Administration, Vol. 22, No. 2, 2002, pp. 146–166.

Ketkar, S. & Sett, P.K., HR flexibility and firm performance: Analysis of a multilevel causal model, in: International Journal of Human Resource Management, 20, 2009, pp. 1009–1038.

Ko, Jaekwon/Seung Uk Hur/Smith-Walter, Aaron, Family-Friendly Work Practices and Job Satisfaction and Organisational Performance: Moderating Effects of Managerial Support and Performance-Oriented Management, in: Public Personnel Management, No. 42(4), 2013, pp. 545–565.

Kuhlmann, Sabine & Wollmann, Hellmut, Verwaltung und Verwaltungsreformen in Europa, Springer, Wiesbaden 2013.

Kurlantzick, J., State-Capitalism – How the return of stateism is transforming the world, Oxford: Oxford University Press 2016.

Kwon, Illoong, Motivation, Discretion and Corruption, in: Journal of Public Administration Research and Theory, No. 24, 2012, pp. 765–794.

Larsen, H. & Brewster, C., Line management responsibility for HRM: What is happening in Europe?, in: Employee Relations, 25, 2003, pp. 228–244.

Lee, Soohoo & Sanders, Robert Mark, Fridays Are Furlough Days: The Impact of Furlough Policy and Strategies for Human Resource Management during a Severe Economic Recession September 2013; in: Review of Public Personnel Administration, Vol. 33, 3, 2013, pp. 299–311.

Levine, Charles H., Organisational Decline and Cutback Management, in: Public Administration Review, Vol. 38, No. 4, 1978, pp. 316–325.

Levine, Charles H., More on Cutback Management: Hard Questions for Hard Times, in: Public Administration Review, Vol. 39, No. 2 (Mar. – Apr., 1979), p. 179–183.

Levine, Charles H./Rubin, Irene S. and Wolohojian, George G., Resource Scarcity and the Reform Model: The Management of Retrenchment in Cincinnati and Oakland, in: Public Administration Review, Vol. 41, No. 6 (Nov. – Dec., 1981), pp. 619–628.

Levinson, Harry, Management by whose objectives?, in: Harvard Business Review, Harvard, MA 2003.

Lodge, Martin & Hood, Christopher, Into an Age of Multiple Austerities? Public Management and Public Service Bargains across OECD Countries, in: Public Governance, Vol. 25, No. 1, 2012, pp. 79–101.

Loewenberger, Pauline, The Role of HRD in Stimulating, Supporting, and Sustaining Creativity and innovation, in: Human Resource Development Review 2013, Vol. 12: 422.

Lowe, Toby, New development: The paradox of outcomes—the more we measure, the less we understand, in: Public Money and Management, 2013, Vol. 33:3, 2013, pp. 213–216.

McLean, L.D., Organisational culture's influence on creativity and innovation: A review of the literature and implications for human resource development. Advances in Developing Human Resources, 7, 2005, pp. 226–246.

Mack, K./Boxall, P., High-involvement work processes, work intensification and employee well-being: A study of New Zealand worker experiences, in: Asia Pacific Journal of Human Resources, 46, 2008, pp. 38–55.

MacLeod, David/Clark, Nita, Engaging for Success: enhancing employee engagement, A report to Government.

Marchington, Mick & Wilkinson, Adrian, Human Resource Management at Work, Chartered Institute of Personnel & Development, 3rd edition 2005.

Marchington, M./Grugulis, I., '"Best practice" human resource management: perfect opportunity or dangerous illusion?', in: International Journal of Human Resource Management, Vol. 11, No. 4, 2000. Pp. 905–925.

Martinko, Mark J./Gundlach, Michael/Douglas, Scott, Towards an integrative theory of counterproductive workplace behaviour: A casual reasoning perspective, in: International Journal of Selection and Assessment, No. 1–2/2002, pp. 36–50.

Marks, M./Mirvis, P./Hackett, E./Grady, J., Employee participation in a quality circle program: Impact on quality of work life, productivity, and absenteeism, in: Journal of Applied Psychology, 71, 1986, pp. 61–69.

Marsden, David & Richardson, Ray, Motivation and Performance Related Pay in the public Sector, Centre for Economic Performance, London School of Economics, Discussion Paper No.75, May 1992.

Martz, Wes (2013), Evaluating Organisational Performance: Rational, Natural, and Open System Models, in: American Journal of Evaluation, Vol. 34 (3), 2013, pp. 385–401.

Martinez, Miguel, L. Introduction: an employment relations perspective to IHRM, in: Martinez M. Lucio (editor), International Human Resource Management, Sage, Thousand Oaks.

Martinko, Mark J./Gundlach, Michael/Douglas, Scott, Towards an integrative theory of counterproductive workplace behaviour: A casual reasoning perspective, in: International Journal of Selection and Assessment, No. 1–2/2002, pp. 36–50.

Mazzucato, Marianna, The Entrepreneural State, Anthem Press, London 2014.

Mc Connell, Allen, Policy Success, Policy Failure and Grey Areas in Between, in: Journal of Public Policy, Vol. 30, 2010, pp. 345–362.

Menzel, Donald, Ethics and Integrity in the public service, in: Donald Menzel/Harvey L White (eds.), The State of Public Administration, Sharpe, London 2011.

Merton, Robert K., The Unintended Consequences of Purposive action, in: American Sociological Review, Vol. 1, Issue 6, 1936, pp. 894–904.

Mungiu-Pippidi, Alina, The Quest for Good Governance, Cambridge University Press 2016.

Myoung Park, Hun/Perry, James L, The Transformation of Governance: Who Are the New Public Servants and What Difference Does It Make for Democratic Governance?, in: The American Review of Public Administration, 43(1), 2012, pp. 26–49.

Neuberger, Oswald, Mikropolitik und Moral in Organisationen, 2. Editions, Lucius & Lucius, Opladen 2006.

Northouse, Peter G. (no year), Leadership, Theory and Practice, Sixth Edition, Sage Publishers.

OECD, OECD Journal on Budgeting – Vol. 3, No. 1, Paris 2003.

OECD (2010), Innovative Workplaces, Paris 2010.

OECD (2011), Divided we stand: Why inequality keeps rising? OECD Publishing, Paris 2011.

OECD (2012), Public Servants as Partners for Growth: Towards a Stronger, Leaner and More Equitable Workforce, OECD Publishing, Paris 2012.

OECD (2012), Restoring Public Finances, 2012 Update, Paris 2012.

OECD (2012), Public Sector Compensation in Times of Austerity, OECD Publishing, Paris 2012.

OECD (2012), Better Skills, better Jobs, better Lifes, OECD Publishing, Paris 2012.

OECD (2014), OECD Economic Outlook 2014, Paris 2014.

OECD (2014), OECD Economic Outlook, Government debt, No. 95, Paris 2014.

OECD (2015), OECD Dataset on managing budgetary constraints: implications for HRM and Employment in Central Public Administration, Paris.

G.R. Oldham/A.Cummings, Employee creativity: Personal and contextual factors at work, in: Academy of Management Journal, 39, 1996, pp. 607–634.

Oliver, A., Nudging, Shoving, and Budging, Behavioural Economic Informed Policy, in: Public Administration, Vol. 93, No. 3, 2015, pp. 700–714.

Papalexandris, N./Panayotopoulou, L., Exploring the partnership between line managers and HRM in Greece. In: Journal of European Industrial Training, 29, 2005, pp. 281–291.

Payne, Jonathan, The unbearable lightness of skill: the changing meaning of skill in UK policy discourses and some implications for education and training, in: Journal of Educational Policy, Vol. 15, 2000, pp. 353–369.

Perry, E./Kulik, P., The devolution of HR to the line: Implications for perceptions of people management effectiveness, in: International Journal of Human Resource Management, 19, 2008, pp. 262–273.

Perry, James E., Measuring Public Service Motivation: An Assessment of Construct Reliability and Validity, in: Journal of Public Administration Research and Theory, Vol. 6, No. 6, 1996, pp. 5–22.

Perry, James L./Hondeghem, Annie (Editors), Motivation in Public Management, Oxford University Press 2008.

Perry, James L./Engbers, T.A./Jun, S.Y., Back to the Future? Performance Related Pay, Empirical research, and the Perils of Persistance, in: Public Administration Review, Vol. 69, No. 1, 2009, pp. 39–51.

Peters, Guy & Pierre, Jon (Editors.), Handbook of Public Administration, First edition, Sage 1995.

Peters, Guy & Pierre, Jon (Editors), Handbook of Public Administration, Second edition, Sage 2003.

Peters, Guy, Advanced Introduction to Public Policy, Edward Elgar 2015.

Pfeffer, J., The Human Equation: Building profits by putting people first. Boston, Harvard Business School Press 1998.

Pfeffer, J., Competitive advantage through people: Unleashing the power of the work force. Boston, MA: Harvard Business School Press 1994.

Pickerty, Thomas, Capital in the Twenty-First Century, Harvard University Press 2014.

Pierre, Jon et al., Measuring Organisational Performance: Methodological Best Practice, in: Journal of Management, Vol. XX, No. X, 2009, pp. 1–86.

Pinnington, Ashly/Macklin, Rob and Campbell, Tom (eds.), Human Resource Management, Ethics and Employment, Oxford University Press, Oxford 2007.

Pollitt, Christopher, Convergence: The Useful Myth?, in: Public Administration, Vol. 79 No. 4, 2001, pp. 933–947.

Pollitt, Christopher, Clarifying convergence, Striking Similarities and durable differences in public management reform in: Public Management Review, No. 4, Issue 1, 2002, pp. 471–492.

Pollitt, Christopher/Bouckaert, Geert, Public Management Reform: A Comparative Analysis – New Public Management, Governance, and the Neo-Weberian State, Third edition, Oxford University Press 2011.

Pollitt, Christopher/Dan, Sorin, The Impacts of the New Public Management in Europe: A Meta-Analysis, Cocops Work package 1, Deliverable 1.1, 14 December 2011.

Pollitt, Christopher, What do we know about Public Management reform? Concepts, Models and some approximate Guidelines, Paper supporting a presentation to the conference and workshop 'Towards a comprehensive reform of Public Governance, Lisbon, 28–30 January 2013.

Posthuma, Richard A./Campion, Michael C./Masimova, Malika/Campion, Michael A., A High Performance Work Practices Taxonomy: Integrating the Literature and Directing Future Research, in: Journal of Management, Vol. 39, No. 5, July 2013, pp. 1184–1220.

Priestland, A./Hanig, R., Developing first level leaders. Harvard Business Review, 83(6), 2005, pp. 113–120.

Purcell, John, 'The search for best practice and best fit in human resource management: chimera or cul-de-sac?', in: Human Resource Management Journal, Vol. 9, No. 3, 1999. pp. 26–41.

Purcell, John, et al, Understanding the People and Performance Link: Unlocking the black box. London, CIPD 2003.

Purcell, John, The limits and possibilities of employee engagement, Warwick Papers in Industrial Relations, University of Warwick, No. 96 2012.

Purcell, John, Disengaging from engagement, in: Human Resource Management Journal, Vol. 24, No. 3, 2014, pp. 241–254.

Rainey, Hal, Understanding and Managing Public Organisations, Fourth Edition, Jossey Bass 2009.

Ramsay, H./Scholarios, D./Harley, B., 'Employees and high-performance work systems: testing inside the black box', in: British Journal of Industrial Relations, Vol. 38, No. 4, 2000. pp. 501–531.

Randma-Liiv, Tiina & Savi, Riin, Introduction to the Special Issue: The Impact of the Fiscal Crisis on Public Administration, in: Administrative Culture, Vol. 15, No. 1, 2014, pp. 4–9.

Renwick, D., Line manager involvement in HRM: An inside view, in: Employee Relations, 25, 2003, pp. 262–280.

Reilly, Thom, Comparing Public-Versus-Private Sector Pay and Benefits: Examining Lifetime Compensation, in: Public Personnel Management 42(4), 2013, pp. 521–544.

Rexed, Knut/Chris Moll/Nick Manning/Jennifer Allain, Governance of Decentralised Pay Setting in Selected OECD Countries, OECD Working Paper, No.3, 2007.

Rifkin, Jeremy, The Zero Marginal Cost-Society: The Internet of Things, The Collaborative Commons and the Eclipse of Capitalism, MacMillan 2015.

Robinson, Dilis, Workforce planning during bleak times, A public sector view, Institute for Employment Studies, Brighton 2010.

Rosa, Hartmut, Resonanz: Eine Soziologie der Weltbeziehung, Suhrkamp. Frankfurt/M 2016.

Rosenbloom, David H./Kravchuk, Robert S./Clerkin, Richard M., Public Administration, Understanding Management, Politics, and Law in the Public Sector, Seventh Edition, Mc Grawhill, Singapore 2009.

Ruel, H.J.M./Bondarouk, T.V./Van der Velde, M., The contribution of e-HRM to HRM effectiveness: Results from a quantitative study in a Dutch ministry, in: Employee Relations, 29, 2007, pp. 280–291.

Sahdev, Kusum/Vinnicombe, Susan and Tyson, Shaun, Downsizing and the changing role of HR, in: The International Journal of Human Resource Management, Vol. 10, 1999, pp. 906–923.

Said, T./Le Louarn, J./Trembly, M., The performance effects of major workforce reductions, in: International Journal of Human Resource Management, Vol. 18 no 12, 2007, pp. 2075–2094.

Sandel, Michael J., What Money Can't Buy: The Moral Limits of Markets, Farrar, Straus and Giroux 2012.

Shafritz, Jay/Hyde, Albert C., Classics of Public Administration, Sixth Edition, Boston 2007.

Schay, Brigitte W./Fisher, Sidney F., The Challenge of Making Performance-Based Pay Systems Work in the Public Sector, in: Public Personnel Management, No. 42(3), 2013, pp. 359–384.

de Schrijver, A./Delbeke, K./Maesschalck, J./Pleysier, S., Fairness perceptions and organisational misbehaviour: An empirical study, in: The American Review of Public Administration, Vol. 40, No. 6/2010, pp. 691–703.

Schuler, Randell/Jackson, Susan E., Human Resource management and organisational effectiveness: yesterday and today, in: Journal of Organisational Effectiveness, People and Performance, Vol. 1, No. 2, 2014, pp. 35–55.

Sheehan, C., A model for HRM strategic integration, in: Personnel Review, 34, 2005, pp. 192–209.

Shih, H. A.& Chiang, Y. H., & Hsu, C. C., Can high performance work systems really lead to better performance?, in: International Journal of Manpower, 27, 2006, pp. 741–763.

Simon, Herbert, Public Administration, Alfred Knopf, New York 1973.

Spencer, David A., Barbarians at the gate: a critical appraisal of the influence of economics on the field and practice of HRM, in: Human Resource Management Journal, Vol. 23, No. 4, 2013, pp. 346–359.

Stewart, Greg L./Brown, Kenneth G., Human Resource Management, Second edition, John Wiley, New Baskerville 2011.

Chan Su Jung & Soo Young Lee, The Hawthorne Experiments Studies Revisited, Evidence from the US Federal Workforce, in: Administration & Society, Vol. 47, 2015, pp. 507–551.

Szabo, Erna, Participative Management and Culture, Peter Lang, Frankfurt/M. et al. 2007.

Taylor, Jeanette/Loo See Beh, The Impact of Pay-for-Performance Schemes on the Performance of Australian and Malaysian Government Employees, in: Public Management Review, Vol. 15, No. 8, 2013, pp. 1090–1115.

Teague, Paul/Roche, William K., Recessionary bundles: HR practices in the Irish economic crisis, in: Human Resource Management Journal, Vol. 24, no. 2, 2014, pp. 176–192.

Thaler, Richard & Sunstein, Cass, Nudge: Improving decisions about Health, Wealth and Happiness, Penguin Books 2009.

Tholen, Berry, Citizen Participation and bureaucratization: the participatory turn seen through a Weberian lens, in: International Review of Administrative Sciences, Vol. 81, 2015, pp. 585–603.

Thompson, Paul, The trouble with HRM, in: Human Resource Management Journal, Vol. 21, no 4, 2011, pp. 355–367.

Thornhill, A./Saunders, M.N.K., What if line managers don't realize they're responsible for HR?, in: Personnel Review, 27, 1998, pp. 460–476.

Tsai, C.J., High performance work systems and organisational performance: An empirical study of Taiwan's semiconductor design firms, in: International Journal of Human Resource Management, 17, 2006, pp. 1512–1530.

Ulrich, Dave/Younger, Jon/Brockbank, Wayne/Ulrich, Mike, HR from the Outside in, Mc Graw Hill 2012.

Ulrich, Dave, Human resource champions: The next agenda for adding value and delivering results. Boston, MA: Harvard Business School Press 1997.

Ulrich, Dave/Brockbank, W., The HR value proposition. Boston, MA: Harvard Business School Press 2005.

Ulrich, Dave/Lake, D., Organisational capability: Competing from the inside out. New York, NY: Wiley 1990.

Vandeberg, R.J./H.A.Richardson/L.J.Eastman, The impact of high involvement work processes on organisational effectiveness: A second order latent variable approach. Group & Organisation Management, 24, 1999, pp. 300–339.

van der Voet, Joris/van de Walle, Steve, How cutbacks and job satisfaction are related: The role of top-level public managers' autonomy, FP7 COCOPS Final Academic Conference: Leuven, Belgium (2014, June, 10–2014, June 11).

van de Walle, Steven/Steijn, Bram/Jilke, S., Extrinsic motivation, PSM and labour market characteristics: A multilevel model of public sector employment preference in 26 countries, in: International Review of Administrative Sciences, *2015, No.* 81(4).

Vaughan-Whitehead, Daniel (Editor), Public Sector Shock: The Impact of Policy Retrenchment in Europe, Edward Elgar Publishing 2013.

Walton, R.E./Allen, C./Gaffney, M. Innovating to compete: Lessons for diffusing and managing change in the workplace. San Francisco, CA: Jossey-Bass.1987.

Weinberg, Hugh (2014), Ethical Leadership in Public Service: A Solid Foundation for Good Government Public, in: Administration Review, 2014, Vol. 74, No. 3, pp. 344–345.

Whittaker, S./Marchington, M. (2003). Devolving HR responsibility to the line: Threat, opportunity or partnership?, in: Employee Relations, 25, 245–261.

Wilke, Helmut, Dezentrierte Demokratie, Frankfurt/M., Suhrkamp. 2016.

Wilkinson, Adrian/Bacon, Nicolas/Redman, Tom/Snell, Scott (2010), The SAGE Handbook of Human Resource Management, London/Thousand Oaks.

Wood, S./De Menezes, L. (1998). High commitment management in the UK: Evidence from the workplace industrial relations survey, and employers' manpower and skills practices survey, in: Human Relations, 51, pp. 485–515.

Wright, P./Dunford, B. B., & Snell, S. A. (2001). Human resources and the resource based view of the firm, in: Journal of Management, 27, pp. 701–721.

Wright, P.M./Haggerty, J.J. (2005). Missing variables in theories of strategic human resource management: Time, cause, and individuals, in: Management Revue, 16, pp. 164–173.

Wright, P.M./Kehoe, R.R. (2008). Human resource practices and organisational commitment: A deeper understanding, in: Asia Pacific Journal of Human Resources, 46, pp. 6–20.

Ziller, Jacques (2001), European Models of Government – Towards a Patchwork with Missing Pieces, in: Parliamentary Affairs, No. 54.

Annex OECD Questionaire

"Managing Budgeting Constraints Implications for HRM and Employment in Central Public Administration" (OECD, 2014/2015)

Objective

Public administration has traditionally been characterised with such bureaucratic features as hierarchical and formalised organisational structure, clear and rigid career paths, lifetime tenure, full-time employment, principle of seniority, specific pension schemes and standardised remuneration systems. These features were introduced in late 19th century to reduce the risk of excessive political influence, corruption, misconduct and instability of government. Today, however, numerous administrative and managerial reforms are affecting these longstanding aspects of public employment. Size and composition of workforce, its working and employment conditions, nature of work, and values and legal status are all undergoing a process of change. So far, budgetary constraints, restructuring programmes and effects of austerity measures have not been a subject of rigorous scrutiny as regards the impact of HR policies and public employment trends. Similarly, the effects of public management reforms have not been studied either and have resulted in national administrations no longer having a single coherent framework. Filling this important gap, this survey attempts to assess the effects of these developments in public employment in the central public administrations of the OECD countries.

Description

On the following pages you will find a questionnaire that consists of different themes split into sub-questions.

Though replies to the questions are necessarily subjective in nature, they should to the extent possible reflect a broad view within your administration or, even better, evidence from national surveys in your administration.

Comment boxes are included at the end of each sections to give you the possibility to provide more general comments on aspects that you think are particularly relevant to your case.

Terminology

The focus of the requested data is core ministries and agencies of central/federal governments. For some governments it will be necessary to include the regional and local branches of central government agencies. However, please note that the survey does not cover sub-national levels of government (regional/local/municipal). The data exclude government-employed doctors and nurses, teachers, police, judiciary, military and staff employed in state owned enterprises. Further definitions are included in this Glossary.

Deadline

9th of June 2014

Contact Information

Dr Christoph Demmke
Christoph.DEMMKE@oecd.org
OECD Headquarter Paris
2, rue André Pascal
75775 Paris Cedex 16
France
Tel: +33 1 45 24 99 83

Daniel Gerson
Daniel.GERSON@oecd.org
OECD Headquarter Paris
2, rue André Pascal
75775 Paris Cedex 16
France
Tel: +33 1 45 24 81 97

1. Employment in Central Administration: Levels and Trends

Q1: Generally speaking, what is the overall trend in central public administration employment in your country?

Select one

□ High decrease
□ Moderate decrease
□ No relevant change
□ Moderate increase
□ High increase

Comments:

Q2: Have the following sectors been subject to personnel changes in the central public administration?

If no other, please click on no "relevant change"

	High decrease	Moderate decrease	No relevant change	Moderate increase	High increase
Ministries, departments	□	□	□	□	□
Central government agencies	□	□	□	□	□
Health sector	□	□	□	□	□
Education sector	□	□	□	□	□
Research sector	□	□	□	□	□
Military sector	□	□	□	□	□
Other (please specify):	□	□	□	□	□

Comments:

Q3: Please indicate which ministries have been the most impacted by personnel reductions since 2008?

If none type "no personnel reductions" in the comment box below

Q4: Please provide the figures of employment in central public administration in total numbers for 2013, annually (or closest year)

If no other, please insert 0

	Indeterminate duration	Fixed-term duration	Other	Total	Comments:
Civil servants					
Other public employees					
Other (please describe)					
Total					

Q4b: Are there any plans to change the current balance of employment in central public administration as indicated in the table above?

□ Yes
□ No

Q4c: Please explain the plans in more details:

Q5: Please provide details regarding the use of following instruments in changing (reducing) public employment levels since 2008.

	No use	Moderate use	Frequent use	Comments:
Dismissals	□	□	□	
Recruitment freezes	□	□	□	
Outsourcing	□	□	□	
Annual productivity targets (e.g. 0.5% personnel reductions)	□	□	□	
Non or partial replacement of retiring staff	□	□	□	
Privatisation	□	□	□	
Decentralisation of employment to lower government level agencies	□	□	□	

Q6: If personnel cuts have taken place since 2008, what is the relation between the reduction of central public administration employees and the reduction of private sector employees?

Select one
□ Stronger reductions in central public administration
□ Equal
□ Stronger reductions in private sector
□ Cannot say

Q6b: If personnel reductions are taking place, to which of the following strategic objectives are they related?

Select all that apply
□ Anticipate the decreasing number of new potential recruits on the labour market
□ Enhance productivity
□ Restructure public administration workforce
□ Other (please specify):

Please provide any comments on the section:

2. Changes in Working Conditions and Remuneration

Q7: Have there been any remuneration reforms implemented in the central public administration in your country since 2008?

□ Yes
□ No

Q7b: Please briefly describe the reforms and their implications and, if possible, include any background document and/or web addresses which contain further information.

If you have any PDF or Word document you would like to provide please email it either to Christoph.DEMMKE@oecd.org or Daniel.GERSON@oecd.org

Q7c: Did the(se) reform(s) contributed to?

Select all that apply
□ Reduction of remuneration specifically for top level
□ Reduction of remuneration for all staff
□ Reduction or abolishment of allowances (e.g., Christmas allowance, 13th salary)
□ Reduction of performance-related-pay/bonuses
□ Pay freeze

□ Other (please specify):

Q8: Are there any remuneration reforms that are expected to be implemented in the next two years?

□ Yes
□ No

Q8b: What remuneration reforms are expected to be implemented in the next two years?

Select all that apply
□ Freezes in increments
□ Changes in indexation of salary increases
□ Reductions in employer's social contributions
□ Increases in employees' social contributions

□ Other (please specify):

Q9: Have training policies been affected since the financial crisis 2008?

□ Yes
□ No

Q9b: How have training policies been affected since the financial crisis 2008?

□ Training budgets
□ Training days
□ Other (please specify):

Q9c: What is the average length of training per year per employee (in days)?

Answer has to be a number (e.g. 3.5)

Q9d: Have you introduced measures in order to raise the efficiency of training policies since 2008?

Select one
□ Yes
□ No

Q9e: What measures were introduced in order to raise the efficiency of training policies since 2008?

Select all that apply
□ Use training needs assessments to ensure that training is only provided when necessary
□ Shift employees training to be readily available at employees' desks (computer-assisted e-training)
□ Reduce travel costs to training events

□ Other (please specify):

Q10: Since 2008, have you introduced cost saving measures in the management of human resources?

Select one
□ Yes
□ No

Q10b: What cost saving measures of human resources were introduced since 2008 in the central public administration?

Select all that apply
□ Use of furloughs (days off without compensation)
□ Reduce/cut hierarchical levels or careers
□ Stop/put on hold promotion opportunities

□ Other (please specify):

Q11: What is the number of statutory regular working hours for central public administration as defined by the law on working hours or collective bargaining agreements (number of hours per week)?

Answer has to be a number (e.g. 35)

Q11b: What is the maximum number of hours of overtime for central public administration as defined by the law on working hours or collective bargaining agreement (number of hours per week)?

Answer has to be a number (e.g. 5)

Q11c: Since 2008, have working hours changed in the central public administration?

□ Yes
□ No

Q11d: To what extent did working hours changed in the central public administration?

Select one
□ High decrease
□ Moderate decrease
□ Moderate increase
□ High increase

Comments:

Q12: How many annual holidays are fulltime employees entitled to take per year (number of days per year)?

Answer has to be a number (e.g. 14.8)

Q12b: Do annual holidays vary by length of services or by position?

□ No

□ Yes (please specify):

Q12c: How many days a year on average are public holidays that apply to the public service?

Answer has to be a number (e.g. 6)

☐

Q12d: Have there been any policies directed to change holiday entitlements or the number of holidays since 2008?

□ Yes
□ No

Q12e: How did the policies introduced changed holiday entitlements or the number of holidays since 2008 in the central public administration?

If no other, please click on stayed the same

	Decreased	Stayed the same	Increased	Comments:
Number of vacation days	□	□	□	
Number of public holidays	□	□	□	
Calculation of paid leave days	□	□	□	
Paid sick leave days	□	□	□	
Other (please specify):	□	□	□	

Q13: Have you introduced any policies directed to reduce absenteeism since 2008?

□ Yes
□ No

Q13b: Which of the following policies directed to reduce absenteeism did you introduce since 2008?

Select all that apply
□ Monetary incentive for unused sick days
□ Incentives for unused sick days (other than monetary)
□ Recommendations for preventive medical care in case of high absence rates
□ Paid sick days (even with doctor's prescription) are limited

□ Reducing number of days allowed to take care of sick children

□ Other (please specify):

Q14: Apart for reasons of misbehaviour, illegal conduct and poor performance, have measures been implemented in order to dismiss central public administration workforce since 2008?

□ Yes
□ No

Q14b: Since 2008, how often do dismissals happen for the following reasons:

	Rarely	Sometimes	Often	Difficult to say	Comments:
In case of restructuring	□	□	□	□	
In case of budgetary constraints	□	□	□	□	
In case of shifting personnel to other administrative levels, organisations, agencies etc.	□	□	□	□	
Other (please specify):	□	□	□	□	

Q14c: Is the government required to propose reallocation possibilities to staff before dismissing them under the terms of the measures introduced since 2008 to reduce central public administration workforce?

□ Yes
□ No
Comments:

Q15: Has the government devised plans since 2008 to encourage voluntary departures in order to implement its plans and targets regarding the allocation of the central public administration workforce?

□ Yes
□ No

Q15b: What kind of plans were introduced since 2008 to encourage voluntary departures in the central public administration workforce?

Select all that apply
□ Leaving allowances
□ Early retirement packages

□ Other (please specify)

Q15c: Did these policies encouraged central public administration staff to leave?

□ Yes
□ No
□ Cannot say

Q15d: Did these policies produce efficiency gains in the central public administration?

□ Yes
□ No
□ Cannot say

***Q15e: Did these policies bring any unintentional side effects?**

Please describe

Q16: Have there been any reforms in the area of fixed term employment?

□ Yes
□ No

Q16b: Overall, what were the reform outcomes in the area of fixed-term employment in the central public administration?

Select one
□ High increase of fixed-term employment
□ Moderate increase of fixed-term employment
□ Moderate decrease of fixed-term employment
□ High decrease of fixed term employment
□ Cannot say

Q16c: In which categories of employees did the proportion of fixed-term employment change?

	High decrease	Moderate decrease	No change	Moderate increase	High increase	Cannot say	Comments
Senior management	□	□	□	□	□	□	
Middle management	□	□	□	□	□	□	
Professional staff	□	□	□	□	□	□	
Technical and administrative staff	□	□	□	□	□	□	

Please provide any comments on the section:

3. Impact of Reforms on Employment Conditions and Employment Status

Q17: Have measures been taken in order to substitute civil servants with public employees under fixed-term contract in central public administration since 2008?

	Yes	No	Cannot say	Comments
For cost-saving measures	□	□	□	
Because of shortages in civil service employment	□	□	□	
Because of recruitment freezes	□	□	□	
Because fixed-term employees perform their tasks	□	□	□	
Other (please specify):	□	□	□	

Q17b: What are the main reasons for the use of fixed-term employment contracts in the central public administration?

	Yes	No	Cannot say	Comments
Need to complete a specific and limited task	□	□	□	
Need for substituting civil servants who are temporarily	□	□	□	
Need for compensation in the case of temporary increase	□	□	□	
Performance of seasonal work	□	□	□	
Need for compensation of temporary and specific needs	□	□	□	
Need for more flexible employment in order to save	□	□	□	
Consequence of budgetary constraints/ austerity measures	□	□	□	
Other (please specify):	□	□	□	

Q18: Have any changes taken place as regards to the level of employment protection since 2008:

	Yes	No	Cannot say	Comments
It has become easier to dismiss civil servants	□	□	□	
It has become easier to dismiss public employees	□	□	□	
Notice periods have been shortened	□	□	□	
Other (please specify):	□	□	□	

Q19: Will budgetary constraints and the subsequent need for stabilising national economies be an extra impetus to abolishing employment as civil servants?

□ Very much
□ Somewhat
□ Fairly little

□ Not at all
□ Cannot say

Please provide any comments on the section:

4. Impact of Reform Policies on Workplace Behaviour and Work Organisation

Q20: Since 2008, in the central public administration of your country, did the introduction of reforms had the following effects:

If no other, please click on "No effect". If more than one other effect, please provide them all in the box. If the different other effects do not have the same importance, just click on the "cannot say" button and provide the information (strong effect, some effect or no effect) in the comments box next to the "other" row.

	Strong effect	Some effect	No effect	Cannot say	Comments
Decrease of trust in the organisation	□	□	□	□	
Decrease of trust in leadership Perception of unfairness compared to how private sector employees are dealt with	□	□	□	□	
Perception of unfairness compared to how colleagues are dealt with	□	□	□	□	
Decline of ethical values	□	□	□	□	
Decrease in workplace commitment	□	□	□	□	
Lowering of job satisfaction	□	□	□	□	
Increase in inappropriate use of resources, e.g., theft and fraud	□	□	□	□	
Unethical behaviour arising from higher stress levels and higher job intensity	□	□	□	□	
Increase in anger	□	□	□	□	
Decrease in loyalty	□	□	□	□	

Greater tendency towards corruption	□	□	□	□	
Other effects (please specify):	□	□	□	□	

Q21: Have sickness levels changed since 2008?

□ Yes
□ No

Q21b: Did they increase or decrease?

□ Increased
□ Decreased
Comments:

Q22: What is the impact of current reform trends on work intensity and stress in central public administration?

	High increase	Moderate increase	No change	Moderate decrease	High decrease	Cannot say
Work/job intensity	□	□	□	□	□	□
Work related stress	□	□	□	□	□	□

Comments:

Q22b: Overall, do you think that the organisation of work and workplace quality has changed since 2008?
e.g. in terms of teamwork, communication, job autonomy, employee involvement in decision-making, skill development opportunities etc.

□ Strongly improved
□ Moderately improved
□ No change
□ Moderately deteriorated
□ Strongly deteriorated

Please provide any comments on the section:

5. The Use of Employee Surveys to Produce Evidence on Reform Outcomes

Q23: Do you conduct employee surveys?

□ Yes
□ No

Q23b: How are these surveys administered?

Select all that apply
□ Centralised surveys across the whole central public administration
□ Administrative sectors conduct their own surveys
□ Each government agency conducts its own survey

□ Other (please specify):

Q23c: How often are these surveys conducted? (if ministries conduct own, please check all that apply and explain variations in the comments section)

Select one
□ On an as-needed basis (please explain in the comment box on the next page)
□ Every year
□ Every two years
□ More seldom than every two years

Comments:

Q23d: Do the surveys aim to assess the following aspects?

Select all that apply
□ Job satisfaction
□ Organisational commitment
□ Stress levels
□ Work intensity
□ Employee motivation
□ Effectiveness of management
□ Effectiveness of HRM systems

□ Impacts on employees of workplace change/transformation
□ Work/life balance
□ Integrity at the workplace

□ Other (please specify):

For each item that you have checked above, can you report recent results/trends:

Q23e: How is the survey data used?

Select all that apply
□ It is reported publicly (if available, please specify website in comments)
□ It is reported to senior management/political level (please specify in the comment box below)
□ It is included in managers' performance assessments

□ Other (please specify):

Q23f: Have the results of data from surveys resulted in changes to and/or the introduction of HRM programs and/or policies?

□ No

□ Yes (please specify):

Please provide any comments on the section:

6. Positive Challenges

Q24: Do you agree with the following statements:

	Totally agree	Rather agree	Rather not agree	Does not agree
The current situation opens the possibility to rethink the division of labour between the public and the private sector	□	□	□	□
The current situation opens the possibility to rethink the need for having differences (or not) in employment and working conditions between civil servants, other public employees and private sector employees	□	□	□	□
The current situation will force public administrations to improve and professionalise workforce planning and improve data management because of the need to reallocate HR resources across sectors resulting from additional demands for staff in other sectors (e.g. health)	□	□	□	□
The need to downsize public employment makes it easier to anticipate future demographic changes and pressures and forces to think more strategically on the structure, composition and size of the future workforce	□	□	□	□

Comments:

Thank you for completing this questionnaire. You will receive an automatic confirmation upon completion via email, along with a summary of final responses for your records.

www.ingramcontent.com/pod-product-compliance
Ingram Content Group UK Ltd.
Pitfield, Milton Keynes, MK11 3LW, UK
UKHW021831100926
8556IPUK00004B/281

9 783631 677001